HAMLYN GUIDE

WILD
FLOWERS

OF BRITAIN AND EUROPE

HAMLYN GUIDE

WILD
FLOWERS
OF BRITAIN AND EUROPE

D. & R. AICHELE
H. W. & A. SCHWEGLER

HAMLYN

Acknowledgements

The publishers wish to thank the following for their permission to reproduce their photographs: D. Aichele (287), R. Aichele (37), J. Apel (9), F.G. Averdieck (1), C. and W Baitinger (10), H. Bechtel (8), W. Bechtle (1), F. Büttner (26), N. Caspers (1), R. Fieselmann (3), K. Frantz (4), E. Garnweidner (4) M. Haberer (9), H. Haeupler (17), D. Herbel (4), E. Humperdinck (1), F. Jantzen (3), W. Käckenmeister (2), R. König (12), P. Kohlhaupt (60), Kullmann (1), H.E. Laux (10), Ch. Lederer (4), E. Müller (37), G. Quedens (1), G.H. Radek (1), G. Rein (1), H. Reinhard (13), S. Sammer (4), W. Schacht (12), J. Schimmitat (13), H. Schmidt (5), T. Schneiders (1), P. Schönfelder (54), H. Schrempp (41), F. Schwäble (12), F. Siedel (16), M. Stellwag (1), K.F. Wolfstetter (9) and P. Zeiniger (1).

The publishers are grateful to Dr Robert Press, Kenneth Beckett and Gillian Beckett for their assistance in the preparation of this edition.

This edition first published in 1992
by The Hamlyn Publishing Group Limited
an imprint of Reed Consumer Books Limited
Michelin House, 81 Fulham Road, London SW3 6RB
and Auckland, Melbourne, Singapore and Toronto

Reprinted 1993

© 1986 Franckh'sche Verlagshandlung, W. Keller & Co Kosmos Verlag, Stuttgart

© 1986 English Translation Ridgmount Books Limited

ISBN 0 600 57510 1

Original title: *Was grünt und blüht in der Natur?*
Translated by Susan Kunze

A CIP catalogue record for this book is available from the British Library

Produced by Mandarin Offset
Printed in Hong Kong

CONTENTS

FOREWORD

Concern for our environment is not just a modern trend, it is vitally important. We must, of course, be able to offer our children and our children's children secure jobs and healthy places to live, but sufficient countryside and other natural landscapes in which to pursue leisure-time activities are also essential.

When we talk about the environment, most of us think of the world of plants: woods, heaths, moors and meadows; valleys, hills and mountains; streams, rivers, lakes and the seashore. When we think of these places we think of the plants, trees and shrubs that grow there. Whenever we try to re-create nature in our cities, parks and greenbelts are planned, landscaped and stocked with an abundance of flowering and non-flowering species. A modern idea in gardening is to plant an area with 'wild' grasses and flowers — an attempt to bring the countryside into our backyards.

Plants, trees and shrubs tell scientists a great deal about the areas in which they can be found. The primrose, for example, does not grow well in soil with lime in it, and so we know that where this plant can be found growing the soil will not contain this element. This is a simple example of how a plant can give us accurate information about its natural habitat. When taken as a whole, the plants in any given area will tell a very revealing story about their landscape. It is not surprising, therefore, that an increasing number of people want to know more about plants and want to be able to identify them when they see them.

The most obviously memorable part of a plant is usually its flower, and this book is arranged so that you can easily look up the flower colour using the coloured band on the edge of the pages. The flower form (that is, the number of petals) then limits the number of possible species within each colour. You should then look through the photographs of the plants that fall into the same categories of colour and form to find the specimen that you wish to identify. Having found it, the symbols and text that accompany each photograph either confirm the identification or direct you to similar species for a correct identification. The text gives a great deal of information on important identification marks, habitat and distribution.

Although this system of identification might be considered unscientific, it has helped a great many amateur naturalists to identify species that they have wanted to learn more about and to increase their knowledge of the natural world. With this system it has been possible to keep the book to a handy size, while at the same time including well over 600 species each with full-colour photographs (only a few species are duplicated because of their differing flower shades). There are also references to similar species so that almost 1000 types are covered, and this far exceeds the usual number of plants described in other popular books on flora.

Amateur botanists nowadays travel extensively throughout Continental Europe, and for this reason certain interesting plants have been included which may be found only in specific places on the Continent. Similarly, plants which may grow wild in one country, some of the mountain flowers for example, may be well-known cultivated rockery

7

plants elsewhere. Quite frequently, cultivated flowers 'escape' and become established in the wild, hence their inclusion in this book.

Also featured are numerous flowering shrubs and trees, some truly wild, others more generally cultivated. Finally it should be mentioned that in some countries certain species are protected due to their rarity, whereas elsewhere they may flourish profusely and not need to be protected. This important point is covered in the Introduction where the system of symbols accompanying each plant description is explained.

INTRODUCTION

The plant descriptions in this book have been arranged in such a way that they form a unit with the photographs directly above them. This simplifies the process of identifying any species.

Identification Marks
The section **IM** (Identification Marks) contains a description of the main features of each specimen. Easily recognizable characteristics that distinguish a plant from any other similar species are given. This information is intended to complement the photographs.

Habitat and distribution
The section **H** (Habitat and distribution) gives valuable data on the plants' soil and climate requirements. Details of the types of landscapes where each species is normally found are also given, as well as the type of vegetation in which the plant is likely to grow.

This section also tells the reader how often he might come across the specimen concerned. A plant is referred to as *common* when it can be found in many different places within its area of distribution, as *local* when it appears only be found here and there, and as *rare* when it can only be found in very few places. No reference is made to the concentration in which the plant can be found in its habitat. It may well be that even rare plants can be found in abundance in one particular area or even only in one individual spot.

Additional Information
The last section of text **AI** (Additional Information) gives distinguishing details of related species or even of particular subspecies, plus general points of interest. Synonyms — additional popular names plus scientific names — are also included where appropriate.

Scientific names
The problem of the correct scientific name is an old one which even today has not been settled satisfactorily. In the mid-eighteenth century the Swedish naturalist Carl von Linné introduced double names for each species: the first name indicates the genus, the second is the name of the species (which is always written with a small initial letter). Often the second part is the name of the person who first identified the species, and after whom the plant has been named. This method should have made it easy to name any plant unmistakeably and clearly. Experience proved that this was not so, however. Often the same species was 'discovered' for the first time by more than one person and named differently by each one. Other species were subdivided or amalgamated using different methods. Some scientists objected to a name on linguistic grounds and quickly created another. Others felt that the old name was not descriptive enough or that it was incorrect. The net result was that many plants had a whole range of names.

Only through the strict application of rules which were worked out laboriously in a series of international congresses has it been possible over the last few decades to bring relative (but not yet final) stability to the situation. The plants in this book are named according to *Flora Europaea*, volumes 1-5 (Cambridge University Press), the most up-to-date single work regarded as authoritative for the whole of Europe. This may mean that some well-known and popular names have not been included, but it is a step towards final standardization.

Common names
The situation with common names is different because these are not governed by any rules. As can be seen from other books on plants, names vary from area to area. The names given here are those recommended by the Botanical Society of the British Isles in *English Names of Wild Flowers*, Dony, Robb and Perring (Butterworths). Whenever a plant was not included in this work, names from other books on wild flowers were used. While the scope of this book is mainly British, it is wide-ranging throughout Europe, and a few species have no common English name.

Family name
The name of the family to which a species belongs is given after the species name itself. Difficulties are far less frequent here. In some cases the old name is given in brackets where this is well known.

Further information
Below the various plant names additional information and symbols are given which are easy to understand and which provide further aids to identification.

FLOWERING TIME   The majority of individual plants of one species are found to be in blossom during a specific period, and the months at the beginning and end of the usual flowering time for each species is quoted. Flowering time does vary somewhat depending on annual climate and geographical position including height above sea level, but within certain tolerances this period is relatively firmly established. It is not usual to find snowdrops for example growing wild in bloom in summer. Individual early or late blossoms are exceptions which do occur occasionally. However, a spring plant may have a late blossoming. With some of these species the start of blossoming depends on the length of the day and in spring this is very short (short-day plants). If the autumn is mild and the days as short as at certain times in spring, then there may well be a widespread second flowering in one year.

HEIGHT OF GROWTH   The figures given after the flowering time indicate to what height a plant will grow under normal conditions. Plants tend to grow to a certain 'level', depending on the type of plant and prevailing conditions. In a meadow, for example, some species remain very close to the ground and even when in flower they are hardly more than 20 cm high. Others grow to the level of the lower grasses, about 50 cm high. The remainder will compete for space and light with the tall grasses.

The height of a plant is a distinguishing feature and should not be ignored for the purposes of identification. In time, the amateur naturalist gets to know whether the conditions in which he finds a plant are its normal habitat, or whether a plant has found itself in a spot which cause it to produce abnormal growth. A lack of light or an excess of nourishment (overfeeding) can lead to abnormally tall examples of species. Where the soil is poor or the plant is in an exposed position, growth may be less than usual, but nevertheless the plant can be quite sturdy. This should not deter anyone from making a positive identification. Compare the conditions in which a plant is found to be growing with those in which it is normally found and an explanation for excessive or reduced growth will often become evident.

CLASSIFICATION   Genuine flowering plants (the angiosperms) are divided into two subclasses. Monocotyledons are plants whose embryos have one cotyledon, and these are indicated by the letter **M**. The more extensive subclass, Dicotyledons, have two cotyledons in the embryos, and are indicated by the letter **D**. These are further divided into three groups: those with flowers with fused petals (gamopetalous), those few flowers without petals (perianth absent), and the large number that have free petals (polypetalous). Gamopetalous species display petals which have to a greater or lesser extent grown together to form a mass.

THE LIFE CYCLE OF PLANTS   Different groups of plants have their own life cycle, that is from germination, through the growing, flowering and fruiting periods, to death.

⊙   This symbol indicates annual plants — those which germinate, flower once, fruit and die completely within one year.

⊙   Biennials produce only leaves in the first year (storage) and blossom, fruit and die in the second.

Plants which live and blossom repeatedly for several years are divided into two groups:

♃   Herbaceous perennials 'die back' each autumn, after flowering and fruiting, which means that the part of the plant that can be seen above the ground withers and dies, but below ground the rhizomes, tubers, bulbs, etc, remain and produce new shoots each year.

♄   Woody plants, such as trees and shrubs, produce woody parts above the ground which remain and grow taller in each vegetation cycle. They either retain their leaves throughout the year (evergreen) or produce new leaves each spring, which wither and fall in the autumn (deciduous).

POISONOUS PLANTS   + indicates plants that are poisonous.

(+) indicates plants which are slightly poisonous or are suspected of being poisonous. Resistance to poison varies from person to person. With some plants contact alone causes allergic rashes (stinging nettles, types of primroses). Even chewing or eating harmless plants can cause ill-effects.

Flower colour and form

The coloured band at the edge of each page indicates the colour of the flowers in each section. These sections have been further divided according to the flower form. Plants with radially symmetrical flowers, such as daisies, are described first and have been further subdivided:

flowers with up to 4 petals

flowers with 5 petals

flowers with more than 5 petals.

Plants with bilaterally symmetrical flowers, such as violets and Lady's Slipper, follow on from the radials.

This indicates flowering trees or shrubs and it precedes the symbol for the flower type itself, to make identification quicker.

A complete and simplified key appears on pages 25–6.

Protected species

Species which ought to be protected in some way are indicated by either a green or black triangle (the latter indicating a species protected by law in Britain, but not necessarily protected in Europe). Protection of plants and animals ensures that we leave our environment in tact for future generations. It is our responsibility therefore to treat the natural world around us with respect. Plants given the triangle symbol may or may not be protected by law in the countries in which we find them, but they have been noted to be in decline by botanists or other scientists and therefore need preserving.

Habitat symbols

The symbols for habitats are wider ranging than for Britain only and have been allocated on a northern European basis. Where British habitats differ from those indicated by the symbols, you will find this information in the Habitat and distribution (**H**) section of the text.

Key to abbreviations and symbols

IM   Identification marks
H   Habitat and distribution
AI   Additional information
M   Monocotyledonous plant
D   Dicotyledonous plant
⊙   Annual
⊚   Biennial
♃   Perennial
♄   Ligneous
+   Poisonous
(+)   Slightly poisonous, or might be poisonous

Radially symmetrical flowers with up to 4 petals

Radially symmetrical flowers with 5 petals

Radially symmetrical flowers with more than 5 petals

Bilaterally symmetrical flowers

Ligneous plant

Plant which should be protected

Weedy and uncultivated areas

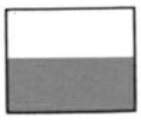

Grasslands

Wooded areas

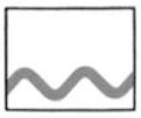

Wetlands

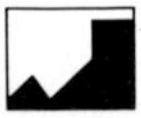

Pioneer communities

13

HABITATS

Weedy and uncultivated areas

Fields, gardens, waysides, embankments, wasteland, fallow fields, rubbish tips.

Cultivated land offers very specific living conditions. The original vegetation has been removed, the soil has been broken down to make it loose, and the ground is enriched, fertilized and sometimes watered. On such soil wild plants quickly establish themselves. These plants are commonly called weeds, and are characterized by their vigorous growth and rapid multiplication. They reproduce not only by the production of many seeds, but also by means of shoots and runners both above and below ground. Many of these plants have adapted to the abundant fertilizer in the ground and have become nitrogen indicators: they only thrive where the soil contains considerable quantities of nitrogenous salts, as well as an abundance of phosphate and potash. Furthermore, in order to thrive they need relatively open ground with little shade and loose soil.

The kind of soil to some extent determines the selection of weeds which will grow in any particular field, as does the abundance of lime or silicic acid in the subsoil. Years of cultivation with planned applications of

An uncultivated field with an abundance of weeds, a rare sight these days.

Thistles grow on piles of rubble in abundance, and in a range of species including some rarities.

fertilizer and herbicides can, however, alter the variety of species to be found anywhere.

Cultivation, beyond steps taken to nurture individual plants, creates conditions appropriate to different groups of weeds, for example fields of root-crops and potatoes harbour different types to those found in grain fields.

The wild plants found in gardens, which are hoed frequently, are similar to those found in fields of root-crops. However, the variety of cultivated plants found in garden beds has created the basis for some very special weeds to establish themselves.

The dry stone walls which enclose some of these highly cultivated areas are a special habitat, and rock plants take root in the nooks and crannies.

The addition to the plants that grow well on loose soil there is a second group, which also likes nitrogen and falls within the category of synanthropic plants, but which grow on compacted ground. Beaten tracks, paths, waysides, embankments, unused corners, rubbish tips, wasteland, grazing land, even the upper reaches of shores or river banks which are flooded (and therefore fertilized) at most once a year are all typical habitats for ruderal flora. Where cultivated land has become neglected there is often a temporary wild growth of annual plants until they give way to the perennials and shrubs which grow very tall, thus shading the ground.

The nutrient content of the soil is the precondition for the occurrence of these plants. Where a large number ensure their survival by means of poisons or thorns there are usually some hardy strays from far-flung continents such as America and Asia. These have developed from previously introduced garden plants which have since become wild. Species spread along rivers, railway lines and major roads. What is currently of particular interest is the progress of various halophytes (plants which thrive on soil rich in sodium chloride) from the seashore along the motorways and major roads that lead inland and which are salted in winter.

Grasslands

Meadows, grazing land, pastures, hillsides, turf.

The prime examples of grassland are the steppes of Asia. This type of land falls between forest and desert. Grasses, with the occasional plant with magnificent blooms, form the main element in the relatively dense vegetation. Plants on the steppes are almost invariably equipped to cope with drought and their annual development is marked by the change from the rainy seasons to longer periods of drought.

In Europe rainfall is far more frequent and not limited to any one season. Meadows and pastures which are used commercially form the greater part of our grassland and the only thing they have in common with the steppe is the high proportion of grasses. In places they are located where previously woods grew and only cutting or animal-grazing ensure that the trees do not begin to grow again.

The ideal meadow for grass for hay-making is the fresh, rich meadow. 'Fresh' refers to the wetness of the ground. Ground can be 'dry', 'fresh', 'damp' or 'wet'. Freshness guarantees that even in years with low rainfall there will be a good grass yield, and in wet years the ground can still be worked with heavy machinery. 'Rich' describes the level of nutrients in the ground. The opposite type of ground is called 'meagre'.

Depending on the degree of dampness and nutrient levels of the soil, and the height above sea level of the location, the flowering plants found in meadows will differ, and with them the nature of the rich meadow. The same meadow can look very different throughout the course of one year: the plants growing there will bloom at different times and so the predominant colour will vary.

The preferences of animals that graze the meadows determines the dominance of certain plants. Fodder which is poisonous, tough or thorny is left and, therefore, increases at the cost of edible plants. If meadows which were previously mown become pasture, many plants that cannot survive being trampled on will disappear. A typical feature of pastureland is the high proportion of trample-resistant white clover.

Top right: Alpine meadows are characterized by their many different blooms.

Right: Even on the plain, there is a colourful selection of flowers.

There is a smooth transition from the types of plants found on wet pasture grounds and damp meadows to the species found in marshes and aquatic areas.

Where the ground is drier with a low level of nutrient, the tall meadow grass gives way to green turf which is usually mown only once a year and is described as 'meagre', 'dry' or 'semi-dry'. The only thing it has in common with garden lawns is the low growth, which in gardens is achieved by frequent mowing. The natural counterpart of the garden lawn is the pasture which is meagre, sparse meadow for grazing small animals.

The turf found in hilly areas is interspersed with stones and rocks. Here the grass is still the main feature. It is also fertilized by cattle. The meagre grassy areas deteriorate into areas where boulders dominate. Where there are streams and rivulets the ground changes and becomes more marshy. In the higher hills and mountains in particular the range of habitats become a closely interwoven patchwork.

Grassy areas of limited size or which occur as verges usually have a certain proportion of weeds. These areas are called balks. These resemble grassland when they are mown. Where they are burnt down they tend to form wasteland. Left alone they soon form hedges and woody areas.

Wooded areas

 Deciduous, mixed and evergreen woods, lowland woods, woods on slopes, heather, bushes, hedges, wood fringes and clearings.

Without human intervention much of our land would still be woodland. Our forebears cleared land to make fields, meadows and settlements. Only a fraction of the original area is still covered by woods, and these are often intersected by major roads. Moreover, natural woodland is now tended and its spread is predetermined so that it is 'cultivated' woodland, a natural unit planned and managed according to economic criteria.

Plants and bushes which grow across the woodland floor are mostly unaffected by artificial fertilizer and pesticides. The main factors influencing their development are climate, soil and light conditions.In this respect, deciduous woods offer far better growing conditions than evergreen woods, which are permanently steeped in deep shadow. Among deciduous trees which start producing their leaves in May, the ground plants have a good opportunity of growing in full sunlight.

Environmental conditions affect which tree species will be present in an area of woodland. Soil type and drainage in particular are often important factors in determining the overall type of wood. On chalk Beech is often the dominant species while on limestone there may be Ash woods. Waterlogged fens can support Alder woods and in riverside woods Willow, Poplars and Alders are common. Richer, dryer soils support a large number of species forming mixed woods, though Oak is usually the dominant tree.

Climate and altitude also influence the type of woodland. At higher altitudes or in colder areas Birch, Hazel and Rowan become more

On sparse heaths of dwarf bushes the prevailing species is often heather.

frequent and important. Coniferous trees flourish in these areas too but are also common in warm, dry areas such as southern heathlands where pines, which can withstand the dry are often the dominant species.

The trees themselves exert a considerable effect on the local environment within the wood and each woodland type has its own characteristic flora. Beech leaves are very slow to rot and Beech woods develop a deep litter of dry fallen leaves which discourages growth of the flowers on the woodland floor. Oak leaves rot faster so oak woods generally have a more prolific ground flora. The practice of coppicing Oak—Hazel woods also encourages the growth of woodland flowers as regular coppicing lets in extra light to reach ground level.

The light conditions prevailing in bush areas are much better than in the woods, but the remaining habitat factors are worse. Heaths form where the climate is too harsh for tree growth, or the soil is too sandy and too peaty. When the ground is covered by only small, low-lying shrubs this is referred to as dwarf bush heaths. Where taller individual bushes rise above the dwarf growth, conditions are somewhat improved.

Hedges are an equivalent of bush areas which have conditions encouraging tree growth. The transitional state is preserved rarely by natural occurrences or more often by occasional clearing, cutting or burning. Compared with wild hedgerows, artificially trimmed hedges are uninteresting as a habitat for ground plants. The woodland margin is a particular type of hedge, nurtured by the forester to provide a wind break and prevented from spreading into nearby fields by the farmer.

In woods where light can penetrate there is an abundance of ground flora.

Clearings also count as a woodland habitat. The first plants to establish themselves there are usually the annuals which are forced out of the wood by shrubs. The plants in the clearing have adapted so well to these conditions that few of them are to be found outside such areas. Occasionally, although rarely, weeds that have come in from the fields can be found in clearings.

Wetlands

 Water, shores, riverbanks, marshland, wet meadows, moorland.

The basic form of non-flowing water is the lake; ponds are usually the result of man-made dams, pools are small and tend to dry out periodically. Often it is hard to distinguish between these three.

Lakes can be divided into three types. Because of the presence of humus materials moorland lakes are brown in colour and the water is poor in nutrients. There are two types of clear-water lakes: that which is poor in nutrients (often good drinking water) and that which is rich in nutrients where there is an abundance of plant life. There is always the danger that the latter type will 'turn': too much plant growth will mean that in autumn, when the plants die off, there are large quantities of rotting matter in water. The result is a lack of oxygen and this can poison the life in the lake.

It is possible to isolate growth zones in lakes. Far out in deep water there are the underwater plants. Then there is a zone of aquatic plants. Further towards the shore are the reeds which give way to a broad band of sedge. The aquatic plants within these zones can sometimes reproduce to such an extent that they temporarily cover the surface of the water.

Running water — streams and rivers — usually display similar flora to the lake, but not in such great quantities and mainly over a smaller area. Only in quiet coves, where the water flows sluggishly, are conditions similar to those on the lake.

Individual trees or bushes may be found along the shores of the water. Where the shore rises away from the water there is a smooth change in the vegetation from those plants which like the moisture to the drier-ground species. If the shores are flat, a wide marshy area can establish itself. The water is then so close to the surface that it will seep out when the ground is stepped on and remain lying in puddles in the footsteps. With the right kind of subsoil marshland can occur some distance from lakes or ponds. When the ground water is stagnant or flows very slowly, the species of plants found are different to those growing in fresh water. Marshland does not have to be made up of grasses, sedge or rushes. Woods can also grow there and are referred to as brush, or river-meadow woods.

Flat moors are bogs which have arisen out of lakes. Every lake silts up

Marsh meadows displaying a magnificent growth of irises are some of the most precious rarities to be found and deserve unlimited protection.

Isolated lakes provide unspoiled habitats for water-lilies and reeds.

eventually, even if the process takes many thousands of years. Flat moors are characterized by a high ground water level and high nutrient content.

High moor can originate as flat bogland but usually it forms independently in areas with heavy rainfall. These moors are usually made up of sphagnum which occurs where the upper part of the plant continues to grow while the lower part dies off and becomes peat. An insulating layer of peat forms between the subsoil and the surface of the high moor. The plants can extract neither nutrients nor water from the ground. They rely on rainwater and dust. High moor habitats are very poor in nutrients.

High moor and flat moor differ greatly from one another, and so does their vegetation. It would be better therefore not to use the same term for both. The word moor describes only the high moor, and marsh or fen is used here for the flat moor.

The transition from marshland to meadow or grassland is a smooth one, and between the two stages there is the wet meadow. Wet habitats can be found anywhere, not only in grassland and woody areas. The only requirement is an abundance of water.

Even though plants cannot survive without water, there are only a few that can cope with a continuous excessive supply. It has a negative effect on the ventilation of the ground and thus on the roots, thereby restricting the plants' breathing. Aquatic plants usually get oxygen to their roots by means of an internal air-pipe system.

Pioneer communities

 Rocks, boulder heaps, scree, steep stony slopes, pebbles, sand, dunes, slag, walls.

Whenever soil, particularly humus, is only found in extremely small amounts, this is the habitat of pioneer plants. Their demands are small and yet they manage to produce large growth. When they die off, they sometimes form the basis for some more demanding plant. These first settlers in habitats alien to vegetation rarely grow in a mass, but are usually found growing sparsely with great gaps between them. This is very evident on rocks where minimal quantities of water and minerals have gathered in the cracks, thereby providing a basis for plant life. With an excretion from their roots, the plants manage frequently to loosen the stony surface still further and thus extend the area in which they can survive. This does, however, lead to weathering and destruction of the rocks. At the start a plant's chances of taking root are very slim. Larger patches of plant life find an opportunity to grow along the wide cracks in the bands of rock or on horizontal ledges, where life-supporting materials can gather.

In the rocks and boulder masses the cushion and trellis plants predominate. These are half-spherical with all their elements huddled together for protection, or spread out but clinging closely to the ground. The picture changes on scree covering ground below rocks, where the roughened chunks can be found on top of each other, each one, on average, the size of a fist. Scree is unstable, and stones are constantly

The flower world in rocky Alpine areas is varied and colourful.

Stony grassland often illustrates the transition of vegetation on scree to turf.

slipping away. Blocks of rock above the scree crumble and tumble down. The plants that survive best are those that have plenty of runners and shoots which simply grow through every new fall of rock. They become a network that eventually enables the mobile mass of rock to establish itself and become stable.

Coarse soils where fine crumbs of earth are few and humus content is low can be divided into two categories: moving and sedentary soils. The size of the crumbs is of little relevance. Whether we are dealing with coarse or fine screes, pebble or slag heaps, or dunes, moving and sedentary soils can be recognized by their vegetation and its growth. The general rule is that sedentary soils produce denser growth and show more resemblance to wastelands or grassland vegetation, except that the plants that grow there demand less humus and nutrients.

Further changes in the vegetation in these habitats are caused by the mineral composition of the coarse material. Limestone and silicates offer different conditions as rock, scree and sand. In the case of limestone, useful nutrients effloresce from the rock itself. It can happen that two types of one species are only marginally different in their form, but one grows on limestone and the other on acid rock.

On steep slopes the ground is rapidly washed away so that the only soil available is undeveloped and 'mountain fresh'. It does not contain any humus and is not a good tilth, so the kind of plants which tend to grow on it are pioneer plants. These experience the same difficulties in becoming established as they would on scree.

24

IDENTIFYING PLANTS

Flower colour

Decide between white, yellow, red, blue, green or brown. Where flowers have several colours, choose the dominant one. A white flower with red dots will be found in the white flower section. In 90 per cent of cases, establishing flower colour is easy but there are two cases where opinions differ as to which colour dominates. Since the colour of the flower may vary slightly in shade from specimen to specimen it is wise to look up both colour sections. The borderline cases are (1) red-violet/blue-violet (p. 305); and (2) light yellow/creamy white/pale green (p. 2).

Flowers which have just started blooming often still bear the greenish bud colour, or have not quite attained their full colour. Flowers which are dying sometimes fade in colour. It is therefore wise to go by the colour of the flower in bloom.

In cold weather the petals often turn red or blue in the bud stage. Sometimes this is just a hint of colour, at other times it is a very intense colouring. The colour change is, however, always restricted to the outside, or underside, so always go by the inner surface.

Flower form

Next decide on the form. The flower will be either clearly bilaterally symmetrical (flower can be divided into identical halves along one line of symmetry only) or more or less radially symmetrical (flower is circular and can be divided into identical halves along any diameter). In the latter case, count how many petals the flower has, or if it has none how many petal tips the corolla displays. The radially symmetrical flowers are divided into three groups:

 Radially symmetrical flowers with up to 4 petals. There are flowers with 3 or 4 petals (2 petals is very rare). Sometimes the petal tips themselves are somewhat unevenly distributed (Speedwell, Mint, for example) so that strictly speaking the flower is not entirely radially symmetrical. Plants with this kind of flower are listed in this section because the amateur will hardly recognize the bilateral symmetry on small flowers.

 Radially symmetrical flowers with 5 petals. Here it should be remembered that certain flowers have 5 split or deeply divided petals (Splendid Pink, and Lesser Stitchwort respectively) which might on superficial examination resemble flowers with many more petals.

 Radially symmetrical flowers with more than 5 petals. This group includes many flowers with more than 6 petals, some even with 7 or 8. The family *Asteraceae (Compositae)* is included as the layman generally considers the capitulum, which is made up of tiny florets, as one flower head. Those with more experience should therefore look up *Asteraceae (Compositae)* in this particular group.

There is only one group of bilaterally symmetrical flowers. Here the number of petals is irrelevant. The corolla is usually bell-shaped or features an upper or lower lip and is thus clearly identifiable as bilateral (campanulate, papilionaceous, labiate, violaceous).

 Woody plants. Only a selection of ligneous plants are listed. They are grouped together at the end of each colour block.

The pages on which each classification can be found are given in the contents list on p. 5, or, even easier, use the key on the next 4 pages. On each of these pages there are photographs of 6 flowers in each colour band which are typical of each of the flower form groups:
    p.28: radially symmetrical flowers with up to 4 petals
    p.29: radially symmetrical flowers with 5 petals
    p.30: radially symmetrical flowers with more than 5 petals
    p.31: bilaterally symmetrical flowers.
What is being illustrated in these 4 pages is flower form, unconnected to flower colour. In the central section of each of the following 4 pages is a 6-part colour band.

Each of the 6 colour blocks contains page numbers which refer to the plant identification section. Refer to the appropriate page numbers for the plant of the particular colour and form of the specimen to be identified.

The page numbers following the ligneous symbol in each colour block refer to trees or bushes with flowers of each form and flower colour.

PICTORIAL KEY
AND PLANT
IDENTIFICATION

 Radially symmetrical flowers with up to 4 petals

| pp. 32–47 | pp. 118–31 | pp. 206–13 | pp. 292–303 | pp. 350–65 |
| pp. 104–5 | pp. 198–9 | pp. 282–5 | | pp. 378–9 |

 Radially symmetrical flowers with 5 petals

pp. 48–77	pp. 132–55	pp. 214–37	pp. 304–21	pp. 366–9
pp. 106–16	pp. 200–1	pp. 286–90		pp. 379–81

 Radially symmetrical flowers with more than 5 petals

pp. 78–93	pp. 156–77	pp. 238–51	pp. 322–9	pp. 370–1
	p. 202	p. 291		

 Bilaterally symmetrical flowers

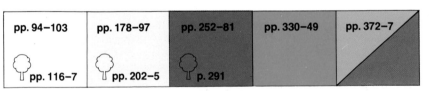

pp. 94–103	pp. 178–97	pp. 252–81	pp. 330–49	pp. 372–7
pp. 116–7	pp. 202–5	p. 291		

Water Plaintain
Alisma plantago-aquatica
Water Plaintain family
Alismataceae

June–Aug.   20–100 cm   M; ♃

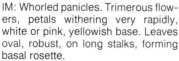

IM: Whorled panicles. Trimerous flowers, petals withering very rapidly, white or pink, yellowish base. Leaves oval, robust, on long stalks, forming basal rosette.
H: Margins of stagnant or slow-flowing waters, in reed beds and sedge, also in ditches. Frequently indicator of muddy ground rich in nutrients. Throughout most of Britain.
AI: Similar to some closely related but much rarer species, which are distinguished by their broad leaves and their habitat: Narrow-leaved Water Plantain (*Alisma lanceolatum*), narrow leaves; Ribbon-leaved Water Plantain (*Alisma gramineum*), leaves ribbon-like, submerged, protected species; both aquatic plants.

Arrowhead
Sagittaria sagittifolia
Water Plaintain family
Alismataceae

July–Aug.   30–90 cm   M; ♃

IM: Erect stem, triangular in cross-section with whorled panicles. Flowers large, up to 2 cm wide, unisexual, the upper ones male, the lower ones female (usually with noticeably shorter stalks). Base of petals has violet tinge. Leaves all basal, some ribbon-like and submerged, some long-stalked, erect with arrow-shaped blade.
H: In reed-beds in still or slow-flowing waters. Likes water rich in nutrients. Local in England, rarer in the North.
AI: The shallow water version develops ribbon-like leaves and petiolate leaves; in deep water only the ribbon-like leaves are present. These are absent on the (stunted) land version.

Water Soldier
Stratiotes aloides
Frog-Bit family
Hydrocharitaceae

June–Aug. 15–50 cm M; ♃

IM: Leaves robust, stiff, triangular in cross-section, long and narrow, margin with spiny teeth. They form a thick funnel-shaped rosette which is usually submerged. Many offshoots. Flowers very large, up to 4 cm wide, males on long stems coming from leaf axils, encircled by a white spathe, females sessile.
H: In lakes, still creeks, ponds and ditches. Mainly floating in the water which must be rich in nutrients but deficient in chalk. Scattered and very local, mainly in eastern England.
AI: Male and female flowers on separate plants. Only female flowers produced in Britain.

Common Frogbit
Hydrocharis morsus-ranae
Frog-Bit family
Hydrocharitaceae

July–Aug. 15–30 cm M; ♃

IM: Plant which floats on water surface. Leaves rounded and long-stalked, heart-shaped at base of stalk, tough, leathery. Flowers one-sexed; males usually in threes, long-stalked, approx. 3 cm wide; female smaller, solitary, short-stalked.
H: In still or slow-flowing waters and in ditches. Likes shady water, low in chalk and not too cool. Scattered throughout England and Wales, sometimes locally common; absent from Scotland.
AI: When not blossoming, similar to even rarer Fringed Water-Lily (*Nymphoides peltata*, flowers yellow, in clusters of 5). However on Frogbit at the base of each leaf-stalk there are 2 large, brownish, oval stipules.

33

Lords and Ladies
Arum maculatum
Arum family
Araceae

April—May   30—45 cm   M; ♃; +

IM: Greenish-white spathe encloses the spadix. Male flowers are above the female. Spadix becomes club-shaped at the top, emits smell of carrion. This feature serves as a fly-trap for the purpose of pollination. Leaves sagittate long-stalked, arrow-shaped and sometimes somewhat spotted.
H: England and Wales, rarer in Scotland. On loose soil rich in nutrients in deciduous or mixed woodland, in thickets and along hedgerows. Prefers not too dry, loamy soil rich in mull. Likes warm situations.
Al: Colour of club can vary from white to violet. Other common names: Cuckoo-pint, Jack-in-the-Pulpit.

Bog Arum
Calla palustris
Arum family
Araceae

June—July   15—30 cm   M; ♃; +

IM: Creeping rhizome below and above ground. Leaves stalked, heart-shaped, leathery, shiny. Flowers in spadix terminating in club-like apex at base of which is large striking spathe. Spadix has coral red berries.
H: In swamps and wet woodlands. Introduced over 100 years ago and now naturalized in a few places in S. England.

May Lily
Maianthemum bifolium
Lily family
Liliaceae

May—June   8—20 cm   M; ♃; +

IM: Usually only 2, stalked, heart-shaped leaves on stem. These are leathery, with entire margin and parallel venation. Flowers small, in a terminal raceme. Fruit globular, red shiny berries (barely 0.5 cm in diameter).
H: Shady woodland, likes thick moss growing over at least surface acidity, low nutrient loamy soil with thick thoroughly decomposed humus layer. Very rare. Only in a few localities in England.

Baneberry
Actaea spicata
Buttercup family
Ranunculaceae

May—June   30—65 cm   D; ♃; +

IM: Straight stem, few branches. Large bi-pinnate leaves with 3 leaflets; when rubbed they give off unpleasant smell. Leaf is divided into hand-shaped toothed segments, margin spiny serrate. Flowers small, in terminal and lateral racemes. Leaves usually extend beyond them.
H: Dense thickets and shady deciduous woodland (especially of Ash), and limestone pavements. Likes porous, well-drained limestone soils. Local in parts of northern England.

White Alpine Poppy
Papaver sendtneri
Poppy family
Papaveraceae

July–Aug.   5–20 cm   D; ♃; (+)

IM: All leaves in basal rosette, asymmetrically pinnate with usually 2 pairs of oval lobes. Flowers solitary on straight stems with no branches; pedicels hairy; flowers approx. 4 cm wide, 2 sepals wither rapidly. Fruit is hairy oval capsule with star-like apex, approx. 1 cm long.
H: Not British. Only in Alpine areas. On scree and rubble in calcareous Alps, rare. Seldom found under 1800 m.
AI: This plant belongs to a whole group of closely related and similar species which grow both on chalk and on gravel scree in Alpine areas. Flowers white, yellow or red.

Garlic Mustard
Alliaria petiolata
Mustard family
Brassicaceae (Cruciferae)

April–June   20–120 cm   D; ☉

IM: Erect stem, leaves alternate, flowers in a false umbel. Lower leaves long-stalked, kidney- or heart-shaped, coarsely crenate. Upper leaves heart-shaped to ovoid, broadly toothed. When rubbed all parts of the plant smell strongly of garlic. Fruit is long pod.
H: Hedgerows, margins of woodland, wayside verges, scree, rubble, walls, fences. Likes nitrogen, needs humidity. Prefers loose, well-drained soils rich in humus. Frequent throughout most of Britain, rare in higher locations.
AI: Also called Hedge Garlic and Jack-by-the-Hedge; scientific name was *A. officinalis.*

Sea Rocket
Cakile maritima
Mustard family
Brassicaceae (Cruciferae)

June–Aug.   15–30 cm   D; ☉

IM: Plant glaucous. Stalk branched, ascending. Leaves fleshy, undivided or deeply lobed, alternate. Flowers scented, a good 0.5 cm wide with approx. 0.5 cm long, nectar-filled tube. Fruit characteristically of two sections, upper mitre-shaped, lower oval-shaped. Section between has pointed protruberances.
H: Occurs along coast, on sandy beaches and in dunes. Can bear high salt concentrations but does not need them to thrive. Rarely spreads inland and does not survive well there.
AI: Plants occur with lilac, purple or white flowers.

Seakale
Crambe maritima
Mustard family
Brassicaceae (Cruciferae)

June–Aug.   40–60 cm   D; ♃

IM: Very branched stem. Lower deciduous leaves large, lobed and wavy, long-stalked, becoming smaller towards the top, the upper ones narrow, linear, short-stalked. Numerous flowers in dense branched clusters. Flowers 1–1.5 cm wide. Fruit is small globular pod. Entire plant glaucous.
H: On sand or between rocks on beach and on primary dunes as far north as Central Scotland. Likes salt; survives flooding and burial in shingle.
AI: It is occasionally grown as a garden vegetable.

Wild Radish
Raphanus raphanistrum
Mustard family
Brassicaceae (Cruciferae)

May–Sept.   20–60 cm   D; ⊙

IM: Erect stem, relatively branched, stiff hairs. Leaves pinnately lobed, upper ones entire, lanceolate. Flowers white or yellow with yellowish or deep violet veins. Sepals erect. Fruit narrow cylindrical; constricted strongly between seeds.
H: Common in fields, also on rubble and in gardens. On light and heavy soil, likes it somewhat acidic.
AI: Plant bears similarities, especially in its yellow version, to Charlock (*Sinapis arvensis*, p. 120), which often grows in the same areas but has horizontal sepals.

Hare's-ear Mustard
Conringia orientalis
Mustard family
Brassicaceae (Cruciferae)

May–July   10–50 cm   D; ⊙

IM: Hairless plant, glaucous. Stalk erect, usually unbranched. Leaves elliptic-ovoid, flattened, clasping stem. Flowers large, in loose umbel; fruit stalked, and spreading, curved and 4-angled.
H: In fields, along wayside and in uncultivated fields. Likes soil not too wet, rich in nutrients and chalk. Casual, quite frequent but rarely becoming established.
AI: Similar: Tower Mustard (*Arabis glabra = Turritis glabra*), another rare introduction. Leaves are pointed and pods are all twisted to one side and down-curved.

Hoary Cress
Cardaria draba
Mustard family
Brassicaceae (Cruciferae)

May–June   30–90 cm   D; ♃

IM: Stem usually branched in inflorescence. Lower leaves stalked, remainder clasping stem, margin entire or serrated. Flowers scented; dense inflorescence. Fruit long-stalked, heart-shaped to globular-inflated pod.
H: Arable land. Prefers exposed chalk areas rich in nutrients in dry warm locations. Throughout England and Wales, spreading.
AI: Often included in Cress family (*Lepidium*) and has many similarities. Its pods are however usually heart-shaped and not split at the tip.

Common Whitlow-grass
Erophila verna
Mustard family
Brassicaceae (Cruciferae)

March–June   3–9 cm   D; ☉

IM: All leaves in basal rosette, lanceolate, margin entire or with 4 teeth. Inflorescence racemose. Petals indented deeply. Fruit is a flat, elliptical pod.
H: On rocks, walls, gravel and railway slag, also among sparse dry turf and semi-dry turf. Mainly spread over warm, not too damp sandy soil with sufficient nutrients. Common, but easily overlooked.
AI: Similar: Shepherd's Cress (*Teesdalia nudicaulis*); strong leaves in rosette shape, pinnatifid. Flower petals of unequal size; throughout Britain. Thale Cress (*Arabidopsis thaliana*), fruit long and thin; in similar habitats throughout Britain.

Cuckoo Flower
Cardamine pratensis
Mustard family
Brassicaceae (Cruciferae)

April–June   15–60 cm   D; ♃

IM: Basal leaves form rosette, pinnate. Leaflets rounded, terminal leaflet usually larger. Stem leaves pinnate with narrow tips. Hollow stem. Inflorescence a raceme. Flowers large, (approx. 1–1.5 cm across), petals longer than sepals. Fruit much longer than wide. Flower colour depends on habitat: white (shady), pink, mauve or deep purple (dry).
H: Mainly in damp meadows and pastures on loamy soil. Indicator of rich ground and ground water. Common.
Al: Similar: Narrow-Leaved Bitter-cress (*C. impatiens*), flowers only 0.5 cm across, petals as long as sepals, whitish; fruit bursts if touched; woods.
40

Hairy Bitter-cress
Cardamine hirsuta
Mustard family
Brassicaceae (Cruciferae)

April–Aug.   7–30 cm   D; ⊙

IM: Basal rosette of pinnate leaflets. Stem usually greatly branched often from base, erect, few or no leaves. Flowers small, under 0.5 cm across, petals considerably longer than sepals. Fruit long thin pod.
H: Bare ground, walls, gardens, newly laid lawns, waysides, hedgerows. Prefers sandy soils, low in chalk but rich in nutrients and not too dry. Likes half-shade. Common.
Al: Similar: Wavy Bitter-cress (*C. flexuosa*); more robust, at least 5 leaves per stem. In damp shady places throughout Britain.

Large Bitter-cress
Cardamine amara
Mustard family
Brassicaceae (Cruciferae)

April–June   10–60 cm   D; ♃

IM: Stalk filled with pulp, slightly pentagonal, usually ascending. Leaves simple or double pinnate. Racemose inflorescence. Flowers large, approx. 1 cm diameter. Anthers purple violet.
H: In streams and ditches, fens and other wet places. Likes wet soil rich in nutrients. Somewhat calcifugous. Scattered throughout Britain up to heights of about 500 m in Scotland. Woodland in N. Europe.
AI: Similar, and often confused with: True Watercress (*Nasturtium officinale*, see right), with hollow stem and yellow anthers. Makes sharper but not so bitter 'wild' salad.

Watercress
Nasturtium officinale
Mustard family
Brassicaceae (Cruciferae)

May–Oct.   10–38 cm   D; ♃

IM: Stem hollow, ascending, lower part often prostrate with roots; sometimes submerged. Very lowest leaves divided into 3 leaflets, upper leaves alternate, pinnate, terminal leaflet usually larger. Flowers in clusters; anthers yellow.
H: In springs, ditches and streams with clear, cool, fast-flowing water. On sandy or muddy ground rich in nutrients. Common throughout lowland Britain but becoming less common as a result of water pollution.
AI: One-rowed Watercress (*N. microphyllum*): more delicate, has longer pods; greenery tinged red-brown in winter; Watercress (*N. officinale*) remains deep green all year round.

Shepherd's Purse
Capsella bursa-pastoris
Mustard family
Brassicaceae (Cruciferae)

All year   7–45 cm   D; ☉ – ☉

IM: Rosette of long dentate basal leaves. Stem branched. Upper leaves margin entire, clasping stem. Flowers in loose racemes. Fruit triangular, slightly heart-shaped, flat, projecting erect. Stalks spreading.
H: Grows well on soils not too dry, not too shady but rich in nutrients. In gardens, fields, on grassy areas, embankments, along paths, on waste ground. Common throughout Britain.
AI: Through self-pollination many local populations have occurred, so variations common from area to area.

Field Penny-cress
Thlaspi arvense
Mustard family
Brassicaceae (Cruciferae)

May–July   10–60 cm   D; ☉ – ☉

IM: Stem erect, angular, often branched at top. Stem lanceolate, leaves usually broadly toothed, with sagittate base. Flowers small, initially racemose, elongating greatly in fruit. Fruit over 1 cm wide, flat, round, broadly winged, with a deep notch apically. When rubbed the plant smells strongly of leek.
H: Arable land, gardens, waysides and rubbish dumps. Frequent. Likes loose loamy soil rich in nutrients.
AI: Similar: Perfoliate Penny-cress (*T. perfoliatum*); more delicate, stem smooth, leaves usually have margin entire. Likes calcareous soils and confined to a few places in Midlands, though occurs as a casual elsewhere.

Round-leaved Penny-cress
Thlaspi rotundifolium
Mustard family
Brassicaceae (Cruciferae)

July–Sept.   5–15 cm   D; ♃

IM: Stem creeping, producing erect or ascending flowering shoots which bear many leaves. Leaves glaucous, ovoid, margin entire or serrate. Flowers in compressed corymbs. Fruit oval, somewhat flattened, slightly winged at edge, approx. twice as long as wide.
H: Not British. Only in Alpine areas over 1000–1500 m.
AI: Prevalent form is distinguished by its blue-tinged corolla with darker veins. White-flowered form is rare.

Water Chestnut
Trapa natans
Water Chestnut family
Trapaceae

July–Aug.   50–300 cm   D; ☉

IM: Stem submerged, floating rosette of many rhomboid, leathery and spreading leaves. Longer leaf-stalks have hollow swelling below the blade. Single flowers in leaf axil, easily overlooked, very perishable. Fruit plus woody sepals forms thorn-bearing 'nut' 2–4 cm wide.
H: Not British. Mostly planted. In stagnant waters rich in nutrients, low in chalk. Rare, but where it occurs it is usually in large numbers. Often planted but rarely thrives.
AI: The many forms of this now widespread plant are distinguished by the shape of the nut.

Enchanter's-nightshade
Circaea lutetiana
Willow-herb family
Onagraceae (Oenotheraceae)

June—Aug.   20–70 cm   D; ♃

IM: Stem usually upright, often branched, hairy. Leaves opposite, ovoid-lanceolate, dull, hairy. Terminal racemes. Flowers small, sometimes faintly pink. Peduncles without subtending leaves.
H: In all types of woodland, even in clearings, provided the soil is damp enough. Likes heavy loamy soil rich in nutrients. Common; usually in large numbers.
AI: Similar: the rarer and more delicate Alpine Enchanter's-nightshade (*C. alpina*), with smooth glossy leaves and bristle-shaped bracteoles under flower stems. More common is the hybrid: Upland Enchanter's-nightshade (*C. intermedia*).
44

Thyme-leaved Speedwell
Veronica serpyllifolia
Figwort family
Scrophulariaceae

March—Oct.   10–30 cm   D; ♃

IM: Stalk creeping, ascendent or erect. Leaves round to ovoid, upper ones smaller and narrower, weakly toothed. Flowers single in axils of upper leaves, small, white, with blue-violet veins. One petal smaller than the other three.
H: Fields, paths, riverbanks, heaths, grassy area communities on meadow paths and pastures. Prefers moist, heavy (compressed), loamy soil, deficient in lime but nitrogenous. Widespread.
AI: Subspecies *V. humifusa*, long, creeping, rooting stem; large, blue flowers; occurs locally in damp, mountainous places in Wales, N. England and Scotland.

Buck's-horn Plantain
Plantago coronopus
Plantain family
Plantaginaceae

June–Aug.   5–10 cm   D; ⅄

IM: All leaves in basal rosette, almost entire, coarsely serrate or most usually 1–2 pinnatifid. Usually many flower stems, ascending, with terminal, linear spikes. Flowers very small, stamens extend beyond them.
H: Seashore, dunes, saline meadows. Sometimes only along the littoral; absent from some inland areas. Likes highly compressed, salty, moist (loamy) soil.
AI: Inflorescence is similar on other plantains (see pp. 302, 365), but this type has divided leaves.

Sweet Woodruff
Galium odoratum
Madder family
Rubiaceae

May–June   10–30 cm   D; ⅄

IM: Stem erect, unbranched, quadrangular in cross-section. Leaves lanceolate to elliptic, dark green, in whorls of 6–8. Terminal cymes with funnel-shaped flowers. Releases characteristic hay smell when plant dying down.
H: In all woodlands but clear preference for deciduous forests. Common; but only on soils which are porous, not too dry, rich in nutrients and mull. Usually in large numbers.
AI: The plant was for a long while classed by systematists as *Asperula odorata* from which it got its well-known popular name: that of 'Our Lady's Bedstraw' will not replace it.

45

Wood Bedstraw
Galium sylvaticum
Madder family
Rubiaceae

June–Aug.   30–100 cm   D; ⧠

IM: Stem erect, usually branched, round. Leaves linear-lanceolate, bluish-green, in whorls of 6–8. Flowers in loose projecting panicles. Plant often has reddish tinge, especially on stem parts and leaf ribs.
H: Not British. In deciduous and mixed woodland on calcareous, slightly moist but warm, loamy soil containing mull. Frequent; up to around 1000 m.

Round-leaved Bedstraw
Galium rotundifolium
Madder family
Rubiaceae

June–Sept.   10–25 cm   D; ⧠

IM: Stem prostrate to ascending, thin, quadrangular, rarely branched. Leaves always in whorls of 4, oval to round, short hooked bristles. Few flowers, clustered panicles. Fruit made up of two globular parts, hairy.
H: Not British. Originally in shady coniferous forests in higher altitudes. Likes well moistened rather poor soils, low in lime and with abundant (acidic) humus layer. Often found in the Alps and Mittelgebirge in Germany, otherwise often introduced with young pine trees (and thrives). Only rare in northern Europe nowadays.
AI: In older botanical works the species is still listed under the scientific name of *G. scabrum*.

Cleavers
Galium aparine
Madder family
Rubiaceae

June–Aug.   15–120 cm   D; ♃

IM: Stem quadrangular in cross-section, climbs with the aid of hooked prickles. Leaves linear, cuneate, 6–8 in a whorl (help support stem when climbing), rough. Inflorescence in leaf axils, few flowers, longer than the leaves.
H: In fields, gardens and hedgerows, on rubbish dumps, also in thickets, woodland margins and scrub along river banks. Common. Nitrogen indicator; likes moist loamy soils rich in nutrients.
Al: Similar but much less widespread: Corn Cleavers (*G. tricornutum*). Usually its inflorescences only comprise three flowers and are shorter than the leaves. In cornfields; likes soil containing lime.

Hedge Bedstraw
Galium mollugo
Madder family
Rubiaceae

June–Sept.   25–120 cm   D; ♃

IM: Stem ascending or erect, quadrangular in cross-section, smooth or hairy, usually branched. Leaves narrow, pointed, mostly in whorls of 8. Many-flowered panicle. Tips of flowers rounded with fine point.
H: Meadows, dry grassy slopes, waysides, thickets. Often on rich loamy soil. More or less throughout Britain.
Al: Similar: in wetter habitats: Common Marsh Bedstraw (*G. palustre*) with red anthers, Fen Bedstraw (*G. uliginosum*) with yellow anthers. Both have rough, bristled stem. Common. On poor soil low in lime: Heath Bedstraw (*G. saxatile*) on heaths, moors and in grassy areas — the flower tips are pointed but without a prickle.

47

Pyrenean Bastard Toadflax
Thesium pyrenaicum
Sandalwood family
Santalaceae

June–Sept. 20–60 cm D; ♃

IM: Bushy but without stolons. Stem erect, branched above. Leaves narrow, bluish-green with 3, sometimes 5, veins. Many-flowered panicle; below each blossom 3 small bracts. Small fruit, round-ovoid, short flower remnant at the top.
H: Not British. Sunny forest margins, open woodland, mountain heaths. Found on rather dry and often stony ground containing lime. Scattered but absent in areas where summer is cool and rainfall heavy.
Al: Synonym: (*T. montanum*).

Black Bindweed
Fallopia convolvulus
Dock family
Polygonaceae

July–Oct. 10–100 cm D; ☉

IM: Stem thin, angular, bent or climbing up on other plants; stem and underside of leaves are mealy. Leaves stalked, triangular/arrow-shaped. Blossoms triangular, 2–5 in leaf axils and clustered to form a false spike.
H: Arable fields, wasteland, gardens, thickets. Common. Likes loamy soils, not too dry and rich in nutrients.
Al: Similar: Copse Bindweed (*F. dumetorium*), more robust, 1–2 m, stem smooth. Scattered in moist thickets and hedges. Both previously belonged first to the genus *Polygonum* and then *Bilderdykia*.

Pale Persicaria
Polygonum lapathifolium
Dock family
Polygonaceae

June–Oct.   25–75 cm   D; ☉

IM: Stem erect or ascending in bends, usually richly branched, with thickened nodes. Leaves oval, broadest over the basal third, often with dark spots. Leaf sheath (ochra) membranous, cornet-shaped, the uppermost with short cilia. Flower spikes at ends of branches, many-flowered, white or rarely pink.
H: Weedy places in fields, on banks of rivers and ponds, less common along paths or in water. Likes moisture and plenty of nutrients. Common.
Al: Similar: Redshank (*P. persicaria*, page 214), all leaf sheaths have fringe of cilia, often grow together in similar habitats. Flowers also white but usually pink.

Knotgrass
Polygonum aviculare
Dock family
Polygonaceae

June–Oct.   3–200 cm   D; ☉

IM: Stem prostrate, richly branched, ascending from branch bases. Branches bear leaves up to the apex. Membranous leaf sheath embracing stem. Flowers axillary, single or in small numbers, greenish with white or red edge, small, barely 3 mm long, but numerous.
H: Fields, rubbish tips, wasteland, verges, roadsides. Very common everywhere. Nitrogen indicator.
Al: Often overlooked, but cannot be mistaken. An aggregate of different species in differing habitats. The true *P. aviculare* is commonest.

Chickweed
Stellaria media
Pink family
Caryophyllaceae

Jan.–Dec.   5–40 cm   D; ☉

IM: Stem prostrate, much branched, round, hairs in single longitudinal row down each internode. Leaves ovoid, opposite, lower ones petiolate. Flowers few in each axil. Petals usually as long as sepals, deeply indented at tip.
H: Fields, gardens, rubbish tips, path verges, also in woods. Likes well-moistened, nitrogenous (over-fertilized) soils. Very common.
AI: A very variable species showing considerable range of size, hairiness, size and number of petals and seed characters.

Lesser Stitchwort
Stellaria graminea
Pink family
Caryophyllaceae

May–Aug.   20–90 cm   D; ♃

IM: Stem quadrangular, brittle, ascending or scrambling: climbs with help of out-spread leaves. These are narrow linear-lanceolate, opposite, grass-green. Terminal, branched cymes. The 5 petals cleft almost to the base, about as long as the calyx.
H: Prefers grassy habitats: meadows, pastures, banks, less common along edges of fields, pathways and thicket margins. Likes calcifugous, acid soils which are not too moist and not too rich in nutrients. Common throughout most of Britain.
AI: Similar: *Stellaria longifolia* = *S. diffusa*). Leaves yellowish-green, rough at the edges; very rare in wet woodlands. Not British.

Greater Stitchwort
Stellaria holostea
Pink family
Caryophyllaceae

April–June 15–60 cm D; ♃

IM: Stem usually erect growing up from bent base, angular. Leaves opposite, sessile, lanceolate, usually stiff and dark green with rough edges. Branched cymes; flowers large, with leafy bracts. Petals cleft approximately to the middle, 1–1.5 cm long.
H: Especially in deciduous and mixed woodland, woodland margins and hedgerows. Likes calcifugous acid loamy soil rich in nutrients and mixed sand, but tolerates wide range of mull soils. Common throughout Britain.
Al: Distant resemblance; Marsh Stitchwort (*S. palustris*); petals 0.5–1 cm, up to twice as long as calyx, cleft almost to the base. Leaves thickish, glaucous with smooth edges. Marshes; scattered.

Wood Stitchwort
Stellaria nemorum
Pink family
Caryophyllaceae

May–June 15–60 cm D; ♃

IM: Stem weak ascending, round, with soft hairs all round, very brittle. Often has long creeping runners. Leaves opposite, heart-shaped to ovoid, lower ones petiolate. Petals about twice as long as sepals, deeply bifid. 3 styles.
H: Shady deciduous woods, and streams. Likes marshy ground soaked in ground water and rich in nutrients. Scattered, in the north and west of Britain.
Al: Similar: Water Chickweed (*Myosoton aquaticum*), scattered on river banks, in moist woodland, marshes and fens. Flower has 5 styles.

Field Mouse-ear
Cerastium arvense
Pink family
Caryophyllaceae

April–Aug.   10–30 cm   D; ♃

IM: Plant covered with short hairs, and somewhat sticky and glandular. Stem base gnarled, stem erect; barren stems prostrate. Leaves opposite, linear-lanceolate, small-leaved short shoots rooted at the nodes. Terminal cymes. Flowers large; petals about 1 cm long, much longer than the sepals, bifid at tip.
H: Grassland, field margins, path verges, dry banks. Likes calcareous sandy soils low in nitrogen and especially warm. Scattered throughout Britain, mainly in the east.
Al: Similar: Snow-in-summer (*C. tomentosum*). White woolly-haired. Rockery plant, often growing wild.

52

Common Mouse-ear
Cerastium fontanum ssp. *triviale*
Pink family
Caryophyllaceae

April–Sept.   10–45 cm   D; ♃

   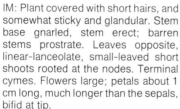

IM: Stem prostrate or erect, densely hairy, rarely glabrous. Leaves narrow-ovoid, opposite. Petals deeply bifid, as long as calyx (around 0.5 cm). Plant usually dark green.
H: Meadows, pastures, waysides, dunes and shingle, less common on fields. Widespread; up to around 1200 m in Scotland. Usually on well-moistened (sandy) loamy soil, rich in nutrients.
Al: Earlier names: *C. caespitosum, C. triviale, C. holosteoides*. Hard to distinguish other species: Sticky Mouse-ear (*C. glomeratum*), arable fields — Little Mouse-ear (*C. semidecandrum*) and Grey Mouse-ear (*C. brachypetalum*) in dry turf.

Corn Spurrey
Spergula arvensis
Pink family
Caryophyllaceae

June–Aug.   7–40 cm   D; ☉

IM: Stem ascending to erect, round, swollen nodes. The leaves are opposite and appear verticillate through short shoots growing out of leaf axils. Linear to awl-like, longitudinal furrow beneath. Forked flower clusters, petals entire, rarely with pink tinge.
H: Root-crop fields, rubbish tips, verges. Scattered, sometimes abundant. Sand indicator; likes acid soil which is not too dry, rich in nutrients, low in lime.
Al: Some types which grow up to 1 m high are cultivated as fodder plants. Similar: *S. pentandra*; leaves without furrow; heaths, sandy areas; rare introduction in Sussex.

Three-nerved Sandwort
Moehringia trinervia
Pink family
Caryophyllaceae

May–June   10–40cm   D; ☉

IM: Stem prostrate, ascending or erect, round, covered with downy hairs. Leaves ovoid, pointed, usually with 3 parallel veins (more rarely 5); opposite, lower ones petiolate. Flowers petiolate, emerging from leaf axils; petals shorter than calyx, sometimes only four petals.
H: All types of woodland but preferably deciduous. Likes moist, loamy soil, superficially acid and rich in nutrients; calcifugous. Frequent.
Al: Similar: Chickweed (*Stellaria media*, see p. 50) with its forest versions. Can be distinguished by its single line of stem hairs.

White Campion
Silene alba
Pink family
Caryophyllaceae

May–Sept.   30–100 cm   D; ☉–♃

IM: Stem erect, forked branching. Leaves opposite, ovoid. Entire plant short-haired to glandular-downy. Three flowers in each leaf axil. Calyx cylindrical-inflated. Petals deeply cleft into two. Flowers unisexual.
H: Weed communities in fields, wasteland, thickets and hedgerows. Likes warmth and nitrogen. Common. Up to 400 m in Scotland.
Al: Synonym: *Melandrium album.* Similar: Night-flowering Catchfly (*S. noctiflorum*); flowers hermaphrodite, petals yellow beneath, pink above, inrolled during the day, only 3 (not 5) styles. Local in sandy arable fields.

Nottingham Catchfly
Silene nutans
Pink family
Caryophyllaceae

May–July   25–80 cm   D; ♃

IM: Stem erect, soft hairs towards the base, glandular-sticky at the top. Leaves opposite, narrow lanceolate, lower ones spatulate, petiolate. Panicles drooping. Calyx gamosepalous, cylindrical to funnel-shaped, with 10 longitudinal veins. Petals deeply cleft. Only spread out in the evening.
H: Dry places, rocks, cliffs, edges of fields. Local. Usually on poor, dry-warm, porous and often stony soil. Woodland in N. Europe.
Al: Similar: Forked Catchfly (*S. dichotoma*); inflorescence clearly two-forked. Frequent as a casual in fields, on balks, rubbish tips and railway embankments.

Bladder Campion
Silene vulgaris
Pink family
Caryophyllaceae

June–Aug.   25–90 cm   D; ⚄

IM: Glaucous, usually glabrous plant. Stem erect to ascending. Leaves opposite, ovoid to lanceolate, pointed. Loose cymes. Calyx gamosepalous, pale, inflated, with a network of 20 longitudinal veins. Main veins usually reddish or blue-green. Petals deeply cleft.
H: Fields, waysides, rocks, dry turf, and thickets. Likes warmth, mainly on calcareous soils rich in nutrients. Common throughout most of Britain, less in the north.
AI: Synonyms: *S. inflata, S. cucubalus.*

Soapwort
Saponaria officinalis
Pink family
Caryophyllaceae

July–Sept.   30–90 cm   D; ⚄; (+)

IM: Leaves opposite, broadly ovoid on erect stem which is often tinged with red. Flowers in dense clusters on main stem and its branches. Petals flat, extending from long cylindrical calyx, slightly notched at tip, each with 2 small teeth in the throat of the corolla.
H: Frequent. A plant of hedgerows and waysides, typically near habitation where it has probably escaped from cultivation. Genuinely wild plants occur next to river banks and in weedy places on porous soil moistened by ground water, further away from bank.
AI: Often white and pink versions in same habitat.

Christmas Rose
Helleborus niger
Buttercup family
Ranunculaceae

Jan.–April   10–30 cm   D; ♃; +

IM: Flowers single; strong round stem with 1–3 scale-like bracteoles. Basal leaves leathery, evergreen, palmate; long petioles. Flowers large, approx. 5–10 cm across, after end of flowering period turn green or reddish.
H: Not British. In mixed woodland or pure coniferous forests (pine) in mountains. Likes stony ground rich in humus with sufficient lime and nutrients. Very rare. Grows wild only in the eastern Alps in Germany; rarely grows wild from gardens and parks.
AI: In gardens the Southern Alpine type 'Snow Rose' is often grown which has flowers around 10 cm in width.

Narcissus-flowered Anemone
Anemone narcissiflora
Buttercup family
Ranunculaceae

May–Aug.   20–40 cm   D; ♃; +

IM: Stem erect, round, hairy. Whorl of narrowly divided stem leaves towards the tip, subtending 3 to 8 pedicellate flowers. Perianth segments 5–60. Basal leaves long-stalked, divided into 3–5 lobes, margins narrow-toothed; dense hairs.
H: Not British. Semi-dry turf, Alpine tussocks and bushy slopes. Very rare. Only in Schwäbisches Alb and in the Alps. Calcicolous; on well-moistened soils between 700 and 2400 m.
AI: On rocky slopes in the High Alps the variation *dubia* (= *oligantha*) can be found. This has a single flower, is small and glabrous and resembles Wood Anemone (p. 85).

Snowdrop Windflower
Anemone sylvestris
Buttercup family
Ranunculaceae

April—June   5—40 cm   D; ♃; +

   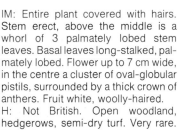

IM: Entire plant covered with hairs. Stem erect, above the middle is a whorl of 3 palmately lobed stem leaves. Basal leaves long-stalked, palmately lobed. Flower up to 7 cm wide, in the centre a cluster of oval-globular pistils, surrounded by a thick crown of anthers. Fruit white, woolly-haired.
H: Not British. Open woodland, hedgerows, semi-dry turf. Very rare. Likes dry-warm soils containing lime.
AI: Similar: Alpine Pasqueflower (*Pulsatilla alpina*, p. 86). Mostly over 5 petals, fruit has tail. Rare under 1000 m.

Aconite-leaved Buttercup
Ranunculus aconitifolius
Buttercup family
Ranunculaceae

May—July   20—120 cm   D; ♃; +

IM: Stem erect, branched. Basal leaves long-stalked. Stem leaves alternate and sessile. Leaves divided into 3—7 lobes. Many flowers. 1—2 cm across, pedicellate.
H: Not British. Wet meadows, banks of streams, marshland round springs, arable land, thickets of high bushes and open canyon forests. Likes damp, nitrogenous (fertilized) slightly acid soils in cool rainy areas. Scattered in mountainous regions up to about 200 m.
AI: Similar (usually only as subspecies): Large White Buttercup (*R. platanifolius*). Leaf lobes similar, central lobe not stalked; flower stems glabrous. More common in shady places (woodland, thicket). 57

River Water-crowfoot
Ranunculus fluitans
Buttercup family
Ranunculaceae

June–Aug.   1–6 m   D; ♃; (+)

IM: Only in running water. Stem low floating, usually without floating leaves. Submerged leaves alternate, repeatedly subdivided into thin wisps; 7–30 cm long, stretched out parallel. Single flowers, on long stalks above the water, 2–3 cm in diameter.
H: Often en masse in clean flowing water containing much oxygen, up to 3 m water depth. Scattered throughout Britain except far north. Likes water to be none too warm.
Al: Often placed in the subgenus *Batrachium* with other white-flowering species of the Buttercup family.

Common Water-crowfoot
Ranunculus aquatilis
Buttercup family
Ranunculaceae

May–June   2.5–120 cm   D; ⊙/♃; (+)

IM: Usually has floating leaves. Submerged leaves alternate, divided into many short wisps. Single flowers, long-stalked, often 1–3 cm across.
H: In stagnant or only slow-flowing water, rich in nutrients (also slightly polluted) up to 1 m or so water depth. Calcifugous. Scattered throughout lowland regions; rarely on land.
Al: Very many variations; also closely related species. Thread-leaved Water-crowfoot (*R. trichophyllus*), flowers less than 1.5 cm wide, usually no floating leaves, repeatedly divided into groups of 3 segments. Similar: Fan-leaved Water-crowfoot (*R. circinatus*); calcicolous, leaves all submerged spread out into flat semi-circle or wheel shape.

Round-leaved Sundew
Drosera rotundifolia
Sundew family
Droseraceae

June–Aug.   6–25 cm   D; ♃

  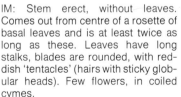

IM: Stem erect, without leaves. Comes out from centre of a rosette of basal leaves and is at least twice as long as these. Leaves have long stalks, blades are rounded, with reddish 'tentacles' (hairs with sticky globular heads). Few flowers, in coiled cymes.
H: On high moors, less common in fens and lower moorland. Restricted to suitable peaty areas, but when it occurs, it often does so in large numbers.
Al: Together with the following species it forms the hybrid *D. obovata*, recognizable by its ovoid leaf blades and the central inflorescence stalks which extend far beyond the rosette of leaves. Sterile. Very rare.

Great Sundew
Drosera anglica
Sundew family
Droseraceae

July–Aug.   10–30 cm   D; ♃

IM: Stem erect, without leaves. Comes out from the centre of a rosette of basal leaves and is up to twice as long as these. Leaves petiolate, leaf blades linear-oblong, with reddish tentacles (hairs with sticky globular heads). Few flowers, in coiled cymes.
H: Moist places on heaths, moors, and fenland. Scattered throughout Britain.
Al: Similar: Oblong-leaved Sundew (*D. intermedia*); inflorescence only slightly longer than the leaves, springs from outside the rosette and bends upwards. Drier areas of heath and moorland than other species. Local with a westerly distribution. Compare also *D. obovata* — see left.

59

Grass-of-Parnassus
Parnassia palustris
Saxifrage family
Saxifragaceae

July–Oct.   10–30 cm   D; ♃

IM: Stem angular, erect with terminal inflorescence and one cordiform leaf on the bottom third of the stem and clasping it. Basal leaves petiolate, heart-shaped. Entire plant glabrous. Flowers 1–3 cm wide, with 5 normal anthers and 5 long glandular fringed formations (staminodes — transmuted stamens; to attract insects).
H: Marshland and wet flushes in moorland, in mountainous areas also on moistened detritus. Calcicolous. Widespread, but local though it often occurs in great abundance.
AI: A shorter, leathery-leaved variety occurs in dune slacks, in north-west Britain.

Meadow Saxifrage
Saxifraga granulata
Saxifrage family
Saxifragaceae

April–June   10–50 cm   D; ♃

  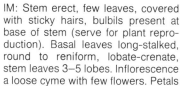

IM: Stem erect, few leaves, covered with sticky hairs, bulbils present at base of stem (serve for plant reproduction). Basal leaves long-stalked, round to reniform, lobate-crenate, stem leaves 3–5 lobes. Inflorescence a loose cyme with few flowers. Petals approx. 1.5 cm.
H: Semi-dry turf, meadows not too damp, grassy slopes, more rarely in light woodland and forest margins. Calcifugous; prefers slightly moist soils rich in nutrients, in lower-lying land. Not usually over 425 m. Local, with easterly distribution.

Livelong Saxifrage
Saxifraga paniculata
Saxifrage family
Saxifragaceae

May–Aug.   10–40 cm   D; ♃

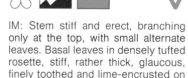

IM: Stem stiff and erect, branching only at the top, with small alternate leaves. Basal leaves in densely tufted rosette, stiff, rather thick, glaucous, finely toothed and lime-encrusted on the edges. Flowers in clusters, often red-spotted.
H: Not British. Rocks, walls, scree and stony ground. Prefers dry-warm locations. Calcicolous.
Al: Older name: *S. aizoon.*

Stone Bramble, Stone Blackberry
Rubus saxatilis
Rose family
Rosaceae

June–Aug.   8–40 cm   D; ⊙

IM: Flowering stem erect, hardly any branches, usually covered with weak prickles. Sterile stems coiled and prostrate to far-creeping with branches which root at the tips. Leaves alternate, petiolate, ternate; leaflets ovoid, margin toothed. Few flowers, in a terminal cyme. Fruit red, bramble-like, but very loose and meagre.
H: In all types of woodland on calcareous soils which are not too dry and contain abundant humus. Local, more common in hilly areas.
Al: Similar: low or creeping versions of the Bramble (*R. fructicosus*, p. 112): stem woody.

Hautbois Strawberry
Fragaria moschata
Rose family
Rosaceae

April—July   10—40 cm   D; ♃

IM: Stem erect, clinging hairs at the top. Leaves ternate, leaflets ovoid, serrate. Cyme with few flowers. Petals pale ivory in colour, margin entire, touching each other. Plant devoid of runners. Fruit (strawberry) greenish to purplish-red and has clinging sepals (hard to remove).
H: Formerly widely cultivated. Reported as an escape in a number of areas but many claims probably erroneous.
Al: Similar: other species of strawberry and Barren Strawberry (see right). All strawberry species easily form hybrids with one another.

Wild Strawberry
Fragaria vesca
Rose family
Rosaceae

April—July   5—30 cm   D; ♃

IM: Flowering stem erect, clinging hairs at the top; runners arching, spreading from the base. Leaves ternate. Leaflets ovoid, serrate margin. Cyme with 3—10 flowers. Petals touch or overlap, with entire margins. Red fruit.
H: All types of woodland, woodland paths, clearings and pastures. Likes rather moist, base-rich soil which is not too shady. Common.
Al: Similar: Hautbois Strawberry (adjacent) and Barren Strawberry (see next page).

Barren Strawberry
Potentilla sterilis
Rose family
Rosaceae

Feb.–May   5–15 cm   D; ♃

IM: Flowering stem, prostrate to ascending, 1–3 flowers, protruding hairs. Leaves ternate, overall similar to strawberry, often bluish-green, hairy. Flowers 1–1.5 cm wide, their petals hardly extend beyond calyx, margin not quite entire at tip, not touching each other.
H: Woodland, thickets, balks, mossy gass pastures. Calcifugous, in drier soils. Common, rarer in the north, reaching to over 700 m.
AI: Synonym: *P. fragariastrum*. Very similar: Wild Strawberry (see left-hand page), note distinguishing features of petals.

White Cinquefoil
Potentilla alba
Rose family
Rosaceae

April–June   5–20 cm   D; ♃

IM: Stem decumbent or more or less erect, few small leaves, usually 3 flowers to each stem. Basal leaves long-stalked, digitate with 5 lobes; lobes lanceolate, serrate at tip, underside covered with dense silver-white hairs. Flowers long-stalked, approx. 2 cm wide.
H: Not British. Open dry woodland, sunny thickets. Rare. Likes warmth.

Goat's-beard Spiraea
Aruncus dioicus
Rose family
Rosaceae

April–July   80–150 cm   D; ♃

IM: Stem stiff erect, glabrous, simple. Leaves up to 0.5 cm long, bi- or tripinnate, when young usually copper-red in colour. Leaflets ovoid, pointed at the tip, double serrate. Panicle up to 50 cm long, many-flowered, usually composes only one sex of flower: male flowers ivory-coloured, around 4 mm wide; female flowers milk-white, aroung 3 mm wide.
H: Not British. Canyon forests, mountain forests, shady banks of steams. Scattered. Likes soils rich in nutrients but low in lime and moist through seepage.
Al: Synonyms: *A. vulgaris, A. sylvestris.*

64

Meadowsweet
Filipendula ulmaria
Rose family
Rosaceae

June–Sept.   60–120 cm   D; ♃

IM: Stem erect, angular, glabrous, often branched at the top. Main stem leaves are numerous, simple pinnate, with 2–5 pairs of large leaflets interrupted by further pairs of much smaller leaflets. Cymose panicle with numerous strongly scented flowers, up to 1 cm wide. Flowers with 6 petals sometimes occur.
H: Marshy meadows, ditches, banks of streams, wet thickets and water meadows. Prefers wet soil rich in nutrients. Common; up to about 1000 m.
Al: Similar: Dropwort (*F. vulgaris*), 8–20 pairs of main leaflets; flowers all white with 6 petals and 6 sepals. Chalky grassland. Widespread but local.

Wood Sorrel
Oxalis acetosella
Wood-Sorrel family
Oxalidaceae

April—May   5—15 cm   D; ♃; (+)

IM: All flowers and leaves long-stalked, basal. Leaves clover-like, ternate with heart-shaped leaflets which are often reddish on the underside. Lower part of peduncle has a pair of scale-like subtending leaves. Petals about 1—1.5 cm long, several times longer than the calyx, fine violet or red veins, with yellow fleck at the base.
H: In hedgerows and all types of woodland on well-moistened, slightly acid and porous soil which is not too heavy or wet. Likes shade. Very common.

Purging Flax
Linum catharticum
Flax family
Linaceae

June—Sept.   5—25 cm   D; ☉ - ☉; +

IM: Stem erect, thin, little or no branching. Stem leaves opposite, entire, narrow oblong, somewhat rough; the upper leaves occasionally alternate. Loose cymes. Petal margins entire, 4—5 mm long.
H: Wet meadows, semi-dry turf, pathways, acid grass meadows. Likes poor soils which are wet in winter and dry in summer. Characteristic of calcareous grassland. Common.
AI: Could be mistaken for a type of Stitchwort (*Stellaria*, p. 50, 51) or Chickweed (*Cerastium*, p. 52), which normally however have cleft petals.

Sanicle
Sanicula europea
Umbellifer family
Apiaceae (Umbelliferae)

May–Sept.   20–60 cm   D; ♃

IM: Stem erect, stiff, sometimes twisted, angular. Few small stem leaves. Basal leaves large, coarse, long-stalked, palmate with 3–5 wide segments. These are in turn lobed and serrate. Compound umbels, the individual small umbels are globular. Flowers occasionally have reddish tinge.
H: Deciduous and mixed woodland. Frequent. Likes wet loamy soil rich in mull. Only found in shady or semi-shady locations. From lowlands to relatively high hilly areas.
AI: The plant was previously used for medicinal purposes and bore a variety of popular names.

Field Eryngo
Eryngium campestre
Umbellifer family
Apiaceae (Umbelliferae)

July–Aug.   30–60 cm   D; ♃

IM: Stem erect, strong, finely furrowed, usually branching in top third. Leaves coarse, light grey-green, net venation and pinnate, thistle-like, with spiny margins. Lower leaves petiolate, upper ones amplexicaule. Almost spherical umbels with narrow or leaf-like, spiny terminal involucres.
H: Dry or semi-dry turf. Likes the warmth, calcicolous. Likes dry, often stony ground in full sunlight. Rare, only in few localities in southern England.

Ground Elder
Aegopodium podagraria
Umbellifer family
Apiaceae (Umbelliferae)

May–July 40–100 cm D; ♃

IM: Stem erect, some branching, furrowed, hollow, few leaves at the top, basal leaves numerous because of subterranean runners, simple or doubly tripartite with large ovoid, deeply serrate leaflets. Compound flat umbels with approx. 15 rays; bracts and bracteoles absent.
H: A common and sometimes troublesome weed of waste places and especially in gardens. Likes nitrogenous soil which is moist with ground water. Widely distributed.
Al: Previously used for medicinal ·ır- poses: Goutweed, Herb G. Bishop's Weed.

Caraway
Carum carvi
Umbellifer family
Apiaceae (Umbelliferae)

June–July 25–60 cm D; ♃

IM: Stem erect, much branched, leafy, fluted. Leaves bi- or tripinnate with very narrow tips. Stem leaves inflated at base where the lowest pinnae are situated. Compound umbel with 5–10 rays. Bracts and bracteoles absent (sometimes 1).
H: In waste places. Prefers soils which are not too dry but rich in nutrients. Scattered and rather rare.
Al: Similar plants of the Umbellifer family (see next page), but the distinguishing feature of this one is the lowest pinnae which have 'slipped' down the stem.

Cow Parsley
Anthriscus sylvestris
Umbellifer family
Apiaceae (Umbelliferae)

April–June   60–100 cm   D; ☉

IM: Stem erect, branched, furrowed, hollow. Leaves bi- or tripinnate; segments coarsely toothed. Compound umbel with 4–10 rays, bract absent, bracteoles ciliate. Petals notched with an inflated tip.
H: Meadows, meadows with trees, hedges, wayside verges. Prefers slightly wet porous soils with plenty of nutrients. Often in great abundance in meadows fertilized with liquid manure. Very common.
AI: Very similar: Golden Chervil (*Chaerophyllum aureum*); stem solid and usually has red or purple flecks. Meadows, in several localities in Scotland.

Hogweed
Heracleum sphondylium
Umbellifer family
Apiaceae (Umbelliferae)

June–Sept.   50–200 cm   D; ☉

IM: Stem erect, angular and grooved, thick, covered with stiff hairs. Leaves usually once pinnate, the segments lobed or further divided, with rough hairs, lower leaves petiolate. Compound umbel with 7–20 rays. Bracts absent or few in number. Bracteoles numerous. Marginal flowers with outer petals enlarged.
H: Meadows, banks, woods, damp thickets, water meadows. Prefers damp soils rich in nutrients. Common. Indicator of over-fertilization.

Wild Carrot
Daucus carota
Umbellifer family
Apiaceae (Umbelliferae)

June–Aug.   30–100 cm   D; ☉

IM: Stem erect, often branched, grooved, hairy, solid. Leaves tri-pinnate. Compound umbels, initially resemble bird's nest, becoming flat when flowering and when in fruit they revert to bird's nest shape. Bracts pinnate. Central flower in umbel usually blackish purple ('Blackamoor Flower').

H: Semi-dry turf, meadows, wayside verges, cliffs and dunes. Frequent. Likes the warmth.

AI: Similar: Cambridge Milk-parsley (*Selinum carvifolia*), bract is usually absent; same applies to Greater Burnet-saxifrage and Burnet-saxifrage (*Pimpinella major* and *P. saxifraga*), where the stem leaves are simple pinnate.

Wild Angelica
Angelica sylvestris
Umbellifer family
Apiaceae (Umbelliferae)

July–Sept.   30–200 cm   D; ♃; (+)

IM: Compound umbel with 20–40 rays. Numerous bracteoles, bracts absent or reduced to a few and falling early. Stem strong, hollow, has whitish tinge, basic colour bluish to reddish. Leaves 2–3 pinnate; segments ovoid, serrate margin. Leaf sheaths striking, light-coloured and inflated.

H: Water meadows, banks, damp meadows or thickets and woods in places on soils rich in nutrients near to ground water. Common.

AI: Wild Angelica is one of those plants in the Umbellifer family which have either white or pink flowers (see p. 229).

69

Marsh Pennywort
Hydrocotyle vulgaris
Umbellifer family
Apiaceae (Umbelliferae)

June–Aug.　　1–25 cm　　　D; ♃; (+)

IM: Leaves round, notched along margin. Petiole comes out of middle of leaf underside. Umbels are small, few flowers, from leaf axils. Peduncle decidedly shorter than petiole. Stem long and creeping, 10–50, sometimes 100, cm long.
H: Bogs, marshes, ditches, banks. Likes soils low in lime and moistened by ground water. Frequent, occurring up to about 600 m.

One-flowered Wintergreen
Moneses uniflora
Wintergreen family
Pyrolaceae

June–Aug.　　1–5 cm　　　D; ♃

IM: Solitary flower on leafless stem, drooping. Petals spread out flat; flower around 1.5 cm in diameter, sweet-scented. Leaves in rosette arrangement, evergreen, leathery, rounded, the blade extending somewhat down the short stalks. Exceptionally 2–3 flowers on one stem.
H: Coniferous woodland. Rare. Likes mossy, somewhat acid soil, dry to slightly moist. Restricted to E. Scotland.
AI: Listed under Wintergreens as *Pyrola (=Pirola) uniflora*.

Serrated Wintergreen
Orthilia secunda
Wintergreen family
Pyrolaceae

July—Aug. 2–10 cm D; ♃

IM: Drooping, campanulate flowers in unilateral racemes. Anthers protrude a little beyond the flower, style noticeably so. Stem ascending. Leaves evergreen, leathery-tough, ovoid, pointed, margin finely serrate. Initially the entire cluster of 20–30 flowers droops.
H: Mixed and coniferous woodland. Rather local in higher areas of N. England, Scotland and Wales as high as 800 m.
AI: This plant also included in other genera as; *Ramischia secunda*, *Pyrola secunda* (= *Pirola secunda*).

Round-leaved Wintergreen
Pyrola rotundifolia
Wintergreen family
Pyrolaceae

July—Sept. 20–35 cm D; ♃

IM: Drooping wide campanulate flowers in multilateral raceme. Only the style projects beyond the flower. Stem erect, obtuse-angled. Leaves almost round, stalked, tough-leathery, finely crenate, in basal rosette. Local with strong easterly distribution, being absent from many parts of the west.
H: Mixed and coniferous woodland. Likes moist somewhat acid loamy soil which is low in lime and rich in humus.
AI: Similar species in the same genus of *Pyrola* (= *Pirola*), all rare and growing in woodland: Intermediate Wintergreen (*P. media*), flowers globular (-campanulate), style projecting; Common Wintergreen (*P. minor*), flowers globular, style hidden.

Milkwhite Rock-jasmine
Androsace lactea
Primrose family
Primulaceae

May—July   5–15 cm   D; ♃

IM: Dense rosette of linear-lanceolate leaves. Out of the middle of leafless erect flower stalk with loose terminal umbel with few flowers. Flowers approx. 1 cm wide, with yellow throat and notched petals. Rosettes usually numerous in porous turf.

H: Not British. Limestone fissures in the Alps up to 2200 m. Scattered. Also found on the Schwäbisches Alb.

Water-violet
Hottonia palustris
Primrose family
Primulaceae

May—June   15–40 cm   D; ♃

  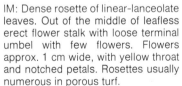

IM: Leaves in whorls/rosettes, pinnate comb-like, usually submerged. Flower stem above water, leafless, erect. Whorls of flowers forming cluster. Flowers approx. 2 cm across with yellow throat, short-stalked, ascending in flower, deflexed in fruit.

H: Stagnant or slow-flowing waters, ponds, ditches. Widespread but local in England, Wales and a few parts of Scotland. Most common in E. England. Prefers soils which are rather poor in nutrients and low in lime and above all likes shallow water.

AI: Occasionally the flowers have a somewhat reddish tinge, especially with the rare flowering deep water types (1–2 m deep), where they are submerged.

Bogbean
Menyanthes trifoliata
Bogbean family
Menyanthaceae

May—July   12–30 cm   D; ♃

           ▽

IM: Leaves divided like Clover, thickish-leathery, on long stalks from a creeping rhizome. Leaflets ovoid, up to 7 cm long. Stem ascending. Dense raceme. Petals have conspicuous hairs on the inner surface, bud usually has red tinge.
H: Bogs, fens and moorland, banks, ditches, ponds; often spreads far out into shallow water. Quite common, sometimes very abundant. Calcifugous; grows up to about 1000 m.
AI: Was an old medicinal plant.

Vincetoxicum
Vincetoxicum hirundinaria
Milkweed family
Asclepiadaceae

May—Aug.   30–120 cm   D; ♃; +

IM: Stem erect, sometimes twining towards the top (see below). Leaves opposite, ovate-cordate, shortly petiolate. Flowers in axillary racemes. Fruit pod-like, with many seeds with hairy heads.
H: Not British. Dry woodland, sunny thickets, balks, rocks and screes. Prefers calcareous stony ground rich in nutrients. Scattered.
AI: The twining version (var. *laxum*) has yellowish-white flowers with green tips. That is the mountain version found in the south of Germany. Synonyms for the entire species are: *V. officinale* and *Cynanchum vincetoxicum*.

73

Hedge Bindweed
Calystegia sepium
Convolvulus family
Convolvulaceae

July–Sept. 1–3 m D: ♃; (+)

IM: Climbing stem. Leaves cordate to sagittate, petiolate, alternate. Flowers funnel-shaped, up to 7 cm long; stems coil in anti-clockwise direction.
H: Hedgerows, waste places, rubbish tips, fences. Frequent on rich soils in mild locations.
AI: Similar species: Large Bindweed (*C. silvatica*), corolla white, about 7 cm long; Hairy Bindweed (*C. pulchra*), corolla about 6 cm, bright pink with light stripes; Sea Bindweed (*C. soldanella*), leaves reniform, flowers pink with 5 white stripes. Found only on dunes, sea shores, rarer in N. Scotland.

Field Gromwell
Buglossoides arvensis
Borage family
Boraginaceae

April–June 10–50 cm D: ☉ - ☉

IM: Plant coarsely hairy. Stem erect, simple or branched. Leaves alternate, lanceolate, with one vein. Flowers small, barely 5 mm wide.
H: Not British. Cornfields, verges of ploughed fields. On sand and loamy soil which is rich in nutrients but not too dry. Scattered, rarely over 1000 m.
AI: Contains a red dye which was previously used as a rouge. Was known for a long time as *Lithospermum arvense*. Similar: Common Gromwell, (*Lithospermum officinale*): flowers more of a dirty or greenish white, leaves have conspicuous lateral veins, plant 0.3–1 m; sunny ridges, thickets; rare.

White Mullein
Verbascum lychnitis
Figwort family
Scrophulariaceae

June–Aug.   50–150 cm   D; ☉

IM: Entire plant covered with fine hairs ('downy'). Stem erect, often somewhat branched, robust. Leaves ovoid, dark green above, lower ones petiolate, upper ones sessile, alternate. Long dense panicle comprising numerous clusters of 2–5 flowers. Flowers 1–2 cm wide, flat. Stamens covered with thick white wool.
H: Dry sunny banks, railway embankments, wayside verges, and waste places. Calcicolous nitrogen indicator. Local in S. England and Wales, casual further north.
Al: Occasionally versions crop up with virtually yellow flowers.

Black Nightshade
Solanum nigrum
Nightshade family
Solanaceae

July–Sept.   30–60 cm   D; ☉ ; +

IM: Stem branched, prostrate to erect, usually glabrous. Leaves ovoid to rhomboid, entire or slightly lobed margin, alternate, stalked. Corolla at first spread out flat then curving backwards, anthers large and inclining towards each other in a cone-shape. Fruit is a berry, green when immature, ripening black.
H: Weedy places in gardens, fields, waste ground, rubbish tips and walls. On loamy soils with abundant nutrients. Common, local in Wales, becoming rarer northwards. Almost absent from Scotland.

Dwarf Elder
Sambucus ebulus
Honeysuckle family
Caprifoliaceae

July–Aug.   60–120 cm   D; ♃; +

IM: Stem stiff and erect, little branching, stout but thoroughly herblike. Leaves opposite, simple or bipinnate. Leaflets of pinnate leaves ovoid, serrate margin. Terminal many-flowered racemes with 3 main branches. Fruits are small, black, globular berries.
H: In waste places and along roadsides. Needs moist soils rich in nutrients. Calcicolous. Very scattered, local in most parts, more so in Scotland.
AI: Also known as Danewort. Similar: Elder (*S. nigra*, see p. 115), usually branched but above all woody.

Three-leaved Valerian
Valeriana tripteris
Valerian family
Valerianaceae

April–June   10–50 cm   D; ♃

IM: Leaves matt, the upper ones three-lobed, the lower ones entire, heart-shaped, toothed. Stem erect, unbranched. Many-flowered paniculate inflorescence.
H: Not British. Rock fissures, scree, stony woodland and thickets in mountainous areas. Calcicolous, needs moisture; likes light and semi-shade. Only found in the area of the Alps and outlying regions (Alb, Black Forest, plateau). Scattered. Up to about 2000 m.

White Bryony
Bryonia cretica ssp. *dioica*
Gourd family
Cucurbitaceae

May–Sept.   0.5–4 m   D; ♃; +

IM: Stem climbs by means of simple tendrils which arise from the side of the deciduous leaves. Leaves coarsely hairy, 5-edged to 5-lobed. Male and female flowers on separate plants, male ones are almost twice as large (approx. 1–2 cm wide), long peduncles. Berries green or whitish when immature, turning red when fully ripe.
H: Paths, fences, walls, hedges, woodland margins. Prefers calcareous soils, not too dry but rich in nutrients in warm location. Scattered but locally common in the south, rare in the north. Absent in C. and N. Scotland.

Spiked Rampion
Phyteuma spicatum
Bellflower family
Campanulaceae

July–Aug.   30–80 cm   D; ♃

IM: Flowers in cylindrical heads, curled up (like a claw) before blossoming. Plant glabrous. Stem erect, simple. Leaves alternate: basal leaves have long stalks, virtually as wide as they are long, cordate; the upper ones narrow ovoid, sessile.
H: Deciduous and mixed woods and thickets. Prefers porous soils which are not too dry but rich in nutrients and containing mull. Rare. Only recorded from Sussex.

False Helleborine
Veratrum album
Lily family
Liliaceae

June–Aug.   50–150 cm   M; ♃; +

IM: Thick, stiff, erect stem with alternate leaves, the undersides covered with downy hairs. Many panicles, terminal, many-flowered. Often over 0.5 m long. Flowers 1–1.5 cm wide.
H: Not British. Frequent in Alpine pastures, rarer in fenland and water meadows. Nitrogen indicator, likes lime. Only in the Alps and outlying areas up to the Mittelgebirge.
AI: Flowers of Alpine variety, ssp. *album* are white inside, greenish outside. Plus, rare, but in outlying regions of Alps common, ssp. *lobelianum*: flowers more or less greenish. Very similar but does not flower: Great Yellow Gentian (*G. lutea*, p. 152) with opposite smooth leaves; also not British.

Star-of-Bethlehem
Ornithogalum umbellatum
Lily family
Liliaceae

April–June   10–30 cm   M; ♃

IM: Loose raceme on stiff stem. Pedicel up to 10 cm long. Petals approx. 2 cm long and at least 4 (to 8) mm wide with green stripe down the back. The grass-like basal leaves with the white central stripe appear only in autumn.
H: Grassy areas. Local in England, more so in Wales and Scotland. Prefers porous loamy soil rich in nutrients in light or semi-shady locations.
AI: Similar: Drooping Star-of Bethlehem (*O. mitans*). Taller, inflorescence unilateral, flowers drooping. Very local in E., C. and N. England.

Branched St. Bernard's Lily
Anthericum ramosum
Lily family
Liliaceae

St. Bernard's Lily
Anthericum liliago
Lily family
Liliaceae

June—Aug.   30—80 cm   M; ♃

May—June   30—70 cm   M; ♃

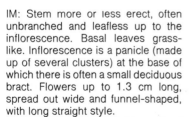

IM: Stem more or less erect, often unbranched and leafless up to the inflorescence. Basal leaves grass-like. Inflorescence is a panicle (made up of several clusters) at the base of which there is often a small deciduous bract. Flowers up to 1.3 cm long, spread out wide and funnel-shaped, with long straight style.
H: Not British. Dry turf, light woodland and thickets. On sunny calcareous soils. Rare, but usually occurs in abundance. Up to over 1500 m.
AI: Sometimes (stunted) varieties occur with cluster-like inflorescence.

IM: Stem erect to ascending, usually unbranched and rarely bears leaves. Basal leaves grass-like, inflorescence a simple raceme. Flowers 1.5—2 cm long, funnel-shaped. Style bent, twisted upwards, no longer than the petals.
H: Not British. Dry turf, light woodland and thickets. Usually on sunny warm ground, low in lime. Rare; absent in the Alps, otherwise up to over 1200 m.
AI: Very rare in habitats rich in minerals and when it grows in well-fertilized gardens the lower part of the inflores-cence has short branches.

Ramsons
Allium ursinum
Lily family
Liliaceae

April–June   10–45 cm   M; ♃

IM: When the plant is rubbed it gives off a garlic smell which is also recognizable even at a distance. Only 2 (or sometimes 3) leaves, ovate-lanceolate and with short stalk. Many-flowered false umbels with obtuse triangular stem, before flowering is enclosed in pale-coloured sheath (the spathe) shaped like narrow onions.
H: Woods and shady places. Likes loose, moist soil containing plenty of humus and nutrients. Often forms dense and diffuse stands.

Streptopus amplexifolius
Lily family
Liliaceae

May–July   40–100 cm   M; ♃; +

IM: Stem slightly zig-zag in shape, erect. Leaves alternate, oval with heart-shaped base clasping the stem. Flowers deeply divided into 6 segments, solitary in leaf axils, drooping under the respective leaf with their bent and jointed pedicels. Fruit: red berries.
H: Not British. Mountain forests and heaths, Alpine thickets. Grows on moist, shady soils containing acid humus. Frequent in the Alps, rare in the Mittelgebirge; hardly found under 700 m.
Al: Similar: Solomon's-seal (*Polygonatum multiflorum*, see next page), with straight, often hanging stem and leaves narrower at base.

Solomon's-seal
Polygonatum multiflorum
Lily family
Liliaceae

May–June   30–80 cm   M; ⁲⵲; +

IM: Stem round, usually hanging a little. Leaves alternate, elliptical, sessile, narrower at base. Often resemble wings stretched out to both sides and pointing slightly upwards. Axillary drooping racemes with 2–5 narrow, funnel-like flowers. Berries globular, blue-black.
H: In woods, especially under deciduous trees. Local in England and Wales, perhaps naturalized in Scotland. Prefers loose, calcareous loamy soil, rich in humus.
AI: Similar: Angular Solomon's-seal (*Polygonatum odoratum = officinale*). Stem angular, flowers usually solitary. Sunny woodland. Very local in N. and W. England and Wales.

Whorled Solomon's-seal
Polygonatum verticillatum
Lily family
Liliaceae

June–July   30–80 cm   M; ⁲⵲; +

IM: Stem thickish, stiff and erect, angular, glabrous. Leaves linear-lanceolate, in whorls of 3–6. Tankard-shaped hanging flowers in leaf axils. Berries first red, when ripe black-blue, globular.
H: Mixed woods in high locations. Very rare, in N. England and S. Scotland only.

Fritillary
Fritillaria meleagris
Lily family
Liliaceae

April—May   20—50 cm   M; ♃; +

IM: Stem erect, with 3—6 very narrow deciduous leaves; these are grooved and blue-green. Flowers solitary (rarely in pairs), drooping, campanulate, up to 4 cm long and 2 cm wide, white and purple chequered like a chess-board, rarely creamy.

H: Very local, in low-lying water meadows rich in nutrients, often flooded in spring. S., E. and C. England.

Al: Often cultivated in gardens and then sometimes escaping. Formerly quite widespread but now disappearing.

Lily-of-the-valley
Convallaria majalis
Lily family
Liliaceae

May—June   8—20 cm   M; ♃; +

IM: Usually 2 (more rarely 1 or 3) short-stemmed basal leaves, ovate-lanceolate, fine bow-shaped veins, long sheath. Flowering stem little longer than the leaves, erect, with unilateral terminal raceme with few flowers. Flowers drooping, bell-shaped, with 6 tips curved outwards. Fruit is a globular red berry.

H: Dry woodland, especially where there are deciduous trees. Likes calcareous soils rich in humus in warm locations. Local but quite widespread in England, less so in Wales and Scotland. Has an easterly distribution.

Al: Popular spring flower often cultivated for the delicate fragrance of the flowers.

Snowdrop
Galanthus nivalis
Daffodil family
Amaryllidaceae

Jan.–March   15–25 cm   M; ♃; (+)

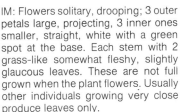

IM: Flowers solitary, drooping; 3 outer petals large, projecting, 3 inner ones smaller, straight, white with a green spot at the base. Each stem with 2 grass-like somewhat fleshy, slightly glaucous leaves. These are not full grown when the plant flowers. Usually other individuals growing very close produce leaves only.
H: Deciduous and mixed woodland. Requires soil saturated in ground water and rich in nutrients and mull. Local. Often escapes from gardens and grows wild, becoming naturalized in many places.

Spring Snowflake
Leucojum vernum
Daffodil family
Amaryllidaceae

Feb.–April   15–20 cm   M; ♃; +

IM: Stem has 1–2 flowers. Flowers drooping, 2–3 cm long; all 6 petals identical, with yellow-green fleck at the tip. Leaves grass-like, bright green, often longer than the peduncle at flowering time.
H: Damp hedges and scrub. Prefers loamy soil rich in nutrients and mull. Very rare, wild only in two places in W. England but often cultivated and many escape.
AI: Similar plant is the related Summer Snowflake (*L. aestivum*), with 3–6 flowers per peduncle; flowers around May. Very local in S. England.

Spring Crocus
Crocus vernus
Iris family
Iridaceae

March—April 5–15 cm M; ♃

IM: Leaves grass-like with white middle stripe appearing with the flowers. Flowers have narrow petals, at least 4 times as long as they are wide. Flowers only a little hairy in their throats.
H: Meadows and fields. Local in England and a very few places in Scotland and Wales. Likes calcareous loamy soil, rich in nutrients and moist in the spring.
Al: The flowers can be white (ssp. *albiflorus*). Various species of spring-flowering Crocus are cultivated and may escape or even persist in old abandoned gardens.

White Water-lily
Nymphaea alba
Water-lily family
Nymphaeaceae

July—Aug. 0.5–2.5 cm D; ♃; (+)

IM: Large round floating leaves with deep heart-shaped indentation on rope-like stalk. Flowers have many petals, wide open, 10–20 cm across. Stamens yellow.
H: Stagnant or slow-flowing warm waters, containing some nutrients. Frequent in suitable habitats.
Al: In cooler (moorland) lakes poor in nutrients the subspecies *occidentalis* is found, its flowers 5–10 cm wide. Found in N. Scotland, rare. Occasionally red-flowering ornamental varieties are planted out. The Yellow Water-lily (*Nuphar luteum*, p. 132) has similar leaves but without the transverse links between the lateral veins.

Wood Anemone
Anemone nemorosa
Buttercup family
Ranunculaceae

March–May   6–30 cm   D; ⚁; +

IM: The flowers emerge individually out of a whorl composed of three, three-lobed leaves about two-thirds of the way up the stem. Flower 1.5–4 cm wide, glabrous or slightly hairy, often tinged with red on the outside — like the parts of the stem. Usually only 1 petiolate basal leaf, palmately lobed, appearing after the flowers are over.
H: Woods, especially deciduous ones, thickets. In all but the poorest and wettest soils. Very common, often forming very large colonies.
AI: Variations in size, degree of hairiness, number and colour of petals (tinged reddish, bluish, greenish) can be found.

Spring Pasqueflower
Pulsatilla vernalis
Buttercup family
Ranunculaceae

April–June   5–35 cm   D; ⚁; (+)

IM: Flowers solitary, more or less erect, open to form a bell, outside usually bluish-violet. The stem bears a sheathed whorl of deeply divided bracts. Flower and stem covered with furry layer of hairs, usually golden yellow, more rarely white. Leaves leathery, evergreen, simple pinnate.
H: Not British. Poor sandy turf, open coniferous forests, Alpine mats. Very rare. Prefers porous slightly acid soil containing plenty of humus.
AI: The lowland variety (var. *vernalis*) is robust and its flowers are approx. 4.5 cm wide. The Alpine variety (var. *alpestris*) is stumpy, its flowers around 5.5 cm wide. In between them is the mountain variety (var. *bidgostiana*).

Yellow Alpine Pasqueflower
Pulsatilla alpina
Buttercup family
Ranunculaceae

June–Aug.   10–40 cm   D; ♃; (+)

IM: The flowers are solitary and emerge from a whorl of bracts which sheathes the otherwise leafless stem. Stem is covered with tufts of hair. Flowers 4–7 cm wide. Basal leaves petiolate, tripinnate, the individual sections being bipinnate and toothed. Small fruits have tufted hairy tail, numerous.
H: Not British. Virtually only in limestone Alps. On mountain meadows, stony mats, rocks; also in thickets and pine areas; scattered, rarely under 1500 m.
AI: Only found at a few points in the central European mountain chain; ssp. *albo*, smaller, flowers approx. 3–4 cm across (Vosges, Harz, Riesengebirge, Carpathians); virtually dying out.

Mountain Avens
Dryas octopetala
Rose family
Rosaceae

June–July   2–8 cm   D; ♄

IM: Stem and branches pressed close to the ground, woody. Pedicals erect, approx 2–8 cm long. Usually 8 petals which wither rapidly. Oblong leaves leathery, evergreen, underside white-woolly, notched along margin and rather curled up. Small fruits with long tufted hairy tails borne in clusters.
H: On rocks, scree, in crevices. Scattered and local. Usually on mountains but coming down to sea level in N. Scotland. Calcicolous.

Dropwort
Filipendula vulgaris
Rose family
Rosaceae

May–Aug. 15–18 cm D; ♃; (+)

IM: Stem erect, may be slightly branched at top. Leaves largely basal, simple pinnate; leaflets approx. 2 cm long, serrate, 8–20 pairs of main leaflets per leaf. Many-flowered branched cymose panicle. Flowers usually have 6 petals, more rarely 5.
H: Meadows and grassland, especially on soils which are wet for a time and then dry again for a while. Calcicolous. Widespread but local, may be quite common in some areas; rarer in Scotland.
AI: This is an old medicinal plant. Synonym: *F. hexapetala.*

Chickweed Wintergreen
Trientalis europaea
Primrose family
Primulaceae

June–July 10–25 cm D; ♃

IM: Stem erect, with small, alternate leaves at the base. At the top a lax rosette of 5–6 large ovoid-lanceolate leaves. Flowers solitary on long slender pedicels, up to 1.5 cm across. Corolla deeply divided into 7 lobes.
H: Damp coniferous forests. Prefers poor, acid, marshy-peaty soil. Scattered and local, rarer in the South.
AI: The only plant in our flora where the flowers virtually always have 7 petals. With other species this is only coincidental and also very rare. An example of this is the Wood Anemone (p. 85) but there can hardly be any confusion here.

White Butterbur
Petasites albus
Daisy family
Asteraceae (Compositae)

March–May   10–30 cm   D; ♃

IM: Stout erect stem with light green leaf scales. Flowers in small narrow racemose capitula. Broad leaves appear only towards end of the flowering time; they are petiolate, round/heart-shaped, their underside is covered with white felt and the margins are irregularly spiny serrate.
H: Woodlands, roadsides and waste places. Likes steep slopes and escarpments on saturated soils rich in nutrients. Local, from the Midlands and mid-Wales northwards.
AI: Without inflorescence similar: Butterbur (*P. hybridus*, p. 243): leaves larger, grey-green on underside. Colt's-foot (*Tussilago farfara*, p. 165): leaves smaller, with short, blackish teeth.

Canadian Fleabane
Conyza canadensis
Daisy family
Asteraceae (Compositae)

Aug.–Sept.   8–100 cm   D; ☉ - ☉

IM: Flowers in numerous small capitula forming a panicled inflorescence. Stem erect, with bristly hairs, often branched, leaves alternate. Stem leaves linear-lanceolate, with bristly hairs.
H: Weedy places in yards, railway track gravel, rubble heaps, paths, also on walls and fences. Likes gardens and clearings, too. Quite widespread but local, becoming rare in the north and Scotland. Likes nitrogen and warmth, hence does not do well in mountains.
AI: This plant was introduced around 200 years ago from North America and its former scientific name was *Erigeron canadensis*.

88

Heath Cudweed
Gnaphalium silvaticum
Daisy family
Asteraceae (Compositae)

July–Sept. 8–60 cm D; ♃

IM: Flowers in narrow-ovoid pointed capitula. Bracts grey-green with wide (usually) golden-brown shiny margins. Inflorescence a long, leafy spike. Stem erect, unbranched. Leaves alternate, lanceolate, hairy, white felt on the undersides, the uppersides glabrous.
H: Light woodland, heaths, clearings, woodland ways, dry turf. Prefers soil which is low in lime, superficially acid and not too dry. Widespread and locally common.

Gallant Soldier
Galinsoga parviflora
Daisy family
Asteraceae (Compositae)

May–Oct. 10–75 cm D; ☉

IM: Stem bushy-branching, more or less bare or with only a few short bristles. Leaves oval, pointed, saw-toothed; alternate. Globular capitula arranged in dichasial cymes; on the outside 4–6 white ligulate florets with 3-toothed apex, on the inside yellow-ish disc florets. Stems of capitula covered with short hairs with a few reddish-brown glandular hairs.
H: Root-crop fields, gardens, and waste ground. Prefers porous nitrogenous soil in mild locations (vulnerable to frost). A fairly common weed in S. England.
Al: Similar: Shaggy Soldier (*G. ciliata = quadriradiata*), stem hairy, with spreading glandular and non-glandular hairs.

Scented Mayweed
Camomilla recutita
Daisy family
Asteraceae (Compositae)

June–July   15–60 cm   D; ☉

IM: Flowers in paniculate capitula; on the outside white ligulate florets, on the inside yellow disc florets. Flower receptacle swollen, hollow, without scales. Stem erect, branched, glabrous. leaves bi- or tripinnate, ultimate segments long and narrow, less than 0.5 mm wide. Strong aromatic smell.
H: Weedy places on fields and waysides. On loamy soils rich in nutrients. Local but often abundant in England and Wales. Also on sandy ground.
Al: Similar: Scentless Mayweed (adjacent) and Corn Chamomile (*Anthemis arvensis*): receptacle with scales among the disc florets. Broad leaves usually bipinnate, ultimate segments shorter, wider (0.5–1 mm). Arable fields. Locally common throughout.

Scentless Mayweed
Matricaria perforata
Daisy family
Asteraceae (Compositae)

July–Sept.   15–60 cm   D; ☉

IM: Flowers in paniculate capitula; on the outside white ligulate florets, on the inside yellow disc florets. Receptacle swollen, without scales. Stem erect, many branches at the top. leaves divided into many fine lobes. Plant smells only slightly aromatic.
H: Weedy places on rubbish tips, pathways and arable fields, also on railway ballast. Needs nitrogenous soils. Common throughout Britain.
Al: Also referred to as *Tripteurospermum inodorum* and *Matricaria inodora*. Similar: (often combined to form one species): Sea Mayweed (*Matricaria maritimum*), leaves somewhat fleshy, stem rather prostrate. On salty ground.

Daisy
Bellis perennis
Daisy family
Asteraceae (Compositae)

Feb.–Nov.   3–12 cm   D; ♃

IM: All leaves in basal rosette, ovoid to spatulate, narrowing to a short wide petiole, margin usually notched. Capitula solitary on leafless scales, the ray florets are pure white or tinged with red on the back, the disc florets are yellow and cylindrical in shape.
H: All types of short grassy areas: meadows, pastures, balks, parks, waysides and field-paths. Needs loamy soil, rich in nutrients and not too dry, in warm light locations. Very common.
AI: This old medicinal plant is also cultivated as an ornamental plant (f. *hortensis*) with many different varieties (usually filled, i.e. capitula contains only ligulate florets.

Stemless Carline Thistle
Carlina acaulis
Daisy family
Asteraceae (Compositae)

June–Sept.   3–40 cm   D; ♃

IM: Leaves thorny, deeply pinnately spiny-lobed. Flowers in a single capitulum 4–7 cm in diameter. Only white to brownish-white cylindrical florets. Inner bracts linear, gleaming white, look like ray florets. Stem very short, prostrate to ascending. leafy.
H: Not British. Semi-dry turf,' heaths, pastures. Likes dry-warm calcareous stony ground. Scattered, in the north very rare, in the Alps up to over 2000 m. Encouraged by grazing.
AI: Plants which have long stems or are heavily branched are only habitat-dependent varieties, like those without stems.

Yarrow
Achillea millefolium
Daisy family
Asteraceae (Compositae)

June–Aug. 8–45 cm D; ♃

IM: Stem erect, leaves alternate, bi- or tripinnate, leaflets divided into 2–5 parts. Flowers in capitula, arranged in loose corymbs: on the inside yellowish-white disc florets, on the outside usually only 4–5 white or rarely red ray florets. Plant with aromatic smell.
H: Common in meadows, semi-dry turf, balks, pastures, arable fields and along waysides and hedgerows. Prefers loose loamy soils which are rich in nutrients and not too moist.
AI: The colour of the ray florets varies from off-white through pure white to reddish pink and deep red.

Sneezewort
Achillea ptarmica
Daisy family
Asteraceae (Compositae)

July–Aug. 20–60 cm D; ♃

IM: Flowers in capitula, arranged in loose corymbs; capitula up to 1.8 cm wide. On the outside wide, short ray florets, pure white to ivory-coloured, on the inside off-white disc florets. Stem erect, many leaves. Leaves undivided, lanceolate, serrate.
H: Wet meadows, ditches, river banks. Prefers loamy soil which is occasionally saturated with ground water and not too poor in nutrients. Common, ascending to 800 m.
AI: Old medicinal plant.

Ox-eye Daisy
Leucanthemum vulgare
Daisy family
Asteraceae (Compositae)

June–Aug   20–70 cm   D; ♃

IM: Stem erect, little branching. At the end of each branch a single capitulum. The ray florets are long, narrow and white, the disc florets are yellow. Unpleasant smell. Lower leaves petiolate, crenate, upper ones sessile and serrate.

H: Meadows, pathways, wasteland, balks; also found in light dry woodland and thickets. Very common, though less so in Scotland. On a variety of soils.

AI: Further names of this popular plant: Moon Daisy, Marguerite. Synonym: *Chrysanthemum leucanthemum*. Many forms.

Scentless Feverfew
Tanacetum corymbosum
Daisy family
Asteraceae (Compositae)

June–Aug.   50–100 cm   D; ♃

IM: Usually 6–20 capitula in flat panicles. Capitulum 1–2 cm wide, outside narrow white ray florets, inside yellow disc florets. No scent. Stem stiff erect, few leaves especially at the top. Leaves tough, bipinnate. Pinnae often themselves coarsely toothed.

H: Not British. Light mixed oak and beech woodland, thickets, forest margins, bushy heaths. Needs summer warmth. Likes calcareous soil rich in nutrients, not too moist. Scattered; very rare in the north.

AI: Difficult to classify systematically, therefore has a variety of names: *Chrysanthemum corymbosum*, *Leucanthemum corymbosum*, *Matricaria corymbosum*.

Marsh Helleborine
Epipactis palustris
Orchid family
Orchidaceae

June—Aug.   15—45 cm   M; ♃

IM: Flower without spur, slightly drooping; lip clearly comprising 2 segments, edge waved and frilled, often has pink veins; remaining petals spread out, slightly greenish to brownish. Raceme unilateral. Stem erect. Leaves linear-lanceolate, sheathed, parallel venation.
H: Fens, dune slacks; woodland in N. Europe. Local, sometimes frequent in England and Wales, as far north as C. Scotland. Needs ground which is at least occasionally wet, calcareous, contains humus.
Al: Similar: Other species, e.g. Broad-leaved Helleborine (*E. helleborine*, p. 372), sometimes have a white lip.

Lesser Butterfly-orchid
Platanthera bifolia
Orchid family
Orchidaceae

May—July   15—45 cm   M; ♃

IM: Stem erect, bearing 2 large oval broad leaves close to one another in the lower part and several small leaves above them. Many-flowered spike. Flowers night-scented. Spur is straight, slender and long, almost horizontal, only slightly curved at the end.
H: Light deciduous or open forests, heaths and sunny balks. Scattered. Indicates slight surface acidity. Likes warmth, but can be found in (limestone) hills up to about 400 m.
Al: Very similar: Great Butterfly-orchid, *P. chlorantha*, on moister soils; in deciduous woods and on damp meadows. Spur thicker at the end, curved downwards. Flowers more greenish-white. Rather more common than its smaller relative.

White Helleborine
Cephalanthera damasonium
Orchid family
Orchidaceae

May–June   15–80 cm   M; ♃

Creeping Lady's-tresses
Goodyera repens
Orchid family
Orchidaceae

July–Aug.   10–25 cm   M; ♃

IM: Flowers without spur, ivory in colour, ovoid as a result of the petals which press together, pointed. 3–12 flowers on spike. Leaves ovoid, spirally twisted, alternate.
H: Woodlands. Prefers porous calcareous soils in none too cold location. Local in England only.
Al: Synonyms: *C. grandiflora, C. alba, C. pallens, C. latifolia.* Similar: Narrow-leaved Helleborine (*C. longifolia = C. ensifolia*); 3–15 pure white flowers, leaves narrow, 2-rowed. Woods. Local, rather rare, from S. England to Scotland.

IM: Rhizome which creeps above ground. Leaves ovoid, thickish, with conspicuous network of veins; rosette formation at the base of erect flower stem. Further up the stem sheathing scale leaves, glandular-hairy like the flowers. Slightly spirally twisted, one-sided spike. Flowers small, whitish, covered with down, sweetish smell.
H: Mossy coniferous forests. Prefers sandy soils, acid humus, not too damp and low in lime. Local becoming more rare, and disappearing from some parts: E. Anglia, N. England and Scotland.
Al: Also referred to as *Satyrium repens.*

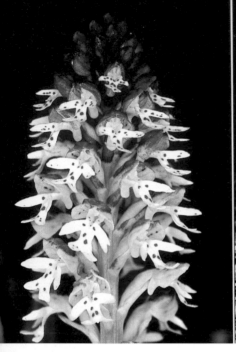

Burnt Orchid
Orchis ustulata
Orchid family
Orchidaceae

May–June   8–20 cm   M; ♃

IM: Dense globular to conical flower spike. Blossoms very small, about 5 mm long, initially brownish-red, later contrasted by the red-spotted white lip. The remaining petals are pressed together to form a helmet shape. Leaves are lanceolate.
H: Widespread but local in England, on grassy hills and dry meadows. Prefers calcareous soil, poor in nutrients but warm and loamy.

Ghost Orchid
Epipogium aphyllum
Orchid family
Orchidaceae

June–Aug.   10–20 cm   M; ♃

IM: Saprophytic plant with no chlorophyll. Stem erect, translucent reddish to yellowish; few leaf scales. Loose cluster of 1–4 flowers. These are drooping, whitish-yellowish-pale reddish, with spur and 3-lobed lip pointing upwards, wax-like and translucent.
H: Oak and beech mixed woodland. Very rare. Prefers shady mossy soil which is well-moistened and contains nutrients and mull. Known only in a few localities in England and the Welsh borders.

Coral-root Orchid
Corallorhiza trifida
Orchid family
Orchidaceae

May–Aug.   7–25 cm   M; ♃

      ▽

IM: Pale green saprophytic plant. Stem narrow, erect, glabrous, usually with 3 somewhat inflated yellowish-green sheaths. No genuine leaves. Approximately 10 yellowish-white flowers without spurs, spreading and upright in lax clusters. Lip points downwards, 3-lobed, white with red spots or lines.

H: Shady woodland, especially birch and pine, alder brake, peat bog spinneys. Likes decaying tree trunks. Rare, N. England and Scotland, in the mountains and occasionally on dunes. Calcifugous, avoids nitrogen. Decidedly a shady plant.

AI: In older works referred to under the name *C. innata*.

Corydalis cava
Fumitory family
Fumariaceae

March–April   10–20 cm   D; ♃; +

        ▽

IM: Stem erect, unbranched, with alternate broad leaves. These are bi- to tripinnate, blue-green, glabrous. Ultimate segments are ovoid, often repeatedly notched. Ten to twenty flowers form a dense raceme, bracts have entire margin. Flowers may be white to purple.

H: A rare escape from gardens which may become established in a few places.

AI: Similar: Solid-tubered Fumitory (*C. solida*, see p. 262).

97

Hare's-foot Clover
Trifolium arvense
Pea family
Fabaceae (Leguminosae)

June–Sept.　　10–40 cm　　D; ☉

IM: Leaves trifoliate; leaflets narrow-oblong. Stem ascending to erect, branched. Flowers white, pink when fading; cylindrical inflorescence, sepals extending beyond petals, reddish and covered with feathery hairs.
H: Dry turf, arable fields, open sandy ground, paths, wasteland. Only found on soils which are free of or low in lime, somewhat acid, loose and warm. Widespread throughout Britain but scattered and rather local.
AI: Weed and worthless as fodder, but as an old medicinal plant it had a variety of names.

White Clover
Trifolium repens
Pea family
Fabaceae (Leguminosae)

June–Sept.　　20–50 cm　　D; ♃

IM: Stem prostrate, rooted. Flowers in pedunculate, erect, round heads. Leaves stalked, pointing upwards, trifoliate; leaflets wedge-shaped to ovoid with almost heart-shaped apices, glabrous on the underside.
H: Pastures, meadows, all types of turf — often sown. Very frequent. Resists trampling, likes nitrogen, reproduces well and therefore suitable for pastures, but also very hard to keep out of cultivated lawns. Up to over 900 m.
AI: Very many varieties; some are cultivated types which have escaped.

Mountain Clover
Trifolium montanum
Pea family
Fabaceae (Leguminosae)

May—July   15—40 cm   D; ♃

IM: Stem erect-ascending, covered with woolly hairs, branched. Leaves trifoliate, toothed margin, underside hairy. Flowers in short globular heads, stalked, white or ivory-coloured.
H: Not British. Balks, thickets, light dry woodland. Requires calcareous dry soil which is occasionally saturated. Must be low in nutrients. Scattered in limestone areas, in mountainous areas up to 1800 m, absent in sandy areas.
AI: Distantly related: Alsike Clover (*Tr. hybridum*), glabrous or only slightly hairy, leaflets ovoid, flowers first white, later pink. Scattered; damp meadows, pathways, wasteland.

White Melilot
Melilotus alba
Pea family
Fabaceae (Leguminosae)

July—Aug.   60—120 cm   D; ☉

IM: Stem erect, many branches. Many long narrow slightly unilateral racemes, erect and bearing large number of flowers. Leaves trifoliate; leaflets ovoid, serrate. At base of leaf-stalk 2 bristle-like stipules.
H: Weedy places along waysides, slopes, railway embankments, gravel banks. Needs rather dry ground rich in nutrients and often stony, but also found on pure loamy soil in warm locations. Frequent in S. England and Wales, but less so elsewhere.
AI: Poor fodder but valuable plant for bees.

Wood Vetch
Vicia sylvatica
Pea family
Fabaceae (Leguminosae)

June–Aug.   60–130 cm   D; ♃

       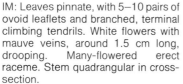

IM: Leaves pinnate, with 5–10 pairs of ovoid leaflets and branched, terminal climbing tendrils. White flowers with mauve veins, around 1.5 cm long, drooping. Many-flowered erect raceme. Stem quadrangular in cross-section.
H: Light deciduous and mixed woodland, wood margins, thickets, grassy areas. Found on dry, warm, loose loamy soils rich in lime and nutrients and often stony. Common throughout Britain.
AI: Similar: Wood Bitter Vetch (*V. orobus*); without tendrils, stem erect, rarely taller than 0.5 m, hairy. Local in woods.

White Deadnettle
Lamium album
Mint family
Lamiaceae (Labiatae)

May–Dec.   20–60 cm   D; ♃

IM: Looks like a nettle, but without the stinging hairs. 5–8 bilabiate flowers in axillary whorls (verticillasters). Stem quadrangular, erect. Leaves opposite and decussate, ovoid, dentate; petiolate.
H: Waysides, waste ground, railway embankments, walls, fences, thickets. Likes nitrogenous soil, thus frequently found on fertilized ground but rarely in fields. Very common in England and Wales, rare in N. Scotland.
AI: May be confused with related plants with yellow and red flowers (p. 192 and 274f. respectively). White Deadnettle always has 3–7 cm long leaves with long pointed teeth and without flecks on them.

Yellow Woundwort
Stachys recta
Mint family
Lamiaceae (Labiatae)

June–Oct.   10–30 cm   D; ♃

IM: Stem erect or ascending, quadrangular. Leaves opposite and decussate, with very short stalks, narrow ovoid. Inflorescence made up of individual whorls where the flowers get smaller towards the top. Flowers yellowish-white, approx. 1.5 cm long; 6–10 per whorl.
H: Naturalized in one locality — in Barry, S. Wales. Rare in N. Europe. Likes stony calcareous ground. Not found in silicate areas or in the mountains over 1000 m.
AI: Old medicinal and magic plant with a variety of popular names. Similar: *S. annua* (see adjacent photo).

Annual Woundwort
Stachys annua
Mint family
Lamiaceae (Labiatae)

June–Oct.   10–30 cm   D; ☉

IM: Stem usually erect and branched, quadrangular. Leaves opposite and decussate, narrow ovoid, short-stalked, the upper one sessile. Inflorescence made up of individual flower whorls. Flowers yellowish-white, around 1–1.5 cm long; 2–6 per whorl.
H: Arable fields and waste places. Likes calcareous and nitrogenous loamy soils in rather warm dry locations. Occurs as a casual in many places but does not become established.

Bastard Balm
Melittis melissophyllum
Mint family
Lamiaceae (*Labiatae*)

May–July   20–50 cm   D; ♃

IM: Stem quadrangular, erect, little branching. Broad leaves opposite and decussate, stalked, ovoid, conspicuously wrinkled, coarsely round-toothed margin. Entire plant has dense covering of soft hairs. Flowers few in numbers in axils of upper leaves, often all favouring one side; smells of honey.
H: Light deciduous forests, woods and hedgerows. Prefers loose calcareous soils, warm but not too dry. Local to rare in Wales and southern parts of England.
Al: The flowers are usually white spotted with pink but may sometimes be more or less completely pink.

Hedge Hyssop
Gratiola officinalis
Figwort family
Scrophulariaceae

June–Aug.   10–50 cm   D; ♃; +

IM: Stem erect to ascending, round, hollow. Leaves opposite and decussate, sessile, lanceolate, margin serrate. Entire plant glabrous. Flowers solitary in leaf axils, pedicellate. Corolla often has reddish veins or the upper lip has a reddish tinge.
H: Not British. In reeds in stagnant or slow-flowing waters, on river banks, ditches and damp meadows. Prefers muddy calcareous and dense soils. Withstands summer drought and excessive salt. Only found on lower levels. Very rare.
Al: Old (poisonous) medicinal plant.

Eyebright
Euphrasia rostkoviana
Figwort family
Scrophulariaceae

July–Aug.   10–40 cm   D; ⊙ ; (+)

IM: Stem ascending, usually little branched. Leaves opposite and decussate, ovoid, small, coarsely round-toothed. Inflorescence has leaflike bracts. Leaves, bracts and calyx are glandular-hairy. Flowers usually about 1 cm long, white with yellow, black-mauve, bluish or reddish spots on the throat of the corolla.
H: Meadows, pastures; tends to avoid lime and reacts badly to fertilizer. Local to rare in N. England, Wales and Border region.
AI: Many different species, hard to determine the limits of the various species in the genus.

Alpine Butterwort
Pinguicula alpina
Butterwort family
Lentibulariaceae

May–July   5–15 cm   D; ♃

IM: Leaves in basal rosette, yellowish-green, lanceolate with upturned margins, sticky on the upperside. Flowers single, stalked, drooping horizontally, spur is curved downwards. Throat of the corolla is wide open and has yellowish flecks on it.
H: Probably extinct in Britain. Flat moorland, areas round springs, Alpine mats which are irrigated or saturated by ground water, rocky fissures. Prefers wet calcareous ground. Scattered up to 2300 m in Alpine regions, very rare in the area of the Lower Alps.
AI: Blue flowering Common Butterwort *P. vulgaris* (p. 347) occasionally produces blossoms with white spots. Even when both species adjacent there is no hybridizing.

103

Traveller's Joy
Clematis vitalba
Buttercup family
Ranunculaceae

July–Aug.   up to 30 m   D; ♄; +

IM: Liana with woody climbing stem. Leaves opposite, pinnate; leaflets ovoid/heart-shaped; petioles tendril-like. Terminal and axillary panicles. Petals absent, sepals petal-like. Fruit has long feathery-hairy style.
H: Hedges, wood margins, thickets. Prefers soil rich in chalk and nutrients. Likes nitrogenous ground, is thus often found near villages. England and Wales as far north as the Midlands and S. Yorkshire. Likes the warmth so is only found in moderately hilly areas.

Holly
Ilex aquifolium
Holly family
Aquifoliaceae

May–Aug.   3–15 m   D; ♄; +

IM: Evergreen, shiny leaves, ovoid, 3–10 cm long, toothed with prickles, slightly waved. Petiole very short. Flowers small, in axillary clusters. Berries round, shiny and red.
H: Deciduous and coniferous woods. On all but very wet soils. Very shade-tolerant. Sometimes found in the garden as a hedge or as an ornamental.
AI: Similar in its foliage: Oregon Grape (*Mahonia aquifolium*); yellow flowers, blue fruit. Decorative shrub, rarely naturalized.

Dogwood
Cornus sanguinea
Dogwood family
Cornaceae

May–July   0.25–4 m   D; ♄

IM: Twigs often have a reddish tinge (blood-red in autumn and winter). Flowers in flat corymbose cymes. Leaves opposite, with curved pinnately branched venation, ovoid, margin entire. Fruit is berry-like, globular, black.
H: Deciduous and mixed woodland, hedges. Prefers calcareous soil rich in nutrients and not too damp in sunny, warm location. Common in England and Wales, rarer in Scotland, where it is introduced.
AI: Has been listed under the genus *Swida* (*S. sanguinea*). Varieties with mottled leaves cultivated (rare; other dogwood species are preferred).

Wild Privet
Ligustrum vulgare
Olive family
Oleaceae

June–July   under 5 m   D; ♄; +

IM: Leaves opposite and decussate, leathery, ovoid-lanceolate, margin entire and glabrous. Short petiole. Many-flowered panicles. Flowers funnel-shaped, with an unpleasant smell. Berries small, globular, shiny and black, very juicy.
H: Thickets, hedges, wood margins. Likes loose calcareous soils, often somewhat stony. Common in England and Wales, introduced in Scotland. Often found in gardens as a hedge, can be cut. Only relative resistance to frost.
AI: In warmer regions the leaves remain green all winter. In gardens it is often replaced by Garden Privet (*L. ovalifolium*), susceptible to frost.

105

Pear
Pyrus communis
Rose family
Rosaceae

April–May   5–15 m   D; ♄

IM: Twigs are glabrous or rapidly become so. Spiny at the tips or on the short lateral twigs. Leaves petiolate, round-ovoid, margin is finely serrated, shiny on the upperside, tough-leathery. Umbel-like corymbs with few flowers at the end of the short shoots. Anthers purple red. Fruit is a small woody pear. Often grows as a large shrub.
H: Typically in hedgerows, usually found as individual trees rather than in large numbers. Widespread in England and Wales but not in large numbers. Prefers loamy soils rich in lime and nutrients. Often cultivated from wild.
AI: Pirus is an old spelling for the generic name.

Crab Apple
Malus sylvestris
Rose family
Rosaceae

May   2–10 m   D; ♄

IM: Twigs sometimes thorny. Leaves petiolate, broadly ovoid, often with off-centre apex, underside glabrous. Corymbs with few flowers. Anthers yellow, petals white or pink, 1–3 cm long. Fruit is a small apple 2–3 cm in diameter, dry and sour, somewhat woody.
H: Deciduous woodland, light thickets, hedgerows. Likes calcareous well-moistened soils rich in nutrients. Common in England and Wales, becoming rarer in Scotland.
AI: Similar to the Crab Apple and partially a hybrid of this is the cultivated apple (*M. domestica*) with its many different varieties. Old types grown wild are hard to distinguish. They generally have leaves with felt-like undersides.

Medlar
Mespilus germanica
Rose family
Rosaceae

May—June   2–3(6) m   D; ♄

IM: Thorny twigs, covered with felt-like hairs when young. Leaves lanceolate, finely serrated, undersides covered with soft hairs. Flowers solitary and terminal on twig tips; the narrow herbaceous calyx lobes are longer than the petals and later crown the rough, leather-brown fruit. Usually grows as a shrub.
H: Hedgerows. Rare. Naturalized in S. England, Midlands and as far north as S. Yorkshire. On dry, warm calcareous ground.
AI: In the Middle Ages, cultivated for its edible fruit.

Snowy Mespil
Amelanchier ovalis
Rose family
Rosaceae

April—May   1–3 m   D; ♄

IM: Small shrub, twigs without thorns. Leaves elliptical, serrate, 2–4 cm long, petiolate. Racemes few-flowered. Petals narrow, 1–2 cm long, covered with tufts of hair on the outside. Fruit the size of a pea, globular, blue-black.
H: Rocky slopes, stony forest margins, sunny thickets. Very rare. Found on stony, flat, dry ground, preferably calcareous. In sunny location up to well over 1500 m.
AI: A North American shrub, planted in parks and gardens, not yet escaped or naturalized in Britain.

Wild Service-tree
Sorbus torminalis
Rose family
Rosaceae

May–June   under 5 m   D; ♄; (+)

IM: Medium-sized tree. Leaves 7–11 lobed, upperside glabrous, underside grey and felt-like when young, later glabrous. Lobes are pointed, coarsely serrate; the lower ones wide-spreading or at right angles to the petiole, the upper ones less so. Flowers in compound corymbs. Petals approx. 5 mm long. Fruit obovoid, brown, covered with light-coloured spots. Autumn foliage conspicuously red in colour.
H: In sunny deciduous and mixed woodland which is warm in summer and relatively dry. Scattered through England and Wales. Calcicolous, likes nitrogenous soil.

Common Whitebeam
Sorbus aria
Rose family
Rosaceae

May–June   under 15 m   D; ♄; (+)

IM: Shrub or small tree. Undersides of leaves are covered with white felt, doubly serrate or slightly lobed. Umbrella-like corymbs. Petals approx. 5 mm long. Fruit ovoid-globular; orange-yellow to red in colour.
H: Dry woodland, stony thicket-covered slopes. Usually on calcareous stony ground. Native in S. England but often planted elsewhere.
AI: Many varieties and often hybrids with other species. A number of closely related and difficult to distinguish species of *Sorbus* are considered to be endemic to the British Isles.

Rowan
Sorbus uncuparia
Rose family
Rosaceae

May–June   5–15 m   D; ♄; (+)

IM: Usually a small tree. Leaves unpaired pinnate; 9–17 oblong leaflets on short stalks with finely serrate margins. Many-flowered corymbs. Petals approx. 5 mm long. Fruit globular, the size of a pea, red.
H: Woodland, thickets, heaths, mountains. Found on dry and moist slightly acid soil, usually free of lime and low in nutrients. Common in north and west, becoming rare in eastern England and parts of the Midlands. Up to about 1000 m.
Al: Is also widely referred to as Mountain Ash. Very many hybrids and varieties.

Hawthorn
Crataegus monogyna
Rose family
Rosaceae

May–June   2–10 m   D; ♄

IM: Usually a shrub or small tree with light grey bark and thorny twigs. Leaves deeply lobed; usually 3–5 lobes, pointed, serrate at the front. Erect lax corymbs. Flowers have strong smell. One style per flower, 1 stone in each red oval fruit. Pedicel hairy.
H: Woods, thickets, hedges. In shallow soil which can be stony. Withstands drought. Very common in almost all parts except N. Scotland. Often used as hedging.
Al: Similar: Midland Hawthorn (*C. laevigata = C. oxyacantha*), pedicel usually glabrous, flower has 2–3 styles, fruit 2–3 stones. Leaves slightly lobed. Somewhat local, mainly in eastern England.

Field Rose
Rosa arvensis
Rose family
Rosaceae

June–July   50–100 cm   D; ♄

IM: Stems green, sometimes tinged purple, curved prostrate or creeping, rarely climbing over another shrub; many thorns. Leaves pinnate, 5–7 leaflets; leaflets ovoid, toothed. Flowers solitary, on pedicels, 3–5 cm wide. Styles united to form a conspicuous column. Small hip.
H: Light- and mixed-deciduous woodland, woodland margins, woodland paths, glades, also rocky hedges. Found on slightly acid ground, not too dry but rich in humus. Common in the south, rarer towards the north, very rare in Scotland.
AI: The creeping growth and the protruding styles distinguish it clearly from other wild roses.

110

Wild Cherry
Prunus avium
Rose family
Rosaceae

Feb.–June   5–25 m   D; ♄

IM: Tree, twigs greyish-brown. Leaves usually appear together with the flowers, obovoid, pointed apex, toothed margin. Petiole has 1–2 brown half-spherical glands at the top. Flowers in umbels of 2–6, long pedicels, 2–3 cm wide. Fruit: small cherry.
H: Woods, hedges, copses, thickets. On well-moistened soils rich in nutrients. Common in England and Wales, becoming rare in Scotland.
AI: Under the name *Cerasus avium* is attributed to a different genus. The Garden Cherry is similar; may have been derived from Wild Cherry by hybridization.

Bird Cherry
Prunus padus
Rose family
Rosaceae

May   3–15 m   D; ♄

IM: Shrub or small tree. Flowers in many-flowered pendulous racemes at the end of leaf twigs; strong smell. Leaves alternate, ovoid, pointed at the apex, somewhat wrinkled, margin doubly serrate. Fruit the size of a pea, cherry-like, black.
H: Moist deciduous woodland, thickets close to the water. Found on deep loamy soil with abundant nutrients. Common in Scotland, N. England and Wales, as far south as the Midlands. Sometimes planted in S. England.

Blackthorn
Prunus spinosa
Rose family
Rosaceae

March–May   1–4 m   D; ♄

IM: Gnarled shrub with blackish bark and thorny twigs. Flowers usually appear before the leaves, solitary (but numerous) on short pedicels. Leaves elliptical, margin sharply serrate. Fruit globular, about 1 cm in length, with bluish bloom, black, dry-sour.
H: Thickets, woodland margins, hedgerows, path verges. Found on ground which is not too dry but rich in minerals. Throughout most of Britain up to about 450 m.
AI: Together with the related Plum the Sloe sometimes forms the hybrid *P. x fruticans*, which baffles anyone trying to classify it. It looks like a Sloe, has no thorns and the fruit is large and sweet.

111

Raspberry
Rubus idaeus
Rose family
Rosaceae

June–Aug.   100–160 cm   D; ♄

IM: Stem covered with fine prickles, erect or arching. Leaves alternate, undersides have thick covering of white hairs, uppersides light green, 3–7 leaflets which are ovoid, upperside wrinkled, toothed margin. Somewhat drooping cyme with few flowers. Compound fruit red.
H: Glades, clearings, woodland margins, heaths, especially in hilly areas. Likes nitrogen. Common. Up to 1000 m. Sometimes occurs in large numbers.
AI: Not always easy to distinguish from the other species of *Rubus* (see p. 61 and adjacent entry) when it is in flower. All characteristics should be examined.
112

Bramble
Rubus fruticosus
Rose family
Rosaceae

May–Sept.   20–200 cm   D; ♄

IM: Stem usually covered with coarse prickles, arching, ascending or creeping. Leaves alternate, ternate or palmately divided into 3–(5)7 leaflets, undersides glabrous or covered with white felt. Inflorescence rather variable. (Compound) fruit black (red).
H: Woodland, hedgerows, wayside verges, fields, gardens, fallow land, heaths. Very common throughout Britain. Usually found on soils which are not too dry but low in lime and containing nutrients.
AI: Sometimes divided into dozens of hard-to-distinguish variants. The fruit and stems of the Dewberry (*R. caesius*) have a bluish tinge. Likes damp habitats; common in England and Wales, less so in Scotland.

Bog Bilberry
Vaccinium uliginosum
Heath family
Ericaceae

May–June   up to 50 cm   D; ♄; (+)

IM: Flat prostrate or erect to ascending shrub with many branches. Bark greyish-brown. Leaves blue-green, obovoid, blunt, margin entire, very short petioles. Several flowers in each leaf axil, drooping, campanulate. Fruit is a globular berry with a blue bloom and colourless juice.

H: Moorland, marshy woodland and heaths. On damp to wet acid soil. Local but sometimes abundant on Bilberry moors.

Cowberry
Vaccinium vitis-idaea
Heath family
Ericaceae

June–Aug.   10–30 cm   D; ♄

IM: Leaves leathery, evergreen; rolled up at the edge. Several flowers in terminal racemes, pink or pure white, slightly drooping. Flowers campanulate, usually 5, rarely 4 fused petals. Fruit: a berry, first white, then shining red when ripe, in dense clusters, usually unilateral.

H: In mixed and coniferous woodland, high moorland, heaths with stunted bushy growth. Common in the mountains and sometimes becoming dominant. Requires acid, meagre soil saturated at intervals and containing coarse humus.

AI: Similar: Bearberry (*Arctostaphylos uva-ursi*), especially when this is not in flower. The leaf edges are flat (see p. 114).

Ledum palustre
Heath family
Ericaceae

June–July   up to 1 m   D; ♄; +

IM: Unpleasant smelling shrub, twigs covered with red felt. Leaves narrow lanceolate, up to about 0.5 cm wide, leathery, evergreen, undersides covered with rust-red hairs. Many-flowered terminal umbel-like racemes. Flowers spread out like rays, corolla often over 1 cm in diameter.
H: Boggy areas. Very rare in a few areas of lowland Scotland. Needs wet peaty soil free of lime and low in nutrients.
Al: Labrador-tea (*L. Groenlandicum*), from North America is a rare escape from cultivation. Laeves wide lanceolate to ovoid, upperside bumpy and rough.

Bearberry
Arctostaphylos uva-ursi
Heath family
Ericaceae

May–July   20–60 cm   D; ♄

IM: Prostrate shrub with ascending twigs. Leaves obovate, glabrous, leathery, evergreen, with smooth flat edges. 5–12 globular-campanulate flowers in terminal racemes; sometimes tinged with pink. Fruit red, floury.
H: High moors. Needs soil which is rich in humus and has at least surface acidity but which must be warm and rather dry. Common in N. England and Scotland, also on high ground in the Midlands.

Elder
Sambucus nigra
Honeysuckle family
Caprifoliaceae

June–July   3–10 m   D; ♄

IM: Shrub with alternate leaves, often long off-shoots from the base; bark has protruding pores; pith is white. Flat umbel-like flowers with 5 main rays, erect, begins to droop when ripe. Rays also turn red. Black berries. Leaves pinnate; 3–7 large serrate leaflets.
H: Woods, glades, hedges, thickets. On disturbed soil rich in humus. Likes nitrogen. Moisture indicator. Common; often found on neglected areas; less so in Scotland.
Al: Old medicinal and berry fruit plant. Sometimes found as an ornamental bush with bipinnate slit foliage (var. *laciniata*).

Wayfaring-tree
Viburnum lantana
Honeysuckle family
Caprifoliaceae

May–June   2–6 m   D; ♄; +

IM: Shrub with many branches; when young the twigs are covered with grey felt-like hairs. Leaves opposite, elliptical, finely serrate margin, undersides wrinkled, with grey felt. Petioles short. Flat terminal umbel-like cymes. Fruit berry-like and red, black in the final stage, ovoid, pressed together laterally.
H: Deciduous and mixed woodland, thickets. Requires sunny, warm loose calcareous soil. Common in S. England, rarer northwards and westwards into Wales. Introduced in Scotland. Scattered; absent in sandy regions.

Guelder-rose
Viburnum opulus
Honeysuckle family
Caprifoliaceae

June–July   2–4 m   D; ♄

IM: Shrub with opposite leaves. Glabrous twigs. Leaves 3–5 lobes. Base of petiole has stipules resembling bristles and cup-like glands. Flat terminal umbel-like cymes. Outer flowers sterile, enlarged. Fruit berry-like, red.
H: Moist deciduous and mixed woodland, scrub and riverbank thickets. On loamy soils saturated by ground water. Moisture indicator. Common in England and Wales, less so in Scotland.
AI: The Snowball Tree (var. *roseum*) is often grown as an ornamental shrub. It has globular heads composed of enlarged sterile flowers. Similar in its leaves: Maple species, e.g. Sycamore (*Acer pseudoplatanus*, p. 381): glands and stipules are absent on petiole.

Fly Honeysuckle
Lonicera xylosteum
Honeysuckle family
Caprifoliaceae

May–June   1–2 m   D; ♄; +

IM: Branched bushy shrub with hollow, rod-shaped twigs. Flowers always in pairs on the peduncle, the ovaries are fused at the base. Corolla hairy. Leaves opposite, margin entire, broadly ovoid. Shiny red paired berries.
H: Deciduous woodland, in hedges. Calcicolous. Needs loose soil rich in humus and nutrients. Scattered in England and Wales, and a few places in Scotland. Introduced in most of these localities.
AI: The flowers are never completely white. In parks and gardens the very similar *L. ruprechtiana* (originates in China) is often planted. Its flowers are snow-white and have no hair on the outside.

Honeysuckle
Lonicera periclymenum
Honeysuckle family
Caprifoliaceae

June–Sept.   up to 6 m   D; ♄; (+)

IM: Woody climber or twining shrub. Leaves opposite, ovoid, the upper ones sessile, the lower ones have short petioles. Terminal whorls of flowers. Flowers scented, cloudy white, often tinged with pink.
H: Deciduous and mixed woodland, forest margins, thickets. Somewhat calcifugous. Likes mild winter climate. Common.
AI: Similar: Perfoliate Honeysuckle, *L. caprifolium*: upper leaves fused in pairs to form oval or round discs with the stem passing through the centres. Old ornamental plant from the Eastern Mediterranean region, often found growing wild in hedgerows in S. and E. England, also in a few parts of the north.

False Acacia
Robinia pseudoacacia
Pea family
Fabaceae (Leguminosae)

June   10–27 m   D; ♄

IM: Tree with light brown bark that has deep longitudinal grooves. Shiny, reddish-brown twigs covered with large double thorns. Leaves pinnate; 9–19 ovoid leaflets, somewhat greyish-green in colour. Many-flowered pendulous racemes. Flowers are scented. Reddish-brown pod.
H: Popular tree in parks and council planting schemes, rarely escaping. Likes warmth.
AI: The tree was first introduced by J. Robin in 1601 and was believed to be an acacia, hence the current name 'False Acacia'.

Branched Bur-reed
Sparganium erectum
Bur-reed family
Sparganiaceae

June—Aug.   50—150 cm   M; ♃

IM: Leaves grass-like, somewhat stiff. Stem branched. Male and female flowers are in separate round heads at the ends of the branches, the male ones at the top and the female ones lower down the stem; fruit is prickly, resembling a bur (hence the name).
H: Frequently found in reed-beds in stagnant or slow-flowing water, in ditches and marshes. Likes soil containing nutrients. Common in almost all areas.
AI: Similar rarer species where the stem is not branched: Unbranched Bur-reed (*S. emersum*), Floating Bur-reed (*S. angustifolium*) with floating leaves, Least Bur-reed (*S. minimum*) with 2—5 small flower heads.

Common Meadow-rue
Thalictrum flavum
Buttercup family
Ranunculaceae

July—Aug.   50—100 cm   D; ♃

IM: Stem erect, glabrous, usually unbranched. Leaves alternate, the lower ones petiolate, the upper ones sessile, bi- or tripinnate. Flowers erect, in bushy clustered panicles, sweet-smelling; petals wither rapidly; many stamens, yellow.
H: Fens, damp meadows, river banks. Likes wet loamy soil which is dry in summer. Frequent, as far north as Inverness.

118

Greater Celandine
Chelidonium majus
Poppy family
Papaveraceae

Drooping Bitter-cress
Cardamine enneaphyllos
Mustard family
Brassicaceae (Cruciferae)

May–Aug.   30–90 cm   D; ♃; +

April–May   20–30 cm   D; ♃

IM: The plant contains an orange-yellow milky juice (latex). Flowers are in clusters or solitary in leaf axils. Leaves almost pinnate, coarsely lobed or toothed, undersides bluish-green. Plant glabrous or with scattered hairs.
H: On rubble areas, pathways, along walls and fences, in gardens, damp light woodland and thickets, forest margins. Nitrogen indicator. Likes warmth but not full sunshine. Common, especially near habitation.

IM: Stem erect but at an angle, no leaves lower down. At the top is a whorl of 3 triple-fingered leaves with short petioles. Flowers in terminal clusters but drooping and thus hanging below the leaf whorl. Flowers pale yellow, 1–2 cm long. Fruits are narrow, 5–8 cm long but erect. When fruit is borne the plant often has long-stemmed basal leaves.
H: Not British. Deciduous and mixed deciduous woodland. On well-moistened loamy soil, rich in nutrients and mull. Rare. Main area of distribution is south-east Germany: the Alps and extensive foreland.
AI: Other scientific name: *Dentaria enneaphyllos.*

Charlock
Sinapis arvensis
Mustard family
Brassicaceae (Cruciferae)

May—July   30—80 cm   D; ☉

IM: Racemes initially short, later becoming extremely long. Flowers deep yellow, 1.5—2 cm wide; narrow, horizontally projecting sepals, yellowish-green in colour. Stem usually erect and unbranched. Leaves undivided but often pronouncedly crenate, the lower ones almost lyre-shaped. Fruits much longer than they are wide.
H: Fields, gardens, wasteland. On calcareous soil rich in nutrients. Common.
AI: Very similar: Wild Radish, *Raphanus raphanistrum*, (p. 38), type which has light yellow flowers; often found in the same habitats but the sepals are erect.

Winter-cress
Barbarea vulgaris
Mustard family
Brassicaceae (Cruciferae)

May—Aug.   30—90 cm   D; ♃

IM: Basal leaves in rosettes, lyre-shaped with small round terminal lobes; stem leaves pinnate, upper ones undivided, sessile, clasping the stem and projecting. Stem angular, usually branched. Inflorescence dense to begin with, elongating later. Petals twice as long as sepals. Ovary long, quadrangular.
H: Weedy areas along pathways, railway embankments, river banks, on gravel banks and sandbanks, waste areas, in clearings. Likes well-moistened stony ground rich in nutrients. Common but less so in north.
AI: Similar: Small-flowered Wintercress (*B. stricta*): sepals c. ⅓ length of petals; Medium-flowered Wintercress (*B. intermedia*): leaves pinnate.

Hedge Mustard
Sisymbrium officinale
Mustard family
Brassicaceae (Cruciferae)

June–July   30–90 cm   D; ☉

IM: Inflorescence initially corymb-like but elongating later. Petals 2–3 mm long. Fruit approx. 1 cm long, narrow, pointed, pressed closely to the stem. Leaves pinnate with rounded terminal lobe, upper leaves with a spear-shaped terminal lobe.
H: A weed of arable land. Pathways, rubble, walls, railway embankments, river banks. On warm soil which is not too damp. Nitrogen indicator. Frequent.
AI: The following also have fruit pressed close to the stem: Tower Mustard (*Arabis glabra*): flowers light yellow, leaves glabrous, bluish-green. Black Mustard (*Brassica nigra*): petals about 1 cm long. *Eruca sativa*: petals about 1.5–2 cm long.

Treacle Mustard
Erysimum cheiranthoides
Mustard family
Brassicaceae (Cruciferae)

June–Aug.   15–90 cm   D; ☉

IM: Flowers small, on relatively long pedicels. Sepals erect, flowers barely 6 mm wide. Inflorescence corymb-like or racemes. All leaves undivided, very coarsely serrate, lanceolate, narrower at the base. Fruit at least 10 times longer than wide.
H: Fields, gardens, pathways, riverbanks, gravel banks and sand banks. Grows on loose slightly damp soil which is somewhat calcareous. Local, sometimes common at low altitudes in the south, rarer in the north.
AI: Yellow cruciform flowers, lanceolate leaves, erect calyx & fruits indicate that this belongs to genus *Erysimum*, if petals less than 2 cm long. Wallflower (*Cheiranthus cheiri*) very similar but flowers over 2 cm wide.   121

Small Alison
Alyssum alyssoides
Mustard family
Brassicaceae (Cruciferae)

May–June   5–25 cm   D; ☉

IM: Bushy plant with erect or cuved ascending stems. Leaves obovoid to narrow-oblanceolate, margin entire, with grey felt-like down. Flowers in dense racemes, approx. 3 mm wide, pale yellow fading to white, with persistent sepals. Small siliculae round, flattened, covered with rough hairs.
H: Fields, both arable and pasture. In sunny dry habitats. Likes lime and a small amount of nitrogen. Scattered in southern and eastern England and parts of eastern Scotland.
AI: Synonym: *A. calycinum.*

Alyssum montanum
Mustard family
Brassicaceae (Cruciferae)

April–June   5–25 cm   D; ♃

IM: Lower part of stem quite woody, many branches. Leaves have entire margin, with grey felt-like covering, narrow, up to 2 cm long. Dense racemes. Flowers golden-yellow, about 5 mm wide. Sepals wither rapidly. Small siliculae oval to round, flattened, grey felt-like covering.
H: Not British. Rocks and dry turf. Needs sunny, warm, sandy or stony ground, dry and calcareous. Very rare but it forms small groups in those localities where it does occur.
AI: Similar: Golden Alison (*A. saxatile*): leaves up to 5 cm long; many-flowered panicle; small siliculae glabrous. Not British. Very rare in rocky areas but widely spread in rockeries as ornamental plant.

Woad
Isatis tinctoria
Mustard family
Brassicaceae (Cruciferae)

July–Aug.   50–120 cm D; ☉-⅔; (+)

IM: Very densely branched, at least at the top, usually with many flowers. Leaves on the stem bluish-green, glabrous, margin usually entire, heart-shaped or sagittate clasping the stem. Fruit flat, broader towards the apex, broadly winged; pendulous, ultimately black-brown-violet, usually 1-seeded.
H: Cultivated in ancient times for the blue pigments (woad) obtained from the partly dried leaves. Nowadays a weed of cornfields and naturalized on cliffs in the Severn Valley.

Ball Mustard
Neslia paniculata
Mustard family
Brasicaceae (Cruciferae)

June–Sept.   15–80 cm   D; ☉

IM: Stem simple or branched from the middle, with hairs towards the base. Leaves lanceolate, the upper ones sessile with arrow-shaped base, the lower ones almost petiolate. Inflorescence elongating in fruit. Flowers golden yellow, approx. 0.5 cm wide. Fruits spherical, 2 mm across, with a network of fine wrinkles, on stalks projecting outwards at an angle.
H: Arable fields, field paths and waste places. On dry warm loamy soils containing lime and nitrogen. Occurring as a casual.
AI: Other name: *Vogelia paniculata*. Similar field weeds (e.g. Gold-of-pleasure, *Camelina sativa*) have virtually been wiped out.

123

Biscutella laevigata
Mustard family
Brassicaceae (Cruciferae)

May–Nov.   15–30 cm   D; ♃

IM: Stem erect, often branched towards top, leaves sparse. Basal leaves are long, margin entire or toothed, usually forming dense rosettes. Loose or dense panicles. Petals pale yellow, 0.5 cm long. Ovaries and fruit (silicula) made up of 2 flat, circular sections resembling spectacles.
H: Not British. Dry stony turf, rocky ledges, Alpine scree, pine and mountain pine forests. Calcicolous; scattered in the Alps, otherwise rare.
AI: Falls into several ecological and geographical categories. Some forms grow on chalky ground and others on limestone moorland. A very variable species with different chromosomal races occupying alpine/lowland habitats. Numerous ssp.

Yellow Whitlow-grass
Draba aizoides
Mustard family
Brassicaceae (Cruciferae)

March–May   5–15 cm   D; ♃

IM: Compact, semi-spherical rosettes of lanceolate leaves, barely 2 cm long, rigid, margin edged with stiff bristle-like hairs. Stems leafless. Corymbose racemes of golden-yellow flowers, relatively large, about 1 cm across. Fruits flat, elliptical, approx. 3 times longer than wide.
H: In Britain only found on limestone in one locality in Glamorgan.

124

Alternate-leaved Golden Saxifrage
Chrysosplenium alternifolium
Saxifrage family
Saxifragaceae

April—July   8—15 cm   D; ♃

IM: Stem, triangular, breaks easily.
Several long-stalked, reniform basal
leaves, 1—3 stem leaves similar to the
lower ones, alternate. Inflorescence
dichotomous, bracts almost sessile,
yellow at the top. Flowers small, rich
yellow in colour.
H: Moist deciduous woods, streams,
around springs, marshy areas, wet
upland meadows. Local in most places
but absent from western parts of England and Wales.
Al: Similar inflorescence: species
from the Spurge genus (*Euphorbia*):
milky juice.

Opposite-leaved Golden Saxifrage
Chrysosplenium oppositifolium
Saxifrage family
Saxifragaceae

April—July   5—15 cm   D; ♃

IM: Stem quadrangular, numerous
leafy, creeping, above-ground stems,
forming a dense flat turf. Flowering
stems ascending. Stem leaves round,
coarsely crenate, short petioles,
opposite. Basal leaves similar, somewhat larger. Inflorescence with yellowish bracts and small rather pale yellow
(also greenish-yellow) flowers.
H: Cool woodland brooks, saturated
rocks, wet ditches, wet areas round
springs. Usually in the shade. Calcifugous. Up to about 1100 m. Common
except in southern and eastern parts.

Wild Mignonette
Reseda lutea
Mignonette family
Resedaceae

June–Aug.   30–75 cm   D; ☉ -♃

IM: Stem branched, ascending to erect. Upper leaves pinnate or bipinnate. Dense racemes of flowers. Flowers pale yellow; usually 4 large deeply lobed petals, plus 2 very small ones.
H: Rubble heaps, paths, railway embankments, arable fields. Calcicolous. Requires loose often stony ground rich in nutrients. Northern England southwards.
AI: Similar: Weld, *R. luteola*: common, in similar habitats. Old dyeing plant. Only 4 petals, all leaves undivided.

Tormentil
Potentilla erecta
Rose family
Rosaceae

June–Sept.   10–30 cm   D; ♃

IM: Stem prostrate to erect. Stem leaves alternate, sessile, with 3 leaflets and 2 large leaflet-like stipules. Basal leaves comprise 3 leaflets, along with thin petioles, often already withered by flowering time. Flowers on pedicels, solitary in leaf axils, about 1 cm wide.
H: Heaths, dry meadows, moorland. On light soils. Calcifugous; indicator of surface acidity and lack of nutrients. Common, up to over 1000 m.
AI: Old medicinal plant with many scientific names: *P. tormentilla*, *Tormentilla erecta*.

Wood Spurge
Euphorbia amygdaloides
Spurge family
Euphorbiaceae

March–May   30–80 cm   D; ♃; +

IM: Plant contains white milky juice (latex). Stem ascending to erect, in 2 conspicuous sections (2-year growth): lower part leathery with a shock of large ovoid-spatulate leaves often covered with fine hairs, upper part herbaceous, few leaves, many-branched inflorescence. Umbels with 5–10 main rays. Glands of cyathium half-moon-shaped: capsule finely spotted (check with magnifying glass). Bracts are fused together in pairs.
H: In deciduous and mixed deciduous woodland on slightly damp loamy soil rich in mull and nutrients and usually calcareous. Common in the south, only local in the north, apparently absent from Scotland.

Euphorbia brittingeri
Spurge family
Euphorbiaceae

May–June   30–50 cm   D; ♃; +

  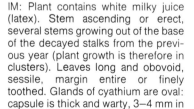

IM: Plant contains white milky juice (latex). Stem ascending or erect, several stems growing out of the base of the decayed stalks from the previous year (plant growth is therefore in clusters). Leaves long and obovoid, sessile, margin entire or finely toothed. Glands of cyathium are oval: capsule is thick and warty, 3–4 mm in diameter.
H: Not British. Balks, meagre turf, sunny thickets. Also on pastures and waysides. Calcicolous. Prefers rather dry deep soils poor in nutrients. Only in southern parts of northern Europe. Scattered. Up to about 1000 m.
AI: Similar: Sweet Spurge (see p. 362). Synonym: *E. verrucosa*.

Broad-leaved Spurge
Euphorbia platyphyllos
Spurge family
Euphorbiaceae

June–Oct.　15–80 cm　D; ⊙ ; +

IM: Plant contains white milky juice (latex). Stem erect or curved at the base. Leaves sessile, finely toothed at the apex: lower ones ovoid with blunt ends, the upper ones rather more lanceolate, pointed. Umbel with 5 (rarely 3) loosely branched main rays. Glands of the cyathium are broadly oval: capsule warty, 2–3 mm in diameter.
H: Fields, gardens: also along paths. On warm, well-fertilized soil which is not too dry. Widespread in England, local in parts and rarer in the north.
Al: Similar: adjacent entry and also *E. stricta*: umbel usually has 2–5 rays, capsule is small, max. 2 mm diameter. In woods on limestone areas of the southern England/Wales border.

Sun Spurge
Euphorbia helioscopia
Spurge family
Euphorbiaceae

May–Oct.　10–50 cm　D; ⊙ ; +

IM: Plant contains white milky juice (latex). Stem usually erect, simple, sometimes with a few branches at the base. Leaf base is wedge-shaped, apex spatulate and finely-toothed, upper leaves enlarged. Umbel usually has 5 main rays. Glands of cyathium are oval: capsule is finely spotted (check with magnifying glass).
H: Cultivated ground and as a wayside weed. On loose soils rich in nutrients and minerals. Nitrogen indicator. Very common throughout.
Al: Similar, often in the same location: Petty-leaved Spurge (*E. peplus*, see p. 362); rather calcifugous. Broad-leaved Spurge (see entry left).

Cypress Spurge
Euphorbia cyparissias
Spurge family
Euphorbiaceae

May–Aug.   10–30 cm   D; ♃; +

Dwarf Spurge
Euphorbia exigua
Spurge family
Euphorbiaceae

June–Oct.   5–30 cm   D; ⊙ ; +

IM: Plant contains white milky juice (latex). Stem erect, many leaves. Leaves narrow-linear, barely 2 mm wide, bluish-green. Umbel with 9–15 rays. Glands of cyathium half-moon-shaped: capsule finely spotted and rough (check with magnifying glass).
H: Grassland, scrubby and open areas and waste places. On sunny warm limestone ground poor in nutrients. Rather scattered, frequently an escape from cultivation or casual.
Al: Yellowish plants with deformed leaf growth have been attacked by uredo (red pustules on the leaf undersides). Similar: Leafy Spurge (*E. esula*): leaves oblanceolate, approx. 3 mm wide. Very rare. The distribution is not fully known.

IM: Plant contains white milky juice (latex). Stem ascending to erect, often with many branches. Leaves linear, 1–4 mm, pointed, sessile. Umbel with 3 (–5) forked main rays. Glands of the cyathium are half-moon-shaped; capsule smooth.
H: Arable fields. Prefers dry calcareous loamy soil rich in nutrients. Likes warmth. Common in England and Wales, also southern Scotland but becoming very rare in the north.
Al: Remotely similar: Sickle Spurge (*E. falcata*): fields: rare (Mediterranean plant). Leaves wider, lanceolate, bluish-green.

129

Common Evening-primrose
Oenothera biennis
Willowherb family
Onagraceae (Oenotheraceae)

June–Sept.   5–100 cm   D; ☉

IM: Flowers large, over 3 cm wide; petals longer than stamens; sepals narrow, folded back. Spikes with many flowers. Stem erect, often unbranched. Leaves long, ovoid, stiff, toothed or entire.

H: Railway embankments, rubble heaps, river banks, quarries, paths, waste places. Usually in dry soil. Once a widespread casual, now decreasing though naturalized in some places.

AI: Many similar types differing in minor characteristics (flower size, hairy growth, red flecks): Small-flowered Evening-primrose (*O. parviflora = muricata*): flowers smaller than 3 cm, stamens long.

Yellow Bird's-nest
Monotropa hypopitys
Wintergreen family
Purolaceae

June–Aug.   10–30 cm   D; ♃

IM: Plant without any chlorophyll, pale yellow to whitish, more rarely reddish or tinged with brown. Leaves scale-like. Stem erect. Flowers in a terminal raceme, initially drooping. Flowers campanulate, 4 lobed, only terminal flower has 5 lobes, all 1–2 cm long, hanging slightly, erect in fruit.

H: Coniferous and mixed woodland, more rarely in pure deciduous woods on poor soil. Needs acid soil rich in mull and well-moistened. Widespread but never common throughout England, in north and south but not central Wales and parts of Scotland.

AI: Two sub-species: Ssp. *hypopitys*: up to 11 flowers, dense inflorescence, usually covered with hairs. Ssp *hypophegea*, 1–6 glabrous flowers.

Crosswort
Galium cruciata
Madder family
Rubiaceae

May–June   15–70 cm   D; ♃

IM: Entire plant covered with short hairs. Stem quadrangular, slender, prostrate to erect. Leaves in whorls of 4, light green, ovoid, with 3 veins. Flowers in leaf axils, small, barely 3 mm wide.
H: Woodland margins, thickets, hedges, waysides, more rarely on meadows near woodland. On well-moistened nitrogenous soil rich in humus and often low in lime. Throughout Britain except the extreme north.
Al: Previously attributed to a different genus under the name of *Cruciata laevipes*. Further synonym: *C. chersonensis*.

Lady's Bedstraw
Galium verum
Madder family
Rubiaceae

July–Aug.   15–100 cm   D; ♃

IM: Stem bluntly 4-angled, ascending to erect. Leaves needle-shaped, single-veined, with short, sharp tips, margins curled up; in whorls of 8–12. Many-flowered terminal panicles. Flowers small, barely 3 mm wide, sweet–smelling.
H: Grassland, hedges, dunes. Likes calcareous soils which are dry and warm in the summer. Very common throughout.
Al: The hybrid *G.* x *pomeranicum* (with Hedge Bedstraw — *G. mollugo*, see p. 47) has pale yellow flowers.

Yellow Water-lily
Nuphar lutea
Water-lily family
Nymphaeaceae

June–Aug.   0.5–2.5 m   D; ♃; (+)

IM: Leaf-blades and flowers floating on the water surface, growing from rope-like stems. Flowers 4–6 cm wide. Leaves broadly ovoid with heart-shaped basal notch, 12–40 cm long; lateral veins forking near the margin, not joining together.
H: Stagnant or slow-flowing water; likes cool water rich in nutrients and occasionally acid. Throughout Britain but rarer in northern Scotland.
AI: Similar: Least Water-lily (*N. pumila*): flowers 1–3 cm wide, leaves 4–14 cm long. Local, mainly in Scotland but also a few in England and Wales, in cold lakes low in nutrients. Leaves of White Water-lily (p. 84) can be identified by lateral veins linking together along leaf margins.
132

Marsh-marigold
Caltha palustris
Buttercup family
Ranunculaceae

March–July   15–50 cm   D; ♃; (+)

IM: Leaves and flowers have glossy sheen. Stem hollow, prostrate to ascending, branched. Leaves reniform, finely toothed margin; the upper ones sessile with conspicuous herbaceous sheaths, the remainder petiolate; petioles grooved. Perianth is composed of only 5 segments (no separate petals and sepals); they measure up to 5 cm in diameter.
H: Wet woodland and meadows, river banks, ditches, streams, areas round springs and reed beds. Likes soil which is rich in nutrients and saturated with ground water. Common throughout. Up to about 1200 m.
AI: Many races; in particular the lowland type, and the type which grows in relatively hilly and mountainous areas.

Yellow Anemone
Anemone ranunculoides
Buttercup family
Ranunculaceae

April   10–20 cm   D; ♃; +

IM: Usually 2 (1–4) stalked flowers emerge from a single whorl of stem leaves. Stem otherwise bare of leaves, erect. Very few basal leaves which appear after flowering, petiolate, palmately compound (3 leaflets). Flowers 1–2 cm wide, layer of downy hairs on the outside.
H: Naturalized in a few places in England.

Goldilocks Buttercup
Ranunculus auricomus
Buttercup family
Ranunculaceae

April–May   10–40 cm   D; ♃; (+)

IM: Stem erect, branched, few hairs. 2–6 basal leaves, petiolate, ranging in shape from undivided with a reniform outline to 5-lobed. Stem leaves conspicuously different from basal leaves: sessile and divided virtually to the base into narrow lobes. Few flowers, 1–2.5 cm across, occasionally with stunted petals or ones which wither rapidly.
H: Deciduous woodland, mixed woodland, lowland forests, thickets, undergrowth along streams. Usually found on calcareous loamy soils saturated with ground water. Common throughout.

Corn Buttercup
Ranunculus arvensis
Buttercup family
Ranunculaceae

June—July   15—60 cm   D; ⊙ ; +

IM: Stem erect, branched. Lower leaves undivided, wedge-shaped, toothed — often dried up by the time the flowers blossom; stem leaves divided into narrow segments. Many sulphur-yellow flowers 0.5—1.5 cm in diameter, on hairy peduncles. Fruit conspicuously prickly.
H: Especially in corn fields but also found on waste land. On loamy soil rich in nitrogen and preferably containing lime. Common in the south, rarer in the north, in some places heavily reduced presence as a result of the use of herbicides.

Meadow Buttercup
Ranunculus acris
Buttercup family
Ranunculaceae

May—July   15—100 cm   D; ♃; +

IM: Stem erect, branched. Lower leaves petiolate, palmately divided, lobes in turn divided or long toothed. Upper stem leaves sessile, less divided, segments narrow. Inflorescence cymose. Peduncles hairy, but not grooved. Calyx spreading but not reflexed.
H: Meadows and pastures which are not too dry. Likes damp nitrogenous loamy soils. Very common; up to about 1300 m.
AI: Similar: in addition to the species on the following page: Wood Buttercup (*R. nemorosus*), peduncles sparsely hairy but with longitudinal grooves. Not British. Light woodland, forest margins, mountain meadows; scattered. Several subspecies.

Bulbous Buttercup
Ranunculus bulbosus
Buttercup family
Ranunculaceae

May–July   15–40 cm   D; ♃; +

IM: Sepals folded back and lying close to the longitudinally grooved peduncle. Stem swollen at the base to form a bulb-like stem-tuber (just below the soil surface). Basal leaves have long petioles and are divided into 3 leaflets, the middle one with a conspicuous stalk. All leaflets may themselves be divided into 3s projecting at base of stem, but clinging towards top.
H: Dry meadows, balks, path verges. Prefers rather poor warm loamy soil, usually calcareous. Throughout Britain, often very common becoming less so in the north.
AI: Similar: Hairy Buttercup (*R. sardous*). Covered with projecting hairs, no bulb; flowers pale yellow. Local, usually as a weed in fields.

Creeping Buttercup
Ranunculus repens
Buttercup family
Ranunculaceae

May–Aug.   15–60 cm   D; ♃; (+)

IM: Stem usually ascending, with creeping runners above the ground, often rooting at the nodes. Basal leaves divided into 3 segments each of which is further divided, middle lobe having a long, conspicuous stalk. Flowers solitary in the leaf axils, on peduncles. Sepals spread out. Peduncles have longitudinal grooves.
H: Edges of banks, wet fields, gardens, path verges, damp meadows, woods. On moist heavy loamy soils. Nitrogen indicator. Common throughout. Often in masses.
AI: Very variable in hair covering, leaf form, flower size (and form) but these variations are apparently only habitat-related (not transmitted through reproduction).   135

Celery-leaved Crowfoot
Ranunculus sceleratus
Buttercup family
Ranunculaceae

May—Sept.   20—60 cm   D; ⊙ ; +

IM: Flowers barely 1 cm across, pale yellow; sepals reflexed but falling off rapidly, as long as or longer than the petals. Peduncles have longitudinal grooves. Stem ascending (also floating in water), hollow, many branches. Leaves somewhat fleshy, divided into 3 narrow lobes, sometimes themselves lobed and toothed. Fruiting head cylindric; 70—100 small fruits.
H: River banks, ditches, mud, shallow pools. Found in soil which is at least occasionally flooded, and must be very wet and rich in nutrients. Rare. Throughout Britain but scattered and rarer in north Scotland. Tolerates salt.
Al: Many habitat-related types: from the stunted growth found on dry soils to the aquatic plant.

136

Woolly Buttercup
Ranunculus lanuginosus
Buttercup family
Ranunculaceae

May—July   30—70 cm   D; ♃; (+)

IM: Entire plant covered with dense projecting hairs. Stem erect, usually branched, hollow at the bottom, with yellow tufts. Basal leaves petiolate, divided into 5 lobes; lobes are wide, ovoid, toothed; stem leaves are similar but with short petioles or sessile. Flowers large, approx. 3—4 cm wide. Sepals spread out; peduncles not longitudinally grooved.
H: Not British. Damp shady deciduous and mixed woodland, thickets, undergrowth along streams. On loamy soils saturated with ground water and rich in nitrogen, lime and mull. Scattered. Eastern parts of C. and S. Europe.
Al: Similar: Wood Buttercup (*R. nemorosus*): more delicate peduncle with longitudinal grooves (p. 134).

Great Spearwort
Ranunculus lingua
Buttercup family
Ranunculaceae

June–Sept.   50–120 cm   D; ♃; (+)

 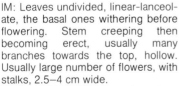 ▽

IM: Leaves undivided, linear-lanceolate, the basal ones withering before flowering. Stem creeping then becoming erect, usually many branches towards the top, hollow. Usually large number of flowers, with stalks, 2.5–4 cm wide.
H: In reed beds in stagnant or slow-flowing waters, also in ditches, marshes and fens. On muddy ground which is occasionally flooded and is rich in nutrients. Local but widespread.
AI: This species grows both on banks and in shallow water up to over 50 cm depth and also grows in different forms depending on the varying conditions.

Lesser Spearwort
Ranunculus flammula
Buttercup family
Ranunculaceae

May–Sept.   8–50 cm   D; ♃; +

IM: Stem fairly thick; prostrate, ascending or erect. Leaves undivided, narrow-lanceolate to ovate, sometimes spoon-shaped with long petioles. Usually numerous flowers, on long peduncles rarely over 2 cm wide.
H: Banks, streams, ponds, ditches, damp meadows, moors, beds of sedge, wet pathways, more rarely in reed beds. Found in wet, muddy or loamy soil, usually acid. Common.
AI: Similar: Creeping Spearwort (*R. reptans*); flowers less than 1 cm, all leaves petiolate in tufts at each point where the creeping stem roots. Prefers soil which is richer in nutrients and more alkaline, rarer.

137

Orpine
Sedum telephium
Stonecrop family
Crassulaceae

July–Sept. 20–60 cm D; ♃

IM: Leaves ovoid, smooth, flat but fleshy. Stem erect. Many flowers in dense cymes at top of stem.
H: In light woodland and hedgerows, often on banks. Likes moderately dry, stony ground rich in nutrients. Scattered and rather local in most parts, rare in northern Scotland; also growing as a garden escape (old ornamental plant).
Al: Various colour types: Ssp. *maximum*, usually with greenish-yellow (more rarely light reddish) flowers; ssp. *telephium*, flowers usually reddish or lilac (more rarely greenish); ssp. *fabaria*, flowers reddish or lilac; ssp. *ruprechtii*, flowers white.

Biting Stonecrop
Sedum acre
Stonecrop family
Crassulaceae

June–July 2–10 cm D; ♃; +

IM: Leaves thick and fleshy, upper sides flat, with ovoid outline, approx. 0.5 cm long. Stem prostrate or ascending. Inflorescence with few flowers. Petals pointed, 0.5–1 cm long.
H: Walls, gravel paths, sand dunes, rock fissures, scree, stony river beds, sandy or stony turf. Found on dry, shallow and often stony calcareous ground.
Al: Also known as Wall-pepper. Similar: Tasteless Stonecrop, *S. sexangulare* (*S. mite*, *S. boloniense*): flowers smaller. Naturalized in some places in England and Wales.

Wood Avens
Geum urbanum
Rose family
Rosaceae

June–Aug.   20–60 cm   D; ♃; (+)

IM: Stem erect, usually unbranched. Basal rosette of 3–7 pinnate leaves with unequal leaflets and short petioles. Stem leaves 3–5 leaflets or entire. Cymes loose and 4-flowered. Sepals about as long as petals, plus 5 shorter epicalyx segments. Fruit has hooked awn.
H: Deciduous and mixed woodland, woodland paths and margins, thickets, balks, hedgerows and shady places. Likes well-moistened nitrogenous soil. Common.
AI: Old medicinal plant. Also called Herb Bennet.

Creeping Avens
Geum reptans
Rose family
Rosaceae

July–Aug.   5–15 cm   D; ♃

IM: Stem mostly erect, flower single. Flowers up to 4 cm wide. Basal leaves form rosette. Leaves pinnate, leaflets deeply cleft, getting larger towards the leaf apex, terminal leaflet is not how- ever exceptionally large. Produces long twisted stolons. Fruits numerous; all have long tufted, hairy style.
H: Not British. Only found in the High Alps between 2000 and 2400 m on damp unstable scree and moraines. Rare.
AI: Similar: Alpine Avens (*G. monta- num*); without stolons, terminal leaflet markedly larger. Alpine turfs and heaths (1500–2300 m). Not British.

Golden Cinquefoil
Potentilla aurea
Rose family
Rosaceae

June–Aug.   5–20 cm   D; ♃

IM: Stem usually curved at the base rising to erect; branched. Flowers in panicles, up to 2 cm across, long peduncles. Leaves palmately 5 lobed — stem leaves sometimes with only 3 lobes. Leaflets wedge-shaped to narrow ovoid, toothed at the apex, margin covered with silky hairs.
H: Not British. Meagre Alpine turf, pastures, snowy valleys, heaths lying between 1000 and 2400 m. Likes acid soil low in lime and not too dry. Only the Alps and Black Forest. Scattered.
AI: Similar Alpine Cinquefoils: Alpine Cinquefoil (*P. crantzii*), see below. *P. brauneana*, leaves have only 3 lobes; stony ground, pastures; calcicolous. Not British.
140

Alpine Cinquefoil
Potentilla crantzii
Rose family
Rosaceae

March–May   5–25 cm   D; ♃

IM: Stem creeping to ascending. Leaves digitate, 5–7 lobes; leaflets toothed, leaf margin does not have silky sheen. Cyme with few flowers. Flowers 1–2 cm across; petals deeply notched, not overlapping at the edge.
H: Sunny balks, dry pastures, sandy slopes. Calcicolous, likes warmth. Very local, usually on high ground. Northern England, north Wales, Scotland.
AI: A very variable species, further confused by the presence of hybrids between it and other cinquefoils.

Creeping Cinquefoil
Potentilla reptans
Rose family
Rosaceae

June–Aug. 30–100 cm D; ♃

IM: Stem prostrate, creeping, stolon-like, rooting at the nodes. Leaves petiolate, palmately divided, usually 5 leaflets (more rarely 3 or 7). Leaflets obovoid or oblong, toothed, sparsely hairy on both sides. Flowers solitary in leaf axils, 1.5–2.5 cm wide.
H: Relatively damp meadows, hedgerows, waste places, also fields and gardens. Likes nitrogenous soil and warmth. Common.
AI: Similar: Trailing Tormentil (*P. anglica = procumbens*): scattered but local, rare in north Scotland. Flowers max. 1.8 cm wide, often only 4 petals. This fertile species is derived from the sterile hybrid of Tormentil (see p. 126) and Creeping Cinquefoil.

Silverweed
Potentilla anserina
Rose family
Rosaceae

June–Aug. 15–50 cm D; ♃

IM: Stem creeping to erect. Leaves pinnate; 7–12 pairs of oblong, deeply serrate main leaflets alternating with smaller leaflets, undersides covered with silky hairs. Flowers solitary, on long peduncles, golden-yellow, approx. 2 cm wide.
H: Path verges, village commons, railway embankments, grassy beaches, fallow land, damp pastures and waste places. Likes warmth and nitrogen, tolerates salt. Prefers compact loamy soils. Common, reaching about 450 m.

Agrimony
Agrimonia eupatoria
Rose family
Rosaceae

June–Aug.   30–60 cm   D; ♃

IM: Many small flowers approx. 1 cm across in spike-like racemes. Stem erect, covered with rough hairs. Leaves pinnate, leaflets serrate; smaller pinnate leaflets growing between the large ones. Fruit with hooked spines.
H: Path balks, sunny slopes, pastures, woodland margins, hedgerows. Likes calcareous humus soil, not too dry but low in nutrients. Likes warmth. Common in most parts up to about 500 m but rare in northern Scotland.
AI: The robust ssp. *grandis* from Europe is larger and hairier than ssp. *eupatoria*.

Upright Yellow Oxalis
Oxalis europaea
Wood-sorrel family
Oxalidaceae

June–Sept.   10–30 cm   D; ☉ – ♃

IM: Stem erect, not rooting at the nodes, hairy. Leaves petiolate, trifoliate like clover, stipules absent. Inflorescence cymose, with 1–6 flowers. Capsules angular, on erect pedicels.
H: Not British. Fields, gardens, paths, rubble heaps. Usually on soil which is low in lime and contains no nitrogen. Frequent as a weed in most parts of Europe except the far north and south.
AI: Synonym: *O. stricta*. Similar: Procumbent Yellow Oxalis (*O. corniculata*): stem creeping, rooting at the nodes, often red. Small stipules at base of leafstalk. Scattered, sometimes common. Gardens, fields, tarmac roads, pavements. Both species are introduced synanthropic plants.

Common Rock-rose
Helianthemum nummularium
Rock-rose family
Cistaceae

June–Sept.   5–30 cm   D; ♃

IM: Stem prostrate to erect, woody at the base. Leaves opposite, oblong or oval, margin entire. Unilateral cymes with few (1–12) flowers. Flowers usually about 2–3 cm wide; 3 larger sepals, 2 very small inner ones.
H: Poor turf, pastures, light thickets. Likes warmth. Prefers stony usually calcareous ground. Common in most parts but absent from the extreme south west of England, Isle of Man and north west Scotland.
AI: Many subspecies: Ssp. *nummularium* (leaf underside has grey felt covering) is main form in lower-lying areas. Ssp. *grandiflorum* (curly hairs) and ssp. *glabrum* (virtually glabrous): Alpine varieties up to 2300 m have large flowers (3–4 cm).

Trailing St. John's-wort
Hypericum humifusum
St. John's-wort family
Hypericaceae

June–Sept.   5–20 cm   D; ☉ – ♃

IM: Stem slender, branched, creeping, curved upwards at the ends; usually has a narrow rib along 2 sides of stem. Leaves opposite, oblong-ovoid. Inflorescence with few flowers. Flowers 1–1.5 cm wide. Plant glabrous.
H: Dry moorland, heaths, open woodland. Likes open soil low in lime. Scattered.

Hairy St. John's-wort
Hypericum hirsutum
St. John's-wort family
Hypericaceae

July—Aug.   40—100 cm   D; ♃

IM: Entire plant has a thick covering of short hairs. Stem twisting at base rising to erect, round. Leaves opposite, margin entire, ovoid, blunt, virtually sessile; leaf surface has translucent spots but no black glands. Inflorescence loose, many flowered. Flowers around 1.5 cm wide. Sepals have black glands around margin, petals have fewer.
H: Somewhat wet open woodland, thickets, grassy areas. Found on calcareous soils rich in nitrogen. Scattered.

Pale St. John's-wort
Hypericum montanum
St. John's-wort family
Hypericaceae

June—Aug.   40—80 cm   D; ♃

IM: Plant slightly hairy. Stem erect, round. Leaves opposite, glabrous above, thinly hairy beneath, sessile, half clasping the stem, with black dots round the edge beneath; only the upper leaves have translucent spots on the leaf blade. Inflorescence dense. Flowers 1—1.5 cm wide. Sepals have black marginal glands. Approx. 40—60 stamens in 3 bundles.
H: Dry thickets and woodland. Found on ground which is rich in nutrients and usually calcareous. Scattered.
AI: In appearance very close to the previous entry; can however be distinguished clearly by the leaves being glabrous above and by the dense, short inflorescence.

Imperforate St. John's-wort
Hypericum maculatum
St. John's-wort family
Hypericaceae

June–Aug.   20–60 cm   D; ♃

IM: Plant glabrous. Stem erect, with 4 narrow longitudinal ribs. Leaves opposite, sessile, barely or not at all translucently spotted, with black marginal glands. Flowers approx. 2.0 cm wide. Sepals and petals often have light-coloured or black spots. Stamens in 3 bundles.
H: Hedgerows and woodland margins. Found on slightly acid ground which is at least occasionally wet. Scattered throughout most of Britain but rather local.
AI: *H. × desetangsii* is similar but the stem has 2 distinct ribs and 2 faint ones. In similar habitats but rare.

Square-stalked St. John's-wort
Hypericum tetrapterum
St. John's-wort family
Hypericaceae

June–Sept.   30–70 cm   D; ♃

IM: Plant glabrous. Stem erect, branched, with 4 wide wing-like longitudinal ribs. Leaves opposite, sessile, half-clasping the stem; leaf blade fine and covered with translucent spots. Additionally the leaves, ribs, petals and sepals have black glandular spots. Inflorescence compact with many flowers. Flowers approx. 1 cm across. Stamens in 3 bundles.
H: Wet meadows, grassy areas around springs, ditches, lakes and ponds. On wet, occasionally flooded soils rich in nutrients and preferably calcareous. Throughout Britain except northern Scotland.
AI: Synonym: *H. acutum*.

Perforate St. John's-wort
Hypericum perforatum
St. John's-wort family
Hypericaceae

June–Sept.   30–90 cm   D; ♃

IM: Plant glabrous. Stem erect, often branched, round, with 2 longitudinal ribs. Leaves opposite, sessile, narrowly oval, spotted with translucent glands. Stamens in 3 bundles.
H: Open woodland, hedges, clearings, poor meadowland and pastures. On various different soils; usually calcareous, low in nitrogen, moderately dry. Common throughout most areas.
AI: Old medicinal magic plant (petals produce a reddish colour when crushed).

Slender St. John's-wort
Hypericum pulchrum
St. John's-wort family
Hypericaceae

June–Aug.   30–60 cm   D; ♃

IM: Plant glabrous. Stem erect or ascending, round. Leaves opposite, sessile, bluntly triangular to heart-shaped, half clasping the stem, translucently spotted. Inflorescence few-flowered. Flowers approx. 1.5 cm wide. Sepals and petals have black marginal glands. Stamens in 3 bundles. Stem, leaves and flowers often tinged with red.
H: Dry open woodland, glades and grassy areas. On acid sandy or loamy soil. Calcifugous. Indicator of poor soil. Avoids wet habitats. Scattered.

Sickle-leaved Hare's-ear
Bupleurum falcatum
Umbellifer family
Apiaceae (Umbelliferae)

July–Oct.   50–130 cm   D; ⌗

IM: Stem erect, hollow. Leaves leathery, usually very narrow, the upper ones sickle-shaped, margin entire. Flowers small, in compound umbels containing 4–10 rays; 2–5 bracts, often unequal, 4–5 large bracteoles which are shorter than the pedicels.
H: Hedgerows and waste places. Found in loose calcareous soils which are low in nitrogen and where the location is warm in the summer. Only in a few places in south-east England.
Al: The Hare's-ear genus is the only one of the Umbelliferae found in Britain to have undivided leaves.

Wild Parsnip
Pastinaca sativa
Umbellifer family
Apiaceae (Umbelliferae)

July–Aug.   30–150 cm   D;⊙

IM: Stem erect, branched at the top, grooved, hairy. Leaves coarsely simple pinnate. Compound umbel with 5–15 rays. Bracts and bracteoles absent, occasionally 1–2 but falling quickly. Flowers barely 2 mm wide. Petals often curled up, golden-yellow.
H: Rubble heaps, path and road verges, fields, railway embankments. Likes nitrogenous deep loamy soil, especially on chalk and limestone. Found throughout England and Wales, sometimes locally common. In Scotland only an escape.
Al: Wild: Ssp. *urens*: grey hairs, stem finely grooved, S., C., E. Europe. Ssp. *sylvestris* (grooved, hairy). C., W., Europe. Wild as an escape. Ssp. *sativa*: almost glabrous, stem grooved.

147

Primrose
Primula vulgaris
Primrose family
Primulaceae

Dec.–May   5–15 cm   D; ♃

IM: Basal leaves oblong to obovoid gradually narrowed at base, occasionally lasting through winter, sometimes killed by frost. Young leaves begin to develop during flowering time; wrinkled, uppersides glabrous, underneath light covering of short hairs. Flowers on hairy pedicels arising from basal rosette. Calyx cleft almost to middle. Corolla 2–3 (+) cm wide, with notched lobes.

H: Woodland, thickets, meadows, balks. On damp soils rich in nutrients and mull but rather low in lime. Common, less so in the north.

Al: Synonyms: *P. acaulis*; meaning without stem. Common ornamental plant (flowers white, yellow, red, brown, blue)

148

Bear's-ear
Primula auricula
Primrose family
Primulaceae

April–July   5–30 cm   D; ♃

IM: Rosette made up of slightly fleshy leaves with cartilaginous margins, hairless and mealy. Many-flowered often one-sided umbel on robust scape. Corolla rather campanulate, approx. 1.5 cm wide, the 5 lobes only slightly notched.

H: Not British. Rocks, stony turf, marshy meadows. Found on very wet ground often low in humus. Calcicolous. In the Alps scattered up to 2400 m, rare in the foreland; found northwards as far as the Schwäbisches Alb and the Black Forest.

Al: Similar: *P. hortensis*. Many-coloured ornamental plant based on hybrid of Auricula and Hairy Primrose (*P. hirsuta*) = *P. × pubescens*. Corolla margin flat, lobes deeply crenate.

Oxlip
Primula elatior
Primrose family
Primulaceae

April–May   10–30 cm   D; ♃

IM: Umbel on tall scape, often one-sided. Flowers sulphur yellow; corolla margin flat, around 2 cm wide; calyx narrow, cylindrical, with green edges. Rosette leaves oblong-ovoid, wrinkled, crenate, with short hairs.
H: Woodland where it occurs on chalky boulder clay. Locally common in small areas. South Midlands eastwards to East Anglia.

Cowslip
Primula veris
Primrose family
Primulaceae

April–May   10–30 cm   D; ♃

IM: One-sided umbel on straight scape. Flowers golden-yellow, with orange flecks on the inside; margin of the corolla approx. 1.5 cm wide, campanulate; calyx inflated, light greyish-yellow. Rosette leaves oblong-ovoid, wrinkled, notched.
H: Balks, meadow slopes, poor turf, thickets, open woodland. Found on soil which is preferably calcareous, not too moist and which contains nutrients. Fairly common, rarer in the north, and absent from some parts of Scotland.

Tufted Loosestrife
Lysimachia thyrsiflora
Primrose family
Primulaceae

May–June   30–70 cm   D; ♃

IM: Stem erect. Leaves opposite and decussate, lanceolate to linear-lanceolate, margin entire, sessile. Many dark gland spots on the leaf blade. Flowers in compressed cylindrical racemes in leaf axils, 3–5 mm wide, occasionally 6 in a raceme. Racemes are stalked but still not as long as the leaves.

H: In marshes, canals and ditches with stagnant or slow-flowing waters. Found in muddy acid ground, not very rich in nutrients and frequently flooded. Rare. Scattered in central England and Scotland and parts of the south.

AI: Has been placed in a genus on its own: *Naumburgia*.

Yellow Loosestrife
Lysimachia vulgaris
Primrose family
Primulaceae

July–Aug.   60–150 cm   D; ♃

IM: Stem erect, slightly angular. Leaves opposite or in whorls of 3–4, large, ovoid, up to 14 cm long with orange or black glands. Terminal panicles with leaves underneath. Flowers 1–2 cm wide; corolla lobes slightly obtuse, smooth margins, calyx lobes with orange margin which is glandular-hairy.

H: Ditches, river banks, marshes, wet land with bushy growth. On wet peaty ground. Scattered throughout, rarer or absent in the north.

AI: Similar: Dotted Loosestrife (*L. punctata*). Flowers 3–3.5 cm wide, corolla lobes pointed, entire margin glandular-hairy; calyx lobes green, margin glandular-hairy. Ornamental plant, sometimes found wild.

Creeping Jenny
Lysimachia nummularia
Primrose family
Primulaceae

June–Aug.   5–60 cm   D; ♃

IM: Stem far-creeping, virtually unbranched, occasionally ascending at the end. Leaves opposite, rounded, 1–3 cm long, short petioles. Flowers on stout pedicels, solitary, axillary; corolla approx. 1.5–2.5 cm across, sometimes spotted with red inside. Calyx lobes pointed. Plant usually glabrous.
H: Meadows, ditches, waysides, fields, hedgerows. Found on heavy (often compressed) damp loamy soil rich in nitrogen. Reasonably tolerant of drought. Scattered throughout but rare in the north.
Al: Varied in the leaf form, number of flowers, scent and length of peduncle. Is occasionally grown in gardens.

Yellow Pimpernel
Lysimachia nemorum
Primrose family
Primulaceae

May–Sept.   10–40 cm   D; ♃

IM: Stem ascending, hardly branched, rooting at the nodes lower down the plant. Leaves opposite and decussate, ovoid, up to 4 cm long, margin entire, on short petioles. Leaf blade densely covered with translucent spots. Flowers solitary in leaf axils, on very slender pedicels. Corolla approx. 1 cm across, lobes ovoid, obtuse, margin entire or toothed.
H: Woods, thickets and hedgerows. On soil which is rich in nutrients but low in lime. Intolerant of drought. Less common in dry areas, otherwise common.

Great Yellow Gentian
Gentiana lutea
Gentian family
Gentianaceae

July–Sept.　　30–60 cm　　D; ♃

IM: Stem robust, erect. Leaves bluish-green, opposite, broadly ovoid, with pronounced curved venation. Clusters of 3–10 flowers in axils of shell-shaped bracts, arranged in several stages above one another at end of stem. Flowers deeply cleft, 5–6 lobes.
H: Not British. Balks, mountain meadows, Alpine mats, open mountain forests. Scattered in the Alps, otherwise very rare. Calcicolous.
AI: Similar in non-flowering state: False Helleborine (*Veratrum album*, see p. 78): leaves alternate; also related Alpine gentians, all very rare with long ovoid-lanceolate leaves: Purple Gentian, Brown Gentian and Spotted Gentian (*G. purpurea, pannonica, punctata*).
152

Smooth Honeywort
Cerinthe glabra
Borage family
Boraginaceae

May–July　　30–50 cm　　D; ♃

IM: Entire plant glabrous, with bluish tinge. Flowers in compact cylindrical clusters drooping at the end of the peduncle. Corolla campanulate-cylindrical, with 5 small somewhat reflexed lobes. Red ring or red spots in the throat of the tubular-shaped corolla. Leaves sessile with heart-shaped base.
H: Not British. Pastures, Alpine mats, weedy places, scrub along brooks. Found on well-moistened ground rich in nitrogen and preferably calcareous. Rare; only in the (western) Alpine region and foreland. Occasionally planted in gardens.

Common Comfrey
Symphytum officinale
Borage family
Boraginaceae

May–June   30–120 cm   D; ♃; (+)

IM: Entire plant covered with rough hairs. Leaves rather narrowly ovoid, distinctly decurrent. Flowers small campanulate, drooping, in scorpioidal cymes.
H: On damp to wet ground, always rich in nutrients. In wet meadows, on river banks and in ditches. Found throughout Britain but less so in the north.

Henbane
Hyoscyamus niger
Nightshade family
Solanaceae

June–Aug. 30–80 cm   D; ☉ - ☉ ; +

IM: Plant covered with sticky hairs. Stem erect, often branched. Leaves oblong to ovoid, entire or with a few large teeth, lower ones petiolate, upper ones sessile and clasping the stem. Corolla funnel-shaped, 5 lobes, dirty yellow with network of violet-coloured veins.
H: Rubble heaps, paths, walls, also in fields. Likes sunny warm loamy soil consistently rich in nitrogen and not too dry. Scattered and local throughout, in some areas only as a casual.

Dark Mullein
Verbascum nigrum
Figwort family
Scrophulariaceae

June–Oct.   50–120 cm   D; ☉

IM: Stamens have violet-coloured woolly hairs. Flowers about 1.5–2.5 cm wide; long terminal racemes with axillary short-stalked clusters of 5–10 flowers. Stem erect, little branching. Leaves elongate-ovoid, crenate, not decurrent, hairy on undersides.
H: Wayside places and open areas. Found on slightly damp nitrogenous soils not always rich in lime but containing abundant nutrients. Southern England, where it is common, the Midlands and Wales, sometimes found further north.
AI: Similar: Moth Mullein (*V. blattaria*): rare; flowers solitary in the axils of bracts, leaves not hairy. White Mullein (*V. lychnitis*, p. 75); corolla smaller, stamens covered with white wool.

154

Aaron's Rod
Verbascum thapsus
Figwort family
Scrophulariaceae

June–Aug.   30–200 cm   D; ☉

IM: Stamens covered with white wool. Flowers 1.5–3 cm wide, in clusters, forming a long dense raceme. Stem erect, usually simple. Leaves oblong, slightly crenate, decurrent as far as the next leaf, (stem therefore looks winged). Covered with dense whitish or greyish felt-like hairs.
H: Pathways, railway embankments, rubble heaps, balks, heaths, forest margins. Likes warmth. Found on loose shallow often somewhat stony ground. Nitrogen indicator. Common in most areas, rarer in northern Scotland.
AI: Similar to the species described in the adjacent entry, which has larger flowers.

Large-flowered Mullein
Verbascum densiflorum
Figwort family
Scrophulariaceae

July–Sept.   30–200 cm   D; ☉

IM: Stamens covered with white wool, flowers 3–4 cm wide. Long dense raceme. Leaves narrowly ovate, strongly decurrent. Thick greyish-yellow felt-like covering of hairs.
H: Wayside places, clearings, sometimes in fields. Likes warmth. Likes dry preferably calcareous soil rich in nitrogen. A rather rare casual.
Al: Synonym: *V. thapsiforme*. Similar: *V. phlomoides*: leaves not or only slightly decurrent (not as far as the next leaf). Rare casual.

Yellow Bellflower
Campanula thyrsoides
Bellflower family
Campanulaceae

July–Sept.   10–40 cm   D; ☉

IM: Flowers approx. 2 cm long, narrow-campanulate. Dense terminal conical-shaped spike. Stem erect, unbranched, many leaves. Leaves narrow, lanceolate, pointed; basal ones blunt, all sessile. Entire plant covered with dense layer of long bristle-like hairs (flowers rather more woolly-haired).
H: Not British. Found exclusively in the Alps upwards of approx. 1500 m on sunny calcareous and often stony ground which contains nutrients and is not too dry. Scattered (but very conspicuous). Only rarely washed down into the valley.

German Asphodel
Tofieldia calyculata
Lily family
Liliaceae

May–July   10–30 cm   M; ♃

IM: Flowers 6-merous on short pedicels in terminal racemes 3–8 cm long. Stem erect, few leaves. Basal leaves grass-like, arranged in two rows, much shorter than the stem. The epicalyx at the base of the flower is 3-lobed and scale-shaped (in addition to the lanceolate bract on the main stem) and is characteristic of this species.
H: Moors, marshy meadowland, damp poor turf, saturated rocks. Calcicolous. Dislikes fertilizer. Very rare, absent in the north.
AI: Similar: Scottish Asphodel, *T. pusilla* (= *palustris*). Local from northern England to Scotland. Does not have an epicalyx, flowers more whitish-green.

156

Bog Asphodel
Narthecium ossifragum
Lily family
Liliaceae

July–Sept.   10–40 cm   M; ♃

IM: Flowers 6-merous in terminal raceme 5–8 cm long, outer flowers greenish. Stem erect, leafy. Leaves grass-like, basal ones arranged in 2 rows, approx. as long as stem and much longer than stem leaves. Young anthers orange; stamens have dense covering of woolly hairs. Stem & petals deep orange after flowering.
H: High moorland, wet heaths, and mountains. Wet peaty soils low in nutrients. Calcifugous. Common where conditions are suitable, rarer in S.E. and absent from some parts of the Midlands and E. England.
AI: Previously classified under the same genus as the previous entry or as *Anthericum* (p. 79) (*Tofieldia ossifraga* or *Anthericum ossifragum*).

Yellow Star-of-Bethlehem
Gagea lutea
Lily family
Liliaceae

March—May   10—25 cm   M; ♃

IM: Single grass-like basal leaf 6—12 mm across. Umbel with 1—5 flowers which emerges from between 2 narrow bracts. Stem leafless. Pedicels glabrous; petals 1—1.5 cm long, with green stripes on the outside.
H: Damp mixed deciduous woodland and grassland. Likes calcareous soil which is acid with humus, close to ground water and always rich in nutrients. Local in most parts, sometimes rare. Mainly in northern and central England.
AI: Similar: *G. pratensis*: Not British, grassy areas, fields, rare. Basal leaf 3—8 mm wide, keeled. *G. villosa = arvensis*: Not British, fields, rare; 2 basal leaves, 1—2 mm wide.

Yellow Iris
Iris pseudacorus
Iris family
Iridaceae

May—July   40—150 cm   M; ♃;

IM: 3 outer petals ovoid, drooping slightly, without a beard of hairs; 3 inner petals smaller, spatulate, erect; stigmas petalloid. Stem erect, robust, leaves almost sheathed. Basal leaves stiff, sword-shaped, up to 3 cm wide, approximately as long as the stem. Capsule large, triangular.
H: Marshy areas; also found in half-shade in damp undergrowth. Likes marshy ground rich in nutrients. Found wherever the right conditions occur.
AI: The yellow-flowered ornamental plants from this genus which are sometimes found growing wild are usually on drier ground and they all have a beard of hair on the inside of the outer petals.

157

Lesser Celandine
Ranunculus ficaria
Buttercup family
Ranunculaceae

March—May   5—15 cm   D; ♃; (+)

IM: Stem hollow, prostrate to ascending. Leaves alternate, heart- to kidney-shaped, crenate, the upper ones smaller; all have relatively long petioles, glossy. There are sometimes bulbils in the leaf axils. Flowers solitary, with long pedicels; 8—12 petals.
H: Damp deciduous woodland and thickets, spring areas, river banks, meadows. Found on damp loamy soil rich in nutrients. Common throughout. Up to around 800 m.
AI: Falls into several sub-species which are not as yet completely defined. Synonym: *Ficaria verna*.

Yellow Pheasant's-eye
Adonis vernalis
Buttercup family
Ranunculaceae

April—May   10—30 cm   D; ♃; +

IM: Flowers usually solitary, terminal, 4—8 cm wide, with 10—20 petals. Stem erect, sheathed scale-like leaves at the base, upper leaves 2—4 pinnately divided and split into many narrow lobes. As well as the peduncles there are also stalks bearing only leaves.
H: Cultivated in Britain. Sunny balks, dry turf, bushy slopes, pine forests. On loose sandy calcareous soils. Very rare and becoming progressively rarer. Only found in lower-lying areas (up to 500 m).
AI: Like most early flowering plants this one may also flower again in autumn.

Globe-flower
Trollius europaeus
Buttercup family
Ranunculaceae

June–Aug.　10–60 cm　D; ♃; (+)

IM: Flower is a closed sphere up to 3 cm in diameter; 6–15 petals. Stem erect, usually only branched at the bottom; flowers solitary and terminal. Leaves palmate, 3–5 lobes. Basal leaves have long petioles.
H: Damp meadows and woods in mountains. Likes a loamy soil slightly acid with humus, rich in minerals and containing some nutrients. Found in mountain regions from south Wales and the Midlands northwards.
AI: This plant used to be very popular as an ornamental plant and as a wild flower for posies.

Wild Mignonette
Reseda lutea
Mignonette family
Resedaceae

June–Aug.　30–75 cm　D; ☉ – ♃

IM: Stem often branched, ascending to erect. Upper leaves pinnate or bipinnate. Dense racemes. Flowers pale yellow; usually 4 large deeply cleft petals, plus 2 very small ones.
H: Rubble heaps, paths, railway embankments, in fields. Calcicolous. Needs disturbed, often stony ground rich in nutrients. Throughout most parts.
AI: Similar to Weld (*R. luteola*), common in similar habitats. Old dye plant. Always has only 4 petals, all leaves undivided.

Goldenrod
Solidago virgaurea
Daisy family
Asteraceae (Compositae)

July–Sept.   5–75 cm   D; ♃

IM: Many small capitula, 7–10 mm long, in an erect raceme or panicle. On the outside 5–12 narrow ray florets, on the inside disc florets. Stem erect, branches rod-like. Lower leaves obovate, toothed, upper ones ovoid-lanceolate.

H: Open woodland, glades, heaths, poor turf, dunes, cliffs. Likes sunny, preferably calcareous soils which are low in nutrients but not too dry. Common; found up to 1200 m.

Canadian Goldenrod
Solidago canadensis
Daisy family
Asteraceae (Compositae)

Aug.–Oct.   50–250 cm   D; ♃

IM: Hundreds of small capitula, about 5 mm long, in curved, 1-sided partial inflorescences, together forming a projecting panicle. Ray florets are hardly longer than disc florets. Stem erect, usually not branched (apart from the projecting flower-bearing branches), hairy. Leaves lanceolate, often somewhat serrate.

H: Widely cultivated and a frequent escape, in many areas. On sunny but damp loamy soils rich in nutrients.

AI: Very similar: Early Goldenrod (*S. gigantea* = *serotina*): equally tall, base of stem hairless, often tinged with red; ray florets clearly longer than disc florets. Somewhat rarer as an escape. Both introduced from N. America and established here as ornamentals.

Irish Fleabane
Inula salicina
Daisy family
Asteraceae (*Compositae*)

July–Aug. 30–50 cm D; ♃

IM: Stem erect, with 1–5 capitula 2.5–3 cm wide. On the outside long ray florets, inside disc florets. Fruit with a pappus of hairs. Leaves alternate, margin entire, usually hairless, or hairy on veins of underside only.
H: Semi-dry turf, thickets, balks, damp meadows. On calcareous sometimes damp soils. This species only found outside continental Europe on the limestone shoreline of Lough Derg in Galway and Tipperary.
AI: Similar: Fleabane, (*Pulicaria dysenterica*); capitula smaller, leaves hairy. Yellow Ox-Eye (p. 162): capitula wider, leaves hairy. Further *Inula* species whose leaves are all conspicuously hairy at least on the undersides.

Ploughman's-spikenard
Inula conyza
Daisy family
Asteraceae (*Compositae*)

July–Sept. 20–130 cm D; ☉ ♃

IM: Numerous capitula approx. 1 cm wide form a terminal corymb. Only disc florets. Bracts have spreading tips. Stem usually erect, reddish-brown. Leaves ovoid–oblong, finely serrated, undersides covered with felt-like downy hairs.
H: Open woods, glades, thickets, high moors, walls, and cliffs. Calcicolous. Found on sunny and rather dry stony ground where the soil is not too poor. Local, occasionally common in England and Wales.
AI: Similar: *I. graveolens* (=*Cupularia graveolens*); annual, unpleasant smell, glandular, sticky, narrow leaves. Very rare in mild locations in salty areas.

161

Yellow Ox-eye
Buphthalmum salicifolium
Daisy family
Asteraceae (Compositae)

July–Sept.   20–60 cm   D; ♃

IM: Capitula 3–6 cm wide, florets, inside disc florets. Pappus a scarious rim with minute teeth. Stem erect, little branching. Leaves alternate, lanceolate, covered with soft hairs; upper leaves sessile.
H: Not British. Open woodland, dry thickets, forest margins, heaths, poor turf. On calcareous and often stony ground.
AI: There are several similar species from the Fleabane genus (*Pulicaria*) and that of *Inula* (see p. 161). However only the Ox-eye has paleae (large scales) in the capitula.

Jerusalem Artichoke
Helianthus tuberosus
Daisy family
Asteraceae (Compositae)

Sept.–Nov.   1–2.5 m   D; ♃

IM: Capitula 3–8 cm wide, erect, terminal. On the outside ray florets, inside disc florets. Stem erect, little branching. Lower leaves opposite, ovoid to heart-shaped, upper ones alternate, narrow-ovoid; all petiolate, toothed margin, leaf blade covered with rough hairs.
H: Widely grown as a vegetable for its edible tubers, often escaping. Grows on sandy or gravelly loamy soil rich in nutrients. Native of North America.
AI: Occasionally other related species (ornamental plants) are found growing wild; definition is very difficult.

Trifid Bur-marigold
Bidens tripartita
Daisy family
Asteraceae (Compositae)

July–Sept.   15–60 cm   D; ☉

IM: Capitula solitary, 1.5–2.5 cm wide and equally long. On the outside occasionally ray florets, inside brownish-yellow disc florets. Fruit usually has 2 barbed bristles. Stem erect, often tinged brownish-red. Leaves opposite, 3–5 lobed.
H: Ditches, river banks, wet meadows and fields. Found on wet sandy or muddy ground rich in nutrients.
Al: Similar: Greater Bur-marigold (*B. radiata*): not British, capitula larger, leaves light green; rare. *B. frondosa* (= *melanocarpa*); leaves pinnate with 3–5 leaflets and long petioles. An American introduction which occasionally becomes established.

Pineappleweed
Chamomilla suaveolens
Daisy family
Asteraceae (Compositae)

June–July   5–40 cm   D; ☉

IM: Capitula semi-spherical, greenish-yellow. Usually only disc florets, very rarely stunted white ray florets. Stem prostate to erect, many branches, glabrous, very leafy. Leaves double pinnate with narrow lobes. The entire plant has an aromatic smell.
H: Paths, fallow land, rubble heaps, railway embankments, walls, sports fields, more rarely in cornfields. Likes rather damp soil rich in nutrients which is not overgrown but is compact as a result of constant passage. Grows well near residential areas. Very common.
Al: Synonyms: *Matricaria matricarioides*, *M. suaveolens*. Introduced into Europe only in 1850.

163

Tansy
Tanacetum vulgare
Daisy family
Asteraceae (Compositae)

July–Sept.   60–120 cm   D; ♃; +

IM: Capitula in corymbs, semi-spherical and flattened, approx. 1 cm wide. All flowers composed only of disc florets, the marginal florets occasionally have very short ligules. Pappus of the fruit a short, papery cup. Stem erect, angled. Leaves alternate, pinnate, with serrate lobes. Slightly harsh aromatic smell.

H: Pathways, rubble heaps, embankments, waste places. Likes loamy soil rich in nutrients in warm summer locations but with adequate rainfall. Common.

AI: Synonyms: *Chrysanthemum tanacetum*, *C. vulgare*.

Mugwort
Artemisia vulgaris
Daisy family
Asteraceae (Compositae)

July–Sept.   60–120 cm   D; ♃; (+)

IM: Capitula narrow, approx. 5 mm long, numerous, in leafy racemose panicles. Disc florets only, virtually entirely enclosed by the somewhat felted involucral bracts. Stem erect, often tinged with dark reddish-violet. Leaves pinnate, undersides covered with white downy hairs. Aromatic smell.

H: Pathways, rubble heaps, embankments, roadsides, waste places. On various different nitrogenous soils. Very common.

AI: Old medicinal and spice plant.

Colt's-foot
Tussilago farfara
Daisy family
Asteraceae (Compositae)

March–April   10–30 cm   D; ♃

IM: Solitary capitula, terminal on stem with scale-like leaves. On the outside several rows of ray florets, on the inside disc florets. Fruit with a pappus of long white hairs. After flowering, stem is longer, and drooping at the top. Basal leaves appear after flowering time: long-stalked, round to heart-shaped, toothed, undersides covered with white felt; teeth slightly black.
H: Arable land, open ground, paths, embankments, walls, waste places. Calcicolous, requires moisture. Very common.
AI: Old medicinal plant. The similar leaves of the Butterbur (*Petasites*, pp. 88 and 243) do not have blackish teeth.

Arnica
Arnica montana
Daisy family
Asteraceae (Compositae)

June–July   20–50 cm   D; ♃

IM: Stem erect, usually unbranched, with 1–2 pairs of opposite leaves, downy. Rosette of leathery, ovoid basal leaves with margin almost entire. All capitula 6–8 cm wide; on the outside long ray florets, on the inside disc florets. Fruit with a pappus of hairs. Slightly harsh aromatic smell.
H: Not British. Poor meadowland, Alpine mats, moorland, heaths. Likes acid loamy soil containing sand and humus; also peaty soil. Calcifugous. Rare. Main area of distribution is the mountains.
AI: Old medicinal plant. Can be distinguished from other yellow *Compositae* by its basal rosette and its opposite leaves.

165

Groundsel
Senecio vulgaris
Daisy family
Asteraceae (Compositae)

Jan.–Dec.   10–45 cm   D; ⊙ - ⊙; +

IM: Capitula arranged in long corymbose clusters. Only disc florets; barely longer than the involucral bracts which have black specks. Fruit with a pappus of hairs. Stem ascending-erect, branched. Leaves alternate, pinnately lobed, often with a cobweb-like covering of hairs.
H: Gardens, fields, paths, rubble heaps, clearings. Found on various soils, all of which are however nitrogenous and slightly damp. Very common throughout.
Al: After flowering the small hairy fruits make the capitula look like a white-haired old man (Latin: Senecio — senex = old man).

Sticky Groundsel
Senecio viscosus
Daisy family
Asteraceae (Compositae)

July–Sept.   10–60 cm   D; ⊙

IM: Capitula arranged in long-ovoid corymb. On the outside narrow ray florets which are usually rolled back, on the inside disc florets. The inflorescence at least is sticky-glandular. Fruit with a pappus of hairs. Stem usually erect. Leaves pinnately lobed with lanceolate coarsely toothed lobes.
H: Rubble heaps, clearings, dunes, railway embankments, pathways. Likes very stony open ground preferably low in lime and not too damp. Scattered, sometimes common throughout lowland areas.
Al: Very similar: Heath Groundsel *S. sylvaticus*: not sticky. Found in similar habitats. Scattered.

Senecio vernalis
Daisy family
Asteraceae (Compositae)

Senecio helenitis
Daisy family
Asteraceae (Compositae)

May–Nov.   15–50 cm   D; ☉

May–June   50–100 cm   D; ♃

IM: Capitula almost campanulate, in a more or less corymbose arrangement. On the inside disc florets, on the outside 13 projecting ray florets. Fruit with a pappus of hairs. Stem erect, little branching. Leaves pinnately lobed, the upper amplexicaul, margin completely serrate.
H: Not British. Fields, paths, rubble heaps, forest margins, railway embankments. Usually found on somewhat dry sandy soil rich in nitrogen but rather low in lime and warm in the summer. Tolerates salt. Rare and usually only temporary but repeatedly introduced (from the East) from approximately 1850 with a steady trend towards a spread westwards in northern Europe.

IM: Capitula campanulate, in a loose corymb. On the outside 13 projecting ray florets, on the inside disc florets. Fruit with a pappus of hairs. Stem stiff and erect. leaves ovoid-spatulate, usually with margin curled up, woolly and cobweb-like; stem leaves very narrow, lower ones amplexicaul.
H: Not British. Marshy meadowland, open woodland. Likes peaty soils which are low in nutrients and free of lime and occasionally wet. Rare, found only in the south and west of northern Europe.
Al: Synonym: *S. spathulifolius.* Many subspecies.

167

Hoary Ragwort
Senecio erucifolius
Daisy family
Asteraceae (Compositae)

July–Aug.　　30–120 cm　　D; ☉-♃

IM: Capitula in terminal and axillary corymbs. On the outside (12–14) projecting ray florets, on the inside disc florets. Fruit with a pappus of hairs. Stem grows erect from short horizontal rootstock. Often reddish-brown, angular. Leaves pinnately lobed, covered with woolly web on the undersides.
H: Balks, pathways, thickets, shingle. Likes nitrogenous loamy soal which is stony and preferably calcareous. Locally common in England and Wales, rarer in a few parts of southern Scotland.
A: Very similar: Common Ragwort, (*S. jacobaea*). Rootstock goes straight into the ground: capitula 15–25 mm wide (instead of 10–15 mm).

Wood Ragwort
Senecio nemorensis
Daisy family
Asteraceae (Compositae)

July–Aug.　　50–150 cm　　D; ♃

IM: Capitula in umbel-like corymbs. On the outside 5 or 7 ray florets, on inside disc florets. Fruit with pappus of hairs. Stem erect, leaves alternate. Leaves ovoid-lanceolate, serrate, at most with short petioles.
H: Not British. Woodland, undergrowth along streams, glades, brush areas in clearings and Alpine regions. Needs well-moistened soil, rich in nutrients and humus. Scattered; rare towards northern Europe.
Al: Ssp. *nemorensis*, type found in moderately mountainous regions of central and eastern Europe: stem green, hairy; leaf margin ciliate. Ssp. *fuchsii*, from the lowlands up to 2000 m; stem red, glabrous, leaves narrow, at least 4 times longer than wide.

Field Marigold
Calendula arvensis
Daisy family
Asteraceae (Compositae)

May—Oct.   10—20 cm   D; ⊙

           ▽

IM: Capitula 1—2 cm wide on long peduncles. On the outside ray florets, on the inside disc florets. Fruit is bent over in the shape of a hook or ring and the back of it is covered with spines. Leaves spatulate to lanceolate, amplexicaul, with covering of downy hairs.
H: Prefers dry soil rich in nutrients and minerals. A frequent casual but not becoming established.
AI: Similar: Pot Marigold (*C. officinalis*), old medicinal and ornamental plant, often escaping. Capitula 2—5 cm across, orange, sometimes yellow.

Carline Thistle
Carlina vulgaris
Daisy family
Asteraceae (Compositae)

July—Oct.   15—60 cm   D; ⊖

                      ▽

IM: Leaves long, margin lobed with prickly thorns. Stem erect, usualy branched. Capitula 2—4 cm wide, in corymbs, occasionally solitary. Bracts thorny, the inner row ray-like and straw-coloured. Only disc florets present. Fruit with a pappus of hairs.
H: Dry grassland. Calcicolous. Likes somewhat dry soil rich in minerals but low in nutrients. Locally common, rarer in the far north and high regions.

Cabbage Thistle
Cirsium oleraceum
Daisy family
Asteraceae (Compositae)

July–Sept.   50–120 cm   D; ♃

IM: Leaves glabrous, serrate with soft prickles, light green; upper ones often undivided, lower ones pinnately divided. Capitula erect, 2–4 cm long growing terminally in small groups and surrounded by pale bracts. Only disc florets present. Fruit with a pappus of hairs.
H: Damp meadows, flat moorland, river banks, ditches, wet woods. Calcicolous. Indicator of wetness. Likes loamy soil rich in nutrients. An introduction from central Europe, established in a few places.

Cirsium spinosissimum
Daisy family
Asteraceae (Compositae)

July–Aug.   20–50 cm   D; ♃

IM: Stem erect, dense foliage. Leaves yellowish-green, pinnately lobed, margin serrate and thorny. Capitula 2–3 cm long; these are usually terminal in small groups and surrounded by pale yellow thorny involucral bracts. Fruit with a pappus of hairs.
H: Not British. Only found in Alpine regions of Europe (France to Yugoslavia). On damp mats and stony turf, grazing land and brush areas near river banks. Likes nitrogen. Found on damp loamy soil. Scattered.
AI: Various habitat-related types: in the shade grows up to over 1 m high; in higher locations single capitulum or very short stem (5 cm). Growth is promoted by grazing.

Rough Hawkbit
Leontodon hispidus
Daisy family
Cichoriaceae (Compositae)

June—Sept. 10–60 cm D; ♃

IM: Capitula terminal, 2.5–4 cm wide.
Ray florets only. Stem slender, pithy,
usually unbranched; scale-like leaves,
1–2 at most. Basal leaves pinnately
lobed or entire. Plant contains a milky
juice (latex).
H: Meadows, balks, pastures. Found
on soil rich in nutrients. Found
throughout Britain, sometimes
common.
AI: Very variable, also in the hair covering. Similar: Autumn Hawkbit (*L.
autumnalis*); usually branched. leaves
mostly glabrous, toothed to pinnately
lobed; meadows. Abundant. Cat's-ear
(*Hypochoeris radicata*): stem bluish-
green. Leaves coarsely serrate, scattered bristles; grassland. Common.

Hawkweed Oxtongue
Picris hieracioides
Daisy family
Cichoriaceae (Compositae)

July—Sept. 15–90 cm D; ☉–♃

IM: Leaves and at least lower part of
stem covered with stiff bristles. Plant
contains milky juice (latex). Stem
usually richly branched and squar-
rose. Leaves long, coarsely toothed.
Capitula in corymbs, 2–3.5 cm wide.
Outer involucral bracts spreading. Ray
florets only. Fruit with a pappus of
hairs.
H: Grassland, wayside and grassy
areas. Grows on calcareous loamy
ground which is not too dry but rich in
nutrients and preferably stony. Local,
sometimes common in the lowlands of
England, Wales and southern Scotland.

Goat's-beard
Tragopogon pratensis
Daisy family
Cichoriaceae (Compositae)

June—July   30—70 cm   D; ⊙ – ⊙; (+)

IM: Capitula 4—6 cm wide. Only ray florets. Fruit with a pappus of hairs. Only 1 row of bracts. Stem erect, little branching, slightly swollen under the capitula. Leaves opposite, margin entire, sheathing stem. Abundant latex.

H: Meadows; rarely along paths. Likes well-moistened loamy soil containing nutrients and minerals. Locally common more or less throughout.

AI: Ssp. *pratensis*, rays pale yellow, as long as the involucral bracts. Common in Europe, less so in Britain. Ssp. *minor*, rays bright yellow, only as long as the involucral bracts. The most common in Britain. Ssp. *orientalis*, rays golden yellow, longer than the involucral bracts. Casual in Britain.

172

Dandelion
Taraxacum officinale
Daisy family
Cichoriaceae (Compositae)

April—June   10—60 cm   D; ♃

IM: Capitula 2—5 cm wide, solitary on leafless, wide, hollow peduncles. Only ray florets. 2 rows of involucral bracts, the outer ones often recurved. Fruit with a pappus of hairs. Basal leaves in a rosette, long, jaggedly serrate. Plant contains milky juice (latex).

H: Everywhere in habitats which are not too wet and shady. Very common; up to around 1900 m.

AI: Collective species or aggregate; numerous micro-species have been recognized.

Perennial Sow-thistle
Sonchus arvensis
Daisy family
Cichoriaceae (Compositae)

July–Oct. 60–150 cm D; ♃; (+)

IM: Capitula up to 5 cm wide, in a loose corymb. Only ray florets. Inflorescence branches and involucral bracts covered with dense layer of yellow glandular hairs. Fruit with a pappus of hairs. Stem only branched at the top, hollow. Leaves jaggedly serrate, the upper ones less so, all spiny serrate. Plant contains abundant milky juice (latex).

H: Fields, gardens, waysides, rubble heaps, salty marshes. Found on nitrogenous soil. Common throughout. Tolerates salt, needs warmth.

AI: Similar: Marsh Thistle (*S. palustris*): glands black, capitula up to 4 cm across. River banks, marshes, etc. Rare, south-east England only.

Smooth Sow-thistle
Sonchus oleraceus
Daisy family
Cichoriaceae (Compositae)

June–Aug. 20–150 cm D; ⊙ ; (+)

IM: Plant is usually glabrous, with abundant milky juice (latex). Capitula 2–2.5 cm wide, in cymose umbels. Only ray florets. Fruit with a pappus of hairs. Stem branched, hollow. Leaves variable, those of the stem usually pinnately divided or serrate, not spiny, with projecting pointed auricles clasping at the stem.

H: A weed of cultivated and waste places. Found on ground which is rich in nitrogen but not too dry. Common throughout.

AI: The flower colour ranges from rich yellow to whitish-yellow. Very similar: Prickly Sow-thistle (*S. asper*): leaf auricles have rounded apices, pressed close to the stem. Common in similar habitats. 173

Wall Lettuce
Mycelis muralis
Daisy family
Cichoriaceae (Compositae)

July–Sept.   30–100 cm   D; ♃

IM: Capitula in panicles, barely 1 cm wide. Only 5 ray florets per capitulum, pale yellow. Fruit with a pappus of hairs. Stem erect, branched towards the top. Leaves frequently tinged with dirty red colour, the lower ones petiolate, the upper ones sessile with large terminal lobe. Plant glabrous and containing abundant milky juice (latex).
H: On shady rocks and walls, occasionally in deciduous woodland. Likes loose loamy soil rich in nutrients with layer of mull. Can also be stony. Scattered in most areas, absent from some parts, notably the Highlands of Scotland.
Al: Synonyms: *Prenanthes muralis*, *Lactuca muralis*.
174

Nipplewort
Lapsana communis
Daisy family
Cichoriaceae (Compositae)

July–Sept.   20–90 cm   D; ☉

IM: Capitula arranged in panicles, approx. 1.5–2 cm wide. Only 8–15 light yellow ray florets per capitulum. Fruit without a pappus. Stem erect, branched towards the top. Lower leaves pinnately lobed, with large terminal lobe, upper ones ovoid, almost all petiolate. Plant contains milky juice (latex) and is usually hairy.
H: Ploughed fields, gardens, rubble heaps, also in thickets, along wood margins, in glades and in light open woodland. Likes somewhat damp soil rich in nutrients. Common throughout.
Al: The plant varies a great deal in its hair covering, its leaf shape and its size.

Rough Hawk's-beard
Crepis biennis
Daisy family
Cichoriaceae (Compositae)

June–July 30–120 cm D; ☉

IM: Capitula 2–3.5 cm wide, in corymbs. Only ray florets. Outer involucral bracts spreading. Fruit with a pappus of hairs. Stem erect, grooved, branched at the top. Leaves pinnately divided, upper ones undivided. Plant contains milky juice (latex).
H: Meadows, path balks, rarely found on fields. Likes loamy soil rich in nutrients. Local, somewhat rarer towards the north.
Al: Similar: Northern Hawk's-beard (*C. mollis*): outer involucral bracts pressed inwards, leaf margin is entire to serrate. Mountain meadows and pastures. Local, rare in the lowlands.

Smooth Hawk's-beard
Crepis capillaris
Daisy family
Cichoriaceae (Compositae)

June–Sept. 20–90 cm D; ☉ - ☉

IM: Capitula 1–1.5 cm wide, arranged in loose corymbs. Only ray florets. Fruit with a pappus of hairs. Stem branched above. Leaves jaggedly serrate to pinnately divided, upper ones narrow, all sagittate at the base, amplexicaul. Plant is usually glabrous and contains milky juice (latex).
H: Meadows, pastures, park lawns, pathway balks. Found on soil which is not too damp and is relatively low in nutrients, preferably also low in lime. Common throughout.
Al: This is the most common of a number of Hawk's-beard species which are small in growth and very difficult to distinguish from one another. Synonym: *C. virens*.

Prickly Lettuce
Lactuca serriola
Daisy family
Cichoriaceae (Compositae)

July–Sept. 30–150 cm D; ☉ – ☉; (+)

IM: Capitula approx. 1 cm wide, in panicles. Only ray florets. Fruit with a pappus of hairs. Stem whitish, often tinged with reddish-violet. Leaves undivided to pinnately divided, sagittate at the base, toothed, prickly beneath; leaves on stem set perpendicularly and arranged in a north–south direction; central rib on leaf underside is prickly. Plant glabrous; contains abundant milky juice (latex).
H: Paths, railway embankments, rubble heaps, wasteland. Found on warm soil rich in nitrogen. South and central England and Wales.
Al: Synonym: *L. scariola.*

Mouse-ear Hawkweed
Hieracium pilosella
Daisy family
Cichoriaceae (Compositae)

May–Aug.   5–30 cm   D; ♃

IM: Capitula solitary on leafless stems, 2–3 cm wide. Only ray florets. Fruit with a pappus of hairs. Leaves basal, ovoid, undersides covered with felt-like hairs, uppersides have individual long bristles. Plant contains milky juice (latex). Has long runners above the ground.
H: Poor turf, dry turf, balks, heaths, open woodland. Found on various soils. Avoids wet and shady localities. Found throughout Britain.

Hieracium murorum group
Daisy family
Cichoriaceae (Compositae)

May–Oct.   20–60 cm   D; ♃

IM: Capitula 2–3 cm wide, corymbosely arranged in small numbers. Only ray florets. Fruit with a pappus of hairs. Stem erect, with no leaves (or up to 2). Remaining leaves are basal, more or less ovoid, usually somewhat toothed, petiolate. No runners. Plant contains milky juice (latex), usually (glandular) hairy. Hairs are black.
H: All types of woodland, less common in the shadow of rocks and walls. Found on soil which is low in lime, not too dry but rich in humus. Common in central and southern England and Wales, rare in southern Scotland.
Al: Synonym: *H. sylvaticum.* Very many closely related species.

Umbellate Hawkweed group
Hieracium umbellatum
Daisy family
Cichoriaceae (Compositae)

July–Sept.   30–80 cm   D; ♃

IM: Capitula 1–3 cm wide, in an umbellate panicle. Only ray florets. Tips of the involucral bracts are recurved. Fruit has ciliate margin. Many narrow stem leaves. Plant contains milky juice (latex)(but often only very little).
H: Wood margins, thickets, heaths, poor turf, dunes. Found on loamy soil low in lime and frequently sandy. Found throughout but chiefly in the lowland areas.
Al: Similar: Species of the *H. sabauda* group: leaves ovoid, involucral bracts pressed inwards.

Lady's-slipper
Cypripedium calceolus
Orchid family
Orchidaceae

May–June   15–45 cm   M; ♃

IM: Stem erect, with 1–2 (rarely as many as 4) flowers. Large yellow labellum, 3–4 cm long inflated and slipper-like; plus 4 lanceolate, purple-brownish outer perianth segments, 4–6 cm long. 3–4 leaves, large, elliptical, with sheathing bases. Leaf margin ciliate.
H: Deciduous woodland. Found on loamy soil rich in lime but not too dry. Very rare, has been wiped out in many areas by collectors. Nowadays found only in one place in Yorkshire.

Pale-flowered Orchid
Orchis pallens
Orchid family
Orchidaceae

April–May   15–40 cm   M; ♃

IM: Short, somewhat dense spike. Outer petals spreading, flower spur at most as long as the ovary, projecting horizontally or curved upwards. Bracts membraneous, pale yellow with a single vein. Leaves broadly ovoid, not spotted.
H: Not British. Deciduous woodland, sunny mixed woodland. Found on somewhat moist calcareous soil containing humus. Likes warmth. Rare. Found in Germany, Austria, Alps and southern Europe; in the Alps up to approx. 1200 m.
AI: Do not confuse with the following entry Elder-flowered Orchid, even though the flowers of the Pale Orchid have similar unpleasantly heavy aroma of elder.

Elder-flowered Orchid
Dactylorhiza sambucina
Orchid family
Orchidaceae

April–June   15–25 cm   M; ♃

IM: Short compressed spike. Outer petals projecting, flower spur longer than ovary. Flower bracts deciduous (not membraneous). Leaves long-ovoid, unspotted.
H: Not British. On sunny balks, poor turf, in open woodland and thickets. Prefers moderately dry, stony, loamy soil low in lime. Very rare.
AI: The spike can be any shade from red to yellow but the yellow plants are more common. Similar: many types of *Orchis* and *Dactylorhiza* (= *Dactylorchis*) with yellow or red flowers.

Bird's-nest Orchid
Neottia nidus-avis
Orchid family
Orchidaceae

June–July   20–45 cm   M; ♃

IM: Entire plant yellowish-brown. Tough stem with narrow-ovoid leaves. Raceme with many flowers, cylindrical. Flowers do not have a spur. Labellum bi-lobed, upper perianth-segments coming together to form a hood.
H: In deciduous and mixed woodland especially in beechwood. Likes loamy soils rich in lime and nutrients and absorbs organic material in the mull with the help of fungi. Throughout Britain but easily overlooked.
AI: The rootstock under the ground bears many tightly interwoven roots. Their nest-like appearance gave the plant its name.

Birthwort
Aristolochia clematitis
Birthwort family
Aristolochiaceae

June–Sept. 20–80 cm D; ♃; +

IM: Stem erect or slightly twining, glabrous. Leaves alternate, the blades about twice as long as the petioles, round-ovoid, with heart-shaped base. Flowers in leaf axils, inflated and globular at the base then becoming a long straight tube terminating in a tongue-shaped lobe; the inside of the tube is covered with hairs pointing inwards (fly-trap).
H: Waysides, walls, thickets. Likes the warmth. Calcicolous. Local in eastern and central England and a few places elsewhere.
Al: Old medicinal and poisonous plant from the Mediterranean region; in Britain it has grown wild from old gardens and has succeeded in establishing itself.

Wolf's-bane
Aconitum vulparia
Buttercup family
Ranunculaceae

June–Aug. 50–150 cm D; ♃; +

IM: Flowers in simple or branched raceme, the topmost petal forming a tall cylindrical helmet 1.5–2 cm long, which is closed off below by 4 smaller oval-shaped petals. Stem erect, with sparse hairs below, more dense further up. Leaves alternate, palmately lobed with 5–7 segments, the lower ones having long petioles. Leaf segments themselves 3-lobed and coarsely serrate.
H: Not British. Moist deciduous woodland, canyon forests, brakes and lowland forests. Likes damp humus soil rich in nutrients. Rare. Main areas of distribution are the higher mountainous regions of C. and S. Europe.
Al: Very many different varieties. Synonym: *A. lycoctonum*.

Yellow Corydalis
Corydalis lutea
Poppy family
Papaveraceae

May—Aug.   10–30 cm   D; ⩛

  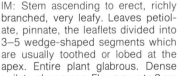

IM: Stem ascending to erect, richly branched, very leafy. Leaves petiolate, pinnate, the leaflets divided into 3–5 wedge-shaped segments which are usually toothed or lobed at the apex. Entire plant glabrous. Dense unilateral racemes. Flowers up to 2 cm long, with a short spur, golden yellow, rich yellow at the tip.

H: On walls and rocks. Ornamental plant from the Mediterranean region which has grown wild and established itself in a number of places. Likes moist calcareous cracks containing some nutrients; does not like full exposure to the sun. Scattered throughout.

Winged Broom
Chamaespartium sagittale
Pea family
Fabaceae (Leguminosae)

May—June   10–30 cm   D; ♄

IM: Branches ascending to erect, with broad wings, sparse foliage. Leaves alternate, sessile, ovoid-lanceolate, margin entire, easily deciduous. Entire plant covered with hairs, but rapidly becoming glabrous, then tough and leathery and woody at the base. Pea flowers 10–15 mm long. Flowers in dense terminal racemes.

H: Not British. Semi-dry turf, poor meadowland, path balks, heaths, open dry woodland, sometimes also on rocks. Somewhat calcifugous. Indicator of surface acidity. Common in central and southern Europe, but rarer in the north.

AI: Has been classified under various different names: *Genista sagitalis*, *Cytisus sagitalis*.

181

Wild Liquorice
Astragalus glycyphyllos
Pea family
Fabaceae (Leguminosae)

July–Aug.   60–100 cm   D: ♃

IM: Stem creeping to ascending, only slightly hairy. Leaves alternate, imparipinnate with 10–20 long-oval leaflets. Flowers pale, (greenish-) yellow to ivory-coloured. Racemes in leaf axils on short peduncles. Fruit is a somewhat puffy pod, curved almost to the point of being spiral.
H: Open dry grassy areas and dry thickets. Likes a loamy soil which is both nitrogenous and calcareous. Scattered throughout Britain.
Al: Medicinal plant rich in sugars.

Ribbed Melilot
Melilotus officinalis
Pea family
Fabaceae (Leguminosae)

July–Sept.   60–120 cm   D; ☉

IM: Stem ascending to erect, heavily branched. Leaves alternate, trifoliate; leaflets long-ovoid, serrate. Dense somewhat unilateral racemes with long peduncles in the axils of the upper leaves. 30–60 flowers, only 5–6 mm long, the wings and standard longer than the keel. Ovary and fruit glabrous.
H: Pathways, railway ballast, fields, wasteland, quarries, river banks, rubble heaps. Nitrogen indicator. Found in somewhat dry sunny places. Southern England only.
Al: Very similar: Tall Melilot (*Melilotus altissima*): fruit hairy (wings, standard and keel more or less the same length). Scattered throughout most areas.

Sickle Medick
Medicago sativa ssp. *falcata*
Pea family
Fabaceae (Leguminosae)

June–July   30–60 cm   D; ♃

IM: Flowers approx. 1 cm long, 6–20 in pedunculate racemes coming out of the axils of the alternate leaves. Stem ascending-erect. Leaves made up of 3 leaflets which are long and emarginate at the apex. Pods are usually sickle-shaped.
H: Dry turf, poor meadowland. Prefers rather dry calcareous soil. Only in the Breckland (East Anglia).
AI: Sometimes separated from Lucerne (p. 332) as a species in its own right.

Black Medick
Medicago lupulina
Pea family
Fabaceae (Leguminosae)

April–Aug.   5–50 cm   D; ☉ – ♃

IM: Stem prostrate to erect, angular. Leaves trifoliate, leaflets have hairy undersides. Flowers 2–3 mm long, initially in compact, globular racemes of 10–50 flowers, approx. 5 mm across. Petals fall off after flowering. Pods are kidney-shaped.
H: Dry meadowland, poor turf, path balks, railway ballast. Calcicolous. Likes warm soil rich in nitrogen. Common in most areas.
AI: Very similar: yellow flowering species of Trefoil (*Trifolium*, see following pages); they usually have less hair and the petals remain brown and dried up in the calyx.

Kidney Vetch
Anthyllis vulneraria
Pea family
Fabaceae (Leguminosae)

Large Hop Trefoil
Trifolium aureum
Pea family
Fabaceae (Leguminosae)

June–Sept.　10–60 cm　D; ♃

July–Aug.　10–50 cm　D; ☉

IM: Stem prostrate to erect. Basal leaves sometimes consisting of the terminal leaflet only. Stem leaves imparipinnate; leaflets long, terminal leaflets much larger than the lateral ones which are sometimes absent. Flowers in dense cymes with pinnately divided bracts.
H: Dry poor turf, balks. Somewhat calcicolous and commoner near the sea. Throughout Britain.
AI: Many subspecies. Ssp. *vulneraria*: hairy, flowers shiny yellow. Ssp. *maritima*: flowers orange-yellow, grows on sand along the North Sea and Baltic coasts. Ssp. *alpestris*: mountain form; flowers large, calyx covered with greyish hairs, flowers golden yellow. Alpine grassland.

IM: Stem usually erect, richly branched right from the bottom. Leaves alternate, trifoliate; leaflets ovoid, all with short, equal petioles. 20–50 flowers in a somewhat long, 7–10 mm wide head. After flowering the petals remain on the flower, dry and yellowish-brown (used for aerial distribution of seeds).
H: Dry turf, poor meadowland, wayside verges, balks. Somewhat calcifugous. Indicator of slight surface acidity. Scattered throughout and somewhat rare.
AI: Synonyms: *T. strepens*, *T. agrarium*.

Hop Trefoil
Trifolium campestre
Pea family
Fabaceae (Leguminosae)

June–Sept. 5–30 cm D; ⊙

IM: Stem prostrate to ascending, branched. Leaves alternate, trifoliate, leaflets obovoid, the middle one having a conspicuously longer petiole than the lateral ones. 20–50 flowers in a globular-ovoid head which is 7–15 mm wide. The petals remain on the flower after blossoming, dry and brownish-yellow (used for aerial distribution of seeds).
H: Balks, dry meadows, railway embankments, paths, roadsides, fallow land. Found on soil which is rich in lime but low in nutrients. Found throughout Britain.
AI: Synonym: *T. procumbens*.

Lesser Trefoil
Trifolium dubium
Pea family
Fabaceae (Leguminosae)

May–Oct. 5–25 cm D; ⊙

IM: Stem thin, round, prostrate to ascending. Leaves trifoliate, alternate, bluish-green. 10–25 flowers usually standing in ascending position and forming a globular head approx. 5 mm wide. Petals later become brown, persistent.
H: Not too dry meadowland and pastures, wayside verges, river banks. Likes soil which contains nutrients and is relatively rich in lime. Common, but rarer in the north or north-west of Scotland.
AI: Synonyms: *T. filiforme, T. minus*.

Common Bird's-foot-trefoil
Lotus corniculatus
Pea family
Fabaceae (Leguminosae)

June–Sept.   10–40 cm   D; ♃

IM: Stem ascending, usually filled with pith. Flowers 6–15 mm long, often tinged with red, 2–7 in cymose head. Leaves have three leaflets plus 2 leafy stipules at the base of the petiole; leaflets are obovoid, and may be glabrous, hairy or ciliate.
H: Dry meadows, balks, moist meadows. Usually calcicolous. Throughout most areas.
AI: A plant with very many different forms varying in degree of hairiness, structure of the calyx and other features. Mountain plants are often dwarf, though similar to lowland forms in other ways.

Greater Bird's-foot-trefoil
Lotus uliginosus
Pea family
Fabaceae (Leguminosae)

June–Aug.   10–60 cm   D; ♃

IM: Stem ascending to erect, with wide tubular hollow stem. Flowers 10–12 mm long, 5–12 of them in a cymose head. Before flowering the 5 calyx teeth are clearly folded back and the flower buds are usually tinged with red. Leaves are made up of 5 segments (3 'genuine' leaflets and the 2 similar stipules at the base of the stem), usually glabrous, bluish on the undersides.
H: Damp meadows, ditches, river banks. On wet soils rich in nutrients and often low in lime. These soils may dry out in the summer. Throughout most areas, less common in the north.
AI: Synonym: *L. pedunculatus*. Very similar: see the entry on the left.

Dragon's-tooth
Tetragonolobus maritimus
Pea family
Fabaceae (Leguminosae)

May–July   10–25 cm   D; ♃

IM: Stem prostrate to ascending, bluish-green like the leaves. Flowers solitary, 2–3 cm long, pale yellow. Leaves trifoliate with 2 large leafy stipules at the base, the lower leaves petiolate, somewhat fleshy, the upper ones with short petioles or sessile. Pods are long (up to 5 cm) and thin, with 4 wide longitudinal ribs.
H: Rough grassland. Calcicolous. Tolerates salt. Local to rare in southern England (except the south west) and a few other places.
Al: Is sometimes attributed to the Trefoil genus: *Lotus siliquosus* (see previous page).

Horseshoe Vetch
Hippocrepis comosa
Pea family
Fabaceae (Leguminosae)

May–July   10–40 cm   D; ♃

IM: Stem prostrate to ascending. Leaves have long petioles, imparipinnate, with 9–15 oblong leaflets. Flowers approx. 1 cm long, 4–10 of them in a capitate head. Base of the petals narrows down conspicuously like a stem. Pods are divided into characteristic horseshoe-shaped segments.
H: Poor turf, sunny balks, cliffs. Likes a warm calcareous soil. Scattered and local as far north as southern Scotland where suitable conditions exist.

Yellow Vetchling
Lathyrus aphaca
Pea family
Fabaceae (Leguminosae)

June–Aug.   15–100 cm   D; ☉

IM: Stem prostrate, ascending or climbing. Leaves opposite, bluish green, heart-shaped to ovoid. Between each pair of 'leaves' is a long tendril (this is the remainder of the actual leaf, whereas the 'leaves' are in fact the much-enlarged stipules). Flowers are usually solitary, axillary, petiolate.
H: Dry places on light soil. Likes calcareous loamy soil rich in nutrients and in a sunny location. Very local in south and south-east England extending to the Midlands and Wales.

Meadow Vetchling
Lathyrus pratensis
Pea family
Fabaceae (Leguminosae)

May–Aug.   30–120 cm   D; ♃

IM: Stem ascending or climbing, quadrangular. Leaves paired pinnate; consisting of 2 lanceolate leaflets and a simple or branched tendril. At the base of the stem 2 pointed leafy stipules. Flowers 1–1.5 cm long. Axillary racemes with long peduncles.
H: Meadows, damp meadows, hedges, woodland margins. Likes a loamy soil which is not too dry and which is rich in humus and nutrients. Common throughout Britain.

Touch-me-not Balsam
Impatiens noli-tangere
Balsam family
Balsaminaceae

July–Sept.   20–60 cm   D; ⊙ ; (+)

IM: Stem erect, glossy; swollen at the nodes, branched towards the top. Leaves alternate, ovoid, coarsely serrate. 2–4 flowers in axillary racemes, hanging, 3–4 cm long, with curved spur; red spots on the inside. Fruit is a somewhat fleshy 5-lobed capsule; if it is touched when ripe it explodes violently (ejecting the seeds).
H: Damp mixed and deciduous woodland, stream sides. Found on wet loamy soil rich in nutrients. Needs shade. Very local, occurring in many places though often only as a casual.
Al: Also called Yellow Balsam.

Small Balsam
Impatiens parviflora
Balsam family
Balsaminaceae

July–Nov.   30–100 cm   D; ⊙ ; (+)

IM: Stem erect, usually branched and leafy at the top; slightly swollen at the nodes. Leaves alternate, ovoid, toothed. 4–10 flowers in erect axillary racemes; approx. 1 cm long, pale yellow; spur straight. Fruit erect; if it is touched when ripe it explodes violently and ejects the seeds.
H: Woods, thickets, rubble heaps, waste places. Found on well-saturated soils rich in nitrogen and low in lime. Likes shady locations. Local in south and east England but also found in other areas; usually in large numbers.

Wild Pansy (Heart's-ease)
Viola tricolor
Violet family
Violaceae

April—Sept. 10—20 cm D; ☉

IM: Stem erect or ascending, usually branched. Leaves longer than wide lower ones usually heart-shaped to ovoid, crenate. Stipules large, palmately lobed. Flowers solitary on long pedicels. Short spur; lower petals usually have blackish stripes on them. H: Fields, path balks, rubble heaps, dunes, mountain meadows. Mostly common but sometimes only local.
Al: Varies in habitat, petal length and colour. Several ssp: 3 in W. Europe. *Tricolor*; flowers bluish, rarely all yellow; throughout. *Curtisii*; low-growing, usually near sea. Flowers various colours. Throughout W. Europe. *Subalpina*; erect. Flowers yellow, sometimes upper petals violet. Mountains from S. and C. Europe.

Yellow Wood Violet
Viola biflora
Violet family
Violaceae

May—Aug. 8—15 cm D; ♃

IM: Stem ascending to erect. Large rosette leaves with long petioles; only 2—4 smaller alternate stem leaves: all heart to kidney-shaped, wider than they are long, crenate margin. Often 2 flowers on pedicels in leaf axil. Petals narrow, 4 pointing upwards, the lower one having a short spur and brown stripes on the front.
H: Not British. Mountain and lowland forests, Alpine pastures, high shrub areas. Likes moist shady locations. Calcicolous. Apart from outlying areas in central Germany is found only in the Alps and their foothills. Scattered in these locations; up to 2500 m. Mountains of central and southern Europe.

Wood Sage
Teucrium scorodonia
Mint family
Lamiaceae (Labiatae)

July–Sept. 15–30 cm D; ♃

IM: Stem erect, quadrangular, leaves opposite and decussate. Entire plant covered with soft hairs. Leaves have short petioles, ovoid, heart-shaped at the base, crenate. Flowers in pairs in a terminal raceme. Flowers approx. 1 cm long, greenish-yellow, without an upper lip. Lower lip has 3 lobes; middle lobe is large spoon-shaped.
H: Open woodland, woodland paths, forest margins, heaths, thickets. Likes acid sandy ground low in nutrients and lime. Common throughout but avoids limestone regions.

Large-flowered Hemp-nettle
Galeopsis speciosa
Mint family
Lamiaceae (Labiatae)

July–Sept. 30–100 cm D; ☉

IM: Stem erect, quadrangular, swollen at the nodes and covered with stiff bristles, hairs bearing yellow glands, especially in the upper half of each internode. Leaves opposite, ovoid, toothed. Petioles 1–4 cm. Verticillasters arranged one above another. Flowers 2.5–4 cm long, pale yellow. Upper lip helmet-shaped. Middle lobe of the lower lip violet-coloured, rarely all yellow.
H: Usually on cultivated land. Scattered throughout.
Al: Similar: Downy Hemp-nettle (*G. segetum*), nodes not swollen, downy, corolla pure yellow. In similar habitats in England and Wales but rare.

Yellow Archangel
Lamiastrum galeobdolon
Mint family
Lamiaceae (Labiatae)

May—June   20—60 cm   D; ⏾

IM: Stem quadrangular, leaves opposite and decussate; sterile stems
prostrate, flowering ones ascending or
erect. Leaves similar to stinging
nettles. Several verticillasters usually
with 6 flowers. Lower lip with brown
lines or markings.
H: Woodland, especially coppiced
areas. Only on moist soil containing
mull and rich in nutrients. Common in
England and Wales, rare in Scotland.
Al: Synonyms: *Galeobdolon luteum*,
Lamium galeobdolon. Ssp. *flavidum*,
with smaller flowers, in mountains of
C. and S.E. Europe. Ssp. *montanum*,
with sharply serrate leaves, more
common in the S. Europe. Ssp. *galeobdolon*, more bluntly toothed leaves,
more common in N. Europe.

192

Jupiter's Distaff
Salvia glutinosa
Mint family
Lamiaceae (Labiatae)

July—Oct.   50—120 cm   D; ⏾

IM: Stem erect, bluntly quadrangular,
usually glabrous at the bottom, at the
top covered with glandular-sticky
hairs. Leaves oblong-ovoid with
spear-shaped base, petiolate to
almost sessile, more or less glandular-
sticky; margin is coarsely toothed.
Flowers 3—5 cm long, (usually) 4—6 in
each verticillaster; up to 16 verticillasters.
H: Not British. Mountain, canyon and
lowland forests, highshrub areas,
bushy slopes. Likes moist loamy soil
containing mull and rich in nutrients
and usually in lime. Prefers semi-
shady location. Only found in the Alps
and outlying foreland. Scattered;
hardly as high as 1500 m. Mountains of
central and southern Europe.

Common Cow-wheat
Melampyrum pratense
Figwort family
Scrophulariaceae

May–Oct.   10–60 cm   D; ⊙ ; (+)

IM: Stem ascending to erect. Leaves opposite linear-lanceolate, rough. Unilateral lax spikes. Flowers 1–2 cm long, bracts green, upper ones toothed. Calyx glabrous.
H: Open woodland, heaths, wet meadows. Found on soil which is always slightly acid, low in nutrients and usually in lime, and slightly dry to damp. Humus indicator. Common throughout.
AI: Very many different forms, to a large extent showing gradual variation from north to south in Europe. Also a number of habitat-related forms.

Small Cow-wheat
Melampyrum sylvaticum
Figwort family
Scrophulariaceae

June–Aug.   5–35 cm   D; ⊙ ; (+)

IM: Stem ascending or erect. Leaves opposite, lanceolate, almost glabrous. Lax unilateral spikes. Flowers up to 1 cm long, usually rich yellow. Bracts green. Calyx glabrous.
H: Mossy woodland acid with humus, thickets and heaths. Found on loamy soils low in lime with surface acidity. Local to somewhat rare in mountainous parts of northern England and Scotland, reaching about 400 m.
AI: A number of habitat/seasonal forms are known, the main ones being spring, autumn and mountain forms.

Leafy Lousewort
Pedicularis foliosa
Figwort family
Scrophulariaceae

June–Aug.   20–50 cm   D; ♃; (+)

IM: Stem erect, unbranched, thick foliage towards the top. Leaves alternate, lobed; lobes are bipinnate. Flowers in a dense spike. Bracts are longer than flowers, similar to the stem leaves. Flowers 2–2.5 cm long, whitish-yellow; upper lip unspotted, covered with rough hairs.

H: Not British. Alpine mats, streams, crook timber areas. Found on stony calcareous ground which is not too dry. Mountains in southern and southern-central Europe to Spain.

Al: Similar: *P. oederi*: bracts shorter than flowers, upper lip of flower glabrous, red spotted. Stony Alpine turf, pebbly ground. Rare. Mountains from Alps and Bulgaria north to the Arctic.

194

Moor-king
Pedicularis sceptrum-carolinum
Figwort family
Scrophulariaceae

June–Aug.   30–100 cm   D; ♃; (+)

IM: Stem erect, unbranched, little foliage, glabrous. Basal leves numerous, pinnately divided with unpaired pinnate lobes. Stem leaves similar, smaller. Long, lax raceme with many flowers. Flowers pale yellow, 3–3.5 cm long; lower lip has red tip. Upper and lower lip come together so that the blossom remains closed.

H: Not British. Wet meadows, river banks, communities in silted areas. Likes very wet peaty and loamy soil usually rich in lime. Very rare and numbers are on the decline. Only found in a few places in north and central Europe.

Greater Yellow Rattle
Rhinanthus alectorolophus
Figwort family
Scrophulariaceae

May–July   10–60 cm   D; ⊙ ; (+)

IM: Stem erect, branched or not. Leaves opposite, oblong, sharply toothed. Axillary flowers, 2 cm long. Calyx wide, tufted hairs. Corolla tube slightly bent; upper lip has blue tooth.
H: Meadows, balks, fields. Semi-parasite. Found on loamy soil rich in nutrients and often calcareous. Common in central Europe; up to over 2000 m; rarer in the north.
AI: Not British. Many different forms. Different summer and autumn forms. Similar: Narrow-leaved Yellow-rattle, *R. angustifolius* (= *serotinus*, = major): calyx glabrous, stem virtually glabrous to hairy. Meadows, fields, hedges. Scattered in Scotland and N. England, rarer in the south. Protected in Britain.

Yellow Rattle
Rhinanthus minor
Figwort family
Scrophulariaceae

May–Aug.   10–40 cm   D; ⊙ ; (+)

IM: Stem erect, slightly hairy, usually with black spots. Leaves opposite, narrow-lanceolate, toothed. Flowers axillary; 1.5 cm long. Calyx glabrous but with hairy margins. Corolla tube straight. Upper-lip tooth white or light blue.
H: Meadows, semi-dry turf. Semi-parasite; likes somewhat moist ground usually low in nutrients and lime. Common throughout.
AI: Very many different forms: not just lowland and mountain forms but also the respective early and (richly branched) late summer forms. Synonyms: *Alectorolophus minor*, *R. crista-galli*.

195

Large Yellow Foxglove
Digitalis grandiflora
Figwort family
Scrophulariaceae

June–July   60–120 cm   D; ♃; +

   ▽

IM: Stem erect, unbranched, at the top glandular-hairy. Leaves alternate, oblong-ovoid, margin ciliate and toothed. Unilateral terminal raceme. Flowers 3–4.5 cm long, campanulate to inflated, drooping, sulphur yellow, brownish spots on the inside; short upper lip, lower lip trilobed.
H: Not British. Mountain forests, deciduous woodland, mixed woodland, thickets, glades; more rarely on mountain meadows and Alpine mats. Found on relatively nutritious soil, often free of lime, but with seepage water. Central Europe to northern Greece.

Small Yellow Foxglove
Digitalis lutea
Figwort family
Scrophulariaceae

June–July   40–80 cm   D; ♃; +

    ▽

IM: Stem erect, unbranched, glabrous. Leaves alternate, glabrous, oblong-ovoid. Unilateral raceme; slightly glandular. Flowers 2–2.5 cm long, tubular, pale yellow, unspotted on the inside. Upper lip 2 lobes, lower lips 3 lobes.
H: Not British. Open woodland, sunny thickets, rocky heaths. Found on not too dry ground moderately rich in nutrients and usually calcareous. Very rare. Eastern and central Europe.
Al: Almost equally common is the hybrid with the Red Foxglove (see p. 280): flowers 3–3.5 cm long, pale yellow, upperside slightly tinged with red; leaves have thin covering of short felt-like hairs (*D.* x *purpurascens*).Not British.

Common Toadflax
Linaria vulgaris
Figwort family
Scrophulariaceae

July–Oct.   30–80 cm   D; ♃

IM: Stem erect, usually unbranched, glabrous. Leaves alternate, sessile, linear-lanceolate, somewhat curled up along the edge. Dense terminal raceme. Flowers 1.5–2.5 cm long with a spur almost as long, pale yellow with orange palate.
H: Weedy areas, paths, walls, fences, railway ballast, waste places, fields, clearings. Likes warmth. Found on loose, not too dry soil which is rich in nutrients and minerals. Needs light. Common in England and Scotland.
Al: Varies especially in the colour of the flowers.

Greater Bladderwort
Utricularia vulgaris
Butterwort family
Lentibulariaceae

July–Aug.   15–45 cm   D; ♃

IM: Free-floating. Leaves divided into hair-like segments, with many (20–200) small bladders 2–4 mm wide (to trap small insects). Leaf segments slightly ciliate. Lax raceme above the water level. Flowers golden-yellow, up to 2 cm long.
H: Stagnant or slow-flowing warm water, low in lime but containing nutrients. Local throughout Britain.
Al: Very similar: *U. australis* (= *neglecta*): flowers pale yelllow; England, Wales, southern Scotland, rare in the east. Other similar species have stems of two kinds, one bearing normal green leaves, the other colourless with reduced leaves and buried in the ground. On some species only these anchoring stems bear bladders.

197

Mistletoe
Viscum album
Mistletoe family
Loranthaceae

Feb.–April   20–100 cm   D; ♄; (+)

IM: Parasite living on trees. Bushy shrub, richly forked branches; whole plant yellowish-green. Leaves opposite, leathery, evergreen, oblong-ovoid, narrower towards base. Flowers in dense cymes, inconspicuous. Plant dioecious. Berries globular, white to yellowish-coloured.

H: Orchards, undergrowth along streams, woodland, also on individual trees. Most common on apples, rarely on conifers. Common in S. England and parts of the Midlands, rarer elsewhere, absent in Scotland.

Al: 3 ssp: *Album*; on apple trees, poplars and other deciduous trees. *Abietis*; on fir trees, and *Austriacum* (= *laxum*) on pines and larches. C. and S. Europe.

198

Box
Buxus sempervirens
Box family
Buxaceae

April–May   2–5 m   D; ♄; +

IM: Low shrub, more rarely small tree. Richly branched. Branches short, usually erect. Leaves approx. 2 cm long, opposite, leathery, tough, evergreen, oblong to elliptical; petioles short. Flowers in axillary clusters; unisexual. Terminal female flower (often more than 4 sepals) forms a cluster with many male flowers (4 sepals).

H: On sunny bushy slopes and in beech woodland on chalk or limestone soils. Very local though sometimes abundant in southern England. Frequently planted elsewhere and very often becoming naturalized.

Al: Ornamental shrub with many variations of growth, leaf shape and leaf colour.

Buckthorn
Rhamnus catharticus
Buckthorn family
Rhamnaceae

May—June   4—6 m   D; ♄; (+)

IM: Branches and leaves opposite. Leaves petiolate, ovoid; margin finely toothed. Many small branches terminating in pointed thorn. Flowers in sparse axillary clusters on the previous year's growth, yellowish-green, inconspicuous, pleasant smelling. Black berries, pea-sized, inedible (or have purging effect).
H: Hedges, dry thickets, oak and ash woods. Prefers calcareous soils. Scattered in England and Wales except for S.W. areas, and Scotland.
AI: Similar: Rock Buckthorn, *R. saxatilis*, more delicate in every respect; leaves only 1—1.5 cm long. The Alder Buckthorn, *Frangula alnus* (see p. 379) has no thorns and leaves are alternate.

Cornelian Cherry
Cornus mas
Dogwood family
Cornaceae

Feb.—March   2—8 m   D; ♄

IM: Flowers in small lateral umbellate clusters, appearing before the leaves. Leaves deciduous, opposite, ovoid to elliptical, margin entire; approx. 10 cm long; petiole approx. 1 cm long; on the underside in the angles of the curved veins there are tufts of hair ('mite nests'). Red oblong drupe, drooping, approx. 1 cm long; edible, somewhat acid taste.
H: Calcicolous, likes warmth. Often planted as a garden ornamental, only rarely escaping and growing wild.

199

Field Maple
Acer campestre
Maple family
Aceraceae

May—June   2—20 m   D; ♄

▽

IM: Small tree or (often) only 2—3 m high shrub. Older bark shows reticulate fissures, young (4—5 years old) twigs often have cork ribs forming wing-like extensions. Leaves opposite, petiolate, 5-lobed, these are in turn bluntly lobed. Flowers in erect corymbose panicles; usually appearing with or just after the foliage. Fruit a pair of winged samaras.
H: Deciduous woodland, thickets, hedges. On soil rich in nutrients and minerals. Common in southerly and central parts of England, especially on basic soils, rarer elsewhere.

Norway Maple
Acer platanoides
Maple family
Aceraceae

April—May   20—35 m   D; ♄

▽

IM: Moderately large tree with wide to ovoid crown. Older bark has numerous short fissures; young twigs glabrous, shiny brown. Leaves opposite, petiolate, 5—15 cm long, 5-lobed; lobes are long-toothed. Flowers in corymbose panicles, usually appearing shortly before the foliage. Fruit a pair of winged samaras.
H: Woods and hedges. Likes damp loose soil often containing pebbles. Fairly common in most areas though often only planted.
AI: There are many other similar maple species, which are particularly well-suited as ornamental trees. The Sycamore (see page 381) is the more common species.

Small-leaved Lime
Tilia cordata
Lime-tree family
Tiliaceae

June   10–25 m   D; ♄

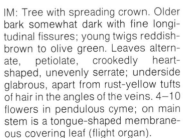

Red-berried Elder
Sambucus racemosa
Honeysuckle family
Caprifoliaceae

April–May   2–4 m   D; ♄

IM: Tree with spreading crown. Older bark somewhat dark with fine longitudinal fissures; young twigs reddish-brown to olive green. Leaves alternate, petiolate, crookedly heart-shaped, unevenly serrate; underside glabrous, apart from rust-yellow tufts of hair in the angles of the veins. 4–10 flowers in pendulous cyme; on main stem is a tongue-shaped membraneous covering leaf (flight organ).
H: Variety of soils, especially common in woods on limestone cliffs. Scattered throughout England and Wales, planted in N. England & Scotland; also often along avenues and in parks.
Al: Similar: Large-leaved Lime (*T. platyphyllos*). Leaves larger, white tufts of hair in angles of veins.

IM: Shrub, very rarely a small tree. Twigs have dark brown bark with coarse pores and brownish-red pith. Leaves opposite, short petioles, pinnate; 3–7 leaflets (usually 5), oblong-ovoid, pointed, margin serrate. Flowers in erect, dense, ovoid panicles, strong smelling. Berries globular, red.
H: Likes somewhat stony ground free of lime. Widely planted, sometimes escaping and becoming naturalized.

201

Barberry
Berberis vulgaris
Barberry family
Berberidaceae

May—June   1—2.5 m   D; ♄; (+)

   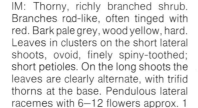

IM: Thorny, richly branched shrub. Branches rod-like, often tinged with red. Bark pale grey, wood yellow, hard. Leaves in clusters on the short lateral shoots, ovoid, finely spiny-toothed; short petioles. On the long shoots the leaves are clearly alternate, with trifid thorns at the base. Pendulous lateral racemes with 6—12 flowers approx. 1 cm long. Berries elongate-cylindrical, scarlet in colour with bitter taste.
H: Open woodland, hedgerows, thickets. On warm calcareous soil rich in nutrients. Scattered throughout Britain but nowhere in large numbers. Planted for ornament and the fruit which has edible pulp (not the stone which is poisonous).
AI: Found in many different species.

202

Gorse
Ulex europaeus
Pea family
Fabaceae (Leguminosae)

May—June   0.5—2 m   D; ♄; +

IM: Very prickly shrub. Stem erect, twigs green, grooved. Leaves of older plants become needle-shaped spines: simple or trifid, the upper ones linear stiff and sharply pointed. 1—3 flowers in the upper leaf axils, 1.5—2 cm long, scented.
H: Rough grassland, open dry woodland, heaths. Somewhat calcicolous, does not withstand frost. Throughout Britain, but planted in parts of the far north.
AI: Also called Furze or Whin.

German Greenweed
Genista germanica
Pea family
Fabaceae (Leguminosae)

May–June   20–50 cm   D; ♄; +

IM: Half-shrub; woody at the bottom, young shoots herbaceous. Ascending or erect, branched at the top, thorny at the bottom. Leaves simple, with rough hairs, elongate-elliptical, 1–2 cm long. Terminal racemes. Flowers 1 cm long, hairy.
H: Not British. heaths, open woodland, path balks. Calcifugous; likes warmth. Scattered, hardly found over 700 m; central and southern Europe.
AI: Similar: Petty Whin (*G. anglica*); also thorny, but entire plant glabrous, bluish-green; heaths and moors on soil low in lime: scattered throughout.

Dyer's Greenweed
Genista tinctoria
Pea family
Fabaceae (Leguminosae)

July–Sept.   30–70 cm   D; ♄; +

IM: Shrub: woody at the bottom, young shoots herbaceous. Prostrate to ascending, more richly branched at the top. Stem and branches do not have thorns. Leaves oblong-lanceolate, 1–3 cm long, with soft hairs along the margin. Flowers axillary, around 1.5 cm long, glabrous.
H: Rough turf and grassy places. Found on loamy soil which is not too dry and preferably low in nutrients. Able to withstand lime. Throughout England and Wales, rare in southern Scotland and absent in the north.
AI: Similar: Hairy Greenweed (*G. pilosa*); also without thorns, but flowers covered with silky hairs, 1–2 in leaf axils. Cliffs and sandy heaths; calcifugous. Rare in S. England and Wales.

Black Broom
Lembotropis nigricans
Pea family
Fabaceae (Leguminosae)

June–Aug.   50–150 cm   D; ♄

IM: Shrub with ascending to erect twigs with brown bark; erect green flower buds, round and finely grooved. Leaves alternate, all made up of 3 leaflets which are ovoid, approx. 2 cm long. Leaves, petioles and twigs covered with short hairs. Erect terminal raceme, 10–30 cm long, without foliage. Flowers around 1 cm long.
H: Not British. Open woodland, forest margins, thickets, path balks, rocks. Likes warmth. Found on shallow stony or sandy ground. Rare. Southern Germany, southern Alps to eastern Europe.
Al: Synonym: *Cytisus nigricans*.

Broom
Cytisus scoparius
Pea family
Fabaceae (Leguminosae)

June–Aug.   50–200 cm   D; ♄; (+)

IM: Shrub with old twigs which usually stand awry; brown bark; rod-like young twigs green in colour and angular. Leaves alternate, falling off rapidly; the lower ones have 3 leaflets which are each approx. 1 cm long, the upper ones are sessile and undivided, elongate-ovoid, flowers approx. 2 cm long, solitary or in twos, short pedicels, in the axils of the upper leaves.
H: Woodland margins, glades, clearings, heaths, path balks, waste places. Calcifugous. Often planted to stop soil erosion and to enrich the soil with nitrogen. Not resistant to frost. Scattered throughout Britain.
Al: Synonym: *Sarothamnus scoparius*.

Shrubby Milkwort
Polygala chamaebuxus
Milkwort family
Polygalaceae

April—June   10—20 cm   D; ♄

IM: Prostrate dwarf shrub with ascending branches. Leaves leathery, evergreen, lanceolate to elliptical, margin entire, the lower leaves ovoid, smaller than the upper ones. 1—2 flowers in the leaf axils, 12—15 mm long, yellow, often brown-reddish tinged. Racemes have few flowers, interspersed with leaves.
H: Not British. Dry pine forests, thickets, heaths, poor stony turf, rocks. On sunny stony ground rich in lime and low in nutrients. Must be dry at least part of the year. Rare; mountains of central and southern Europe.

Fly Honeysuckle
Lonicera xylosteum
Honeysuckle family
Caprifoliaceae

May—June   1—2 m   D; ♄; +

IM: Branched shrub with rod-like hollow twigs. Flowers always in pairs on a stem, the lower globular ovaries having grown together. Corolla hairy. Leaves opposite, simple, wide ovoid, blunt, margin entire. Shiny red (double) berries.
H: Deciduous woodland, in hedges. Calcicolous. Needs loose soil rich in humus and nutrients. Scattered in England and Wales, and a few places in Scotland. Mostly introduced.
AI: The flowers are never pure white. Often the very similar *L. ruprechtiana* from China is planted in parks and gardens. Flowers do not have hairs on the outside, snow-white in colour, changing to yellow.

205

Water-plantain
Alisma plantago-aquatica
Water Plantain family
Alismataceae

June—Aug.   20–100 cm   M; ♃

IM: Flowers in whorls, their parts (petals etc) in threes, the petals withering very rapidly, white or lilac, yellowish base. Leaves oval, robust, on long stalks, forming basal rosette.
H: Banks of stagnant or slow-flowing waters, in reed beds and sedge, also in ditches. Throughout most of Britain, rarer in the north. Indicator of muddy ground rich in nutrients.
AI: Similar to some closely related species. They are distinguished by their leaves and their habitat: Narrow-leaved Water-plantain, *A. lanceolatum*: leaves narrow; Ribbon-leaved Water-plantain (*Alisma gramineum*): leaves ribbon-like, submerged, protected in Britain. Both aquatic plants.

Water-pepper
Polygonum hydropiper
Dock family
Polygonaceae

July—Oct.   25–75 cm   D; ☉ ; (+)

IM: Spike lax, thin and slender. Stem erect. Leaves elongate-lanceolate, narrower towards the base and the tip. Flowers greenish or reddish.
H: Ditches, river banks, damp pathways. Prefers ground low in lime. Withstands temporary flooding. Indicator of nitrogen. Common throughout Britain except northern Scotland.
AI: The plant may be confused with Tasteless Water-pepper (*P. mite*). When chewed this does not taste peppery and sharp. It occurs in the same habitats, but is rarer.

Common Sorrel
Rumex acetosa
Dock family
Polygonaceae

May–June   30–100 cm   D; 24; (+)

IM: Leaves tough and thickish, spear-shaped at the base with backward-pointing lobes. Upper leaves more or less sessile and clasping the stem. Leaves have a somewhat acid taste. Flower panicles slender. Plant dioecious.
H: Meadows and open woodland, on loamy soil rich in nutrients. Common throughout.
AI: This plant is eaten because of its high Vitamin C content. It contains oxalic acid. Large quantities are damaging to one's health. The similar Sheep's Sorrel (*R. acetosella*) rarely grows higher than 30 cm and can be distinguished easily from Common Sorrel by the leaf-lobes and upper leaves, which do not clasp the stem.

Sheep's Sorrel
Rumex acetosella
Dock family
Polygonaceae

May–Aug.   8–30 cm   D; 24; (+)

IM: Plant is smaller than 30 cm. When chewed the leaves have a distinctly bitter taste. All leaves petiolate, the upper ones not clasping the stem. Leaves narrow, often with a spear-shaped base, the lobes forward-pointing.
H: Dry meadows, sandy ground and heaths, more rarely on sandy fields. Indicator of sandy and acid soil. Common.
AI: Various races can be distinguished within the species. On very poor sandy soils is the similar *R. tenuifolius*, with narrower leaves, with inrolled margins.

207

Common Poppy
Papaver rhoeas
Poppy family
Papaveraceae

June–Aug. 20–60 cm D; ☉ – ☉;(+)

IM: Pedicels have projecting bristles. Ovary and capsule glabrous, the capsule more or less globular. Plant contains whitish milky juice (latex). Leaves deeply pinnate, serrate.
H: Cornfields, rubble heaps, roads and wayside places. Prefers calcareous loamy soil. Common in the south, becoming rarer in the north of Scotland.
AI: The similar Long-headed Poppy (*Papaver dubium*) has a club-shaped capsule. It occurs in the same localities as the Common Poppy but prefers soil low in lime. Both species have been reduced in numbers over recent years as a result of weed-killing through herbicides.

Cuckoo Flower
Cardamine pratensis
Mustard family
Brassicaceae (Cruciferae)

April–June   15–60 cm   D; ♃

IM: Basal leaves in rosette arrangement, pinnate, leaflets round, the terminal leaflet usually larger. Stem leaves pinnate with narrow segments. Stem hollow. Flowers in racemes, large (approx. 1–2 cm wide). Ovaries and fruit much longer than wide. Flower colour is very variable ranging from white, pink, lilac to deep blue-violet.
H: Damp meadows and woodland on loamy soil. Common throughout.
AI: Similar: Narrow-leaved Bitter-cress (*C. impatiens*); flowers about 0.5 cm wide, whitish. Local in woodland in the west of Britain.

Coralroot
Cardamine bulbifera
Mustard family
Brassicaceae (Cruciferae)

April—May   30—70 cm   D; ♃

IM: Flowers violet-coloured, usually tending more towards blue than to red. No rosette of leaves. Leaves at least partially pinnate. Upper leaves narrow and undivided. In the axils there are blackish-coloured bulbils.
H: Deciduous and mixed woodland on soil rich in nutrients and usually calcareous. Local in southern England, Midlands to southern Scotland.
AI: The Coralroot reproduces mainly by means of its bulbils. The formation of seeds is rare or totally absent. Ants carry off the bulbils, which explains why there are often only small numbers of the plant in the localities where it occurs. Synonym: *Dentaria bulbifera*.

Sea Rocket
Cakile maritima
Mustard family
Brassicaceae (Cruciferae)

June—Aug.   15—45 cm   D; ☉

IM: Plant tinged with bluish-green. Stem richly branched, ascending. Leaves fleshy, undivided or pinnately divided, alternate. Flowers sweet-smelling, a good 0.5 cm long; dense racemes. Fruit in two sections, the lower one chisel-shaped, the upper one oval-shaped at the joining point with spear-like humps.
H: All around the coasts of Britain, on sandy and shingle beaches and in dunes. Withstands high salt concentration, but does not need it to grow. Rarely carried inland and does not grow well there.

Great Burnet
Sanguisorba officinalis
Rose family
Rosaceae

June–Sept.   30–100 cm   D; ⁤

IM: Dense terminal heads of deep purplish-red or brownish-red flowers. Stem erect and branched in the upper part. Leaves large, pinnate. Leaflets petiolate, ovoid, margin crenate.
H: Moist meadows. Grows on very damp, often peaty soil but also loamy. Does not form very large numbers. Common locally, mainly in western parts of Britain.
AI: The inconspicuous flowers are generally bisexual, i.e. they have both stamens and ovaries. Occasionally however you may find unisexual flowers. The very light seeds of the Great Burnet are dispersed by the wind.

Pale Willowherb
Epilobium roseum
Willow Herb family
Onagraceae

July–Aug.   25–60 cm   D; ⁤

IM: Many-flowered inflorescence. Petals 4–5 mm long, deeply notched, initially almost white, later streaked with pink. Stem glabrous at the bottom, further up slightly hairy. Leaves elongate-lanceolate, fairly long petioles, finely toothed.
H: Woods, river banks, also in ditches. Likes calcareous soil rich in nutrients and wet from seepage. Throughout most of Britain but absent from mountainous areas.
AI: Similar: *E. alpestre*: petals 6–12 mm long, red right from initial flowering. Leaves in threes on lower part of stem, sessile, very clearly toothed. Scattered. Mountains of central and southern Europe.

Rosebay Willowherb
Epilobium angustifolium
Willowherb family
Onagraceae

July–Sept.   30–120 cm   D; ♃

IM: All leaves alternate, 1–2 cm wide and 5–15 cm long. Leaf uppers dark green, undersides bluish-green. Flowers 2–3 cm in diameter. Style curved with 4 clear stigmas.
H: Woodland, old ballast areas, e.g. railway tracks which have been shut down or are used only infrequently. Grows on loose nitrogenous soil. Common throughout though less so in the north.
AI: This plant is sometimes placed in a genus of its own (Fireweed — *Chamaenerion*).

Alpine Fireweed
Epilobium fleischeri
Willowherb family
Onagraceae

July–Aug.   10–30 cm   D; ♃

IM: Stem not erect but prostrate or ascending. Leaves alternate, only 1–3 mm wide. Flowers vivid red.
H: Not British. Only found in central and southern Europe. There it grows on loose gravel and scree. Scattered, sometimes absent in a whole area.
AI: Hybrids between this species and most of the other species in the family have not been found. The Alpine Fireweed is also sometimes placed in the same genus as Fireweed (*Chamaenerion*), as is Rosemary Willowherb (*E. dodonaei*), which also has narrow leaves but an upright stem.

Great Willowherb
Epilobium hirsutum
Willowherb family
Onagraceae

May–Aug.   80–150 cm   D; ♃

IM: Flowers in corymbose racemes at the ends of the stem and main branches. Flowers around 2 cm in diameter. Petals notched, light purplish-red. Middle and lower leaves are between 5–12 cm long. Lower leaves mostly opposite and sessile and slightly decurrent. Stem is hairy lower down.
H: Ditches, reeds, damp woodland, fens. Prefers calcareous soils, withstands or requires occasional flooding. Common in all but the far north west.
AI: Great and Hoary Willowherb are very similar but the Great Willowherb is decidedly the larger. Its flowers grow to twice the size of the Hoary Willowherb (*E. parviflorum*).
212

Hoary Willowherb
Epilobium parviflorum
Willowherb family
Onagraceae

June–Sept.   15–80 cm   D; ♃

IM: Whole stem has projecting hairs, stem usually erect, more rarely only ascending. Leaves elongate or lanceolate, barely over 7 cm long, the lower and middle ones opposite, the upper ones alternate. Flowers fairly large, approx. 1 cm in diameter. Petals deeply notched.
H: Reed beds, ditches, moist woodland. Likes damp loamy soil rich in nutrients.
AI: As the Hoary Willowherb is often found in the same locations as the Great Willowherb, it used to be thought that these were two sexually different examples of the same species.

Broad-leaved Willowherb
Epilobium montanum
Willowherb family
Onagraceae

June–Aug. 20–60 cm D; ♃

IM: Petals 8–10 mm long, pale pink to almost white, deeply notched. Stem usually only branched in the top part, also not too many standing close together. Plant does not, therefore, make a compact effect. Leaves in the lower half of the plant opposite, in the upper half sometimes in whorls of three, 4–8 cm long.

H: Woodland, hedgerows, occasionally also in gardens. Likes moist somewhat stony ground. Frequently found on calcareous soil. Common throughout Britain.

Water Mint
Mentha aquatica
Mint family
Lamiaceae (Labiatae)

July–Oct. 15–90 cm D; ♃

IM: Flowers grow in rounded terminal heads or in verticillasters in the axils of the upper leaves. The 'lip blossom' is so inconspicuous on the Water Mint that for the layman the plant does not even seem to be bilaterally symmetrical. It is taken as having 4 lobes. Stem 4-angled; leaves opposite and decussate, toothed.

H: Reeds, river banks, ditches, wet meadows and fields. Common throughout Britain.

AI: The various types of Mint are hard to distinguish from one another because there are many hybrids. The best-known one is the Peppermint (*M.* x *piperita*). This hybrid is a cross between the Water Mint and the Spear Mint.

213

Knotgrass
Polygonum aviculare
Dock family
Polygonaceae

July–Oct. 10–200 cm D; ⊙

IM: Stem prostrate. Flowers in axillary clusters, pale greenish-white, often tinged with pink.
H: Weedy places on fields and along paths and waste places. Nitrogen indicator. Very common throughout. Resistant to trampling.
AI: Knotgrass can be clearly distinguished from other species in this genus by its prostrate, non-twining stem and the axillary flower clusters.

Redshank
Polygonum persicaria
Dock family
Polygonaceae

June–Oct. 25–75 cm D; ⊙ ; (+)

IM: Stem somewhat branched, each branch terminating in a spike. Petiole projecting from a papery sheath (ochra) surrounding the stem at each node. Ochra fringed along margin. Leaves between petiole and leaf centre often somewhat hairy.
H: Fields, rubble heaps, ditches. Likes nitrogen. Common throughout Britain.
AI: Similar: Pale Persicaria (*P. lapathifolium*). Leaf sheaths not fringed. Fields, ditches. Likes nitrogen.

Common Bistort
Polygonum bistorta
Dock family
Polygonaceae

June—Aug.   25—50 cm   D; ♃

IM: Stem unbranched, bearing only a single spike at the end. The flowers on the spike are usually dense and thus create a compact cylindrical effect when the flowers are open. Leaves ovoid, greyish-green underneath. Rootstock twisted like a snake (hence the name).
H: Damp meadows, damp woodland, occasionally on roadsides. Moisture indicator. Common. Usually forms large groups.
AI: Especially on damp meadows Common Bistort may form large colonies. Then it becomes a nuisance. In hay it does not dry well. Drainage and liming help to reduce numbers.

Wall Gipsy Weed
Gypsophila muralis
Pink family
Caryophyllaceae

June—Oct.   5—20 cm   D; ☉

IM: Flowers only 6—10 mm in diameter, pink, with darker veins. Calyx has dry membraneous stripes, toothed, teeth only approx. 1/3 of length calyx. Stem ascending or stiffly erect, with forked branching. Leaves opposite, narrow linear, barely 1 mm wide.
H: Most of Europe. In Britain only as a rare casual.
AI: Similar: Creeping Gypsophila (*G. repens*). Not British. Perennial plant. Flowers white, at most tinged with purple. Limestone scree and damp rubble heaps. Mountains of central and southern Europe. Creeping Gypsophila dams up scree.

Deptford Pink
Dianthus armeria
Pink family
Caryophyllaceae

July–Aug.   30–60 cm   D; ☉ – ☉

IM: 2–10 flowers in terminal cluster surrounded by narrow, densely packed bracts. Flowers approx. 1 cm in diameter. Epicalyx of 2 scales. Uppersides of the petals light purplish-red to dark pink, with numerous white spots; towards the throat of the corolla there are individual darker spots and individual hairs.
H: Dry turf, hedgerows. Calcifugous. Rare, in lowland habitats in England, Wales and a few places in Scotland.
AI: Sweet-William (*D. barbatus*): Epicalyx of 4 scales. Flowers larger. Calcareous soil. Popular garden plant sometimes found growing wild.

Carthusian Pink
Dianthus carthusianorum
Pink family
Caryophyllaceae

June–Sept.   15–40 cm   D; ☉ – ♃

IM: 4–10 flowers in a terminal cluster, but usually only one or two flowers blossom at a time. Petals dark red or deep pinkish-red. Calyx glabrous with hairy pointed epicalyx scales at the base, approx. $1/12$ length of the calyx. Leaf sheaths on the stem at least twice as long as the leaves are wide.
H: Dry turf, open woodland and dry thickets. Scattered.
AI: The Carthusian Pink is a rare escape from cultivation in Britain.

Maiden Pink
Dianthus deltoides
Pink family
Caryophyllaceae

June–Sept.   15–45 cm   D; ♃

IM: Stem erect or ascending, covered with rough, short hairs, branched at the top. Petals purplish-red, with clear white spots and relatively long white hairs. A dark line running parallel to the outer petal margin is usually clearly visible. Calyx cylindrical, glabrous, at the base with 2 epicalyx scales which are only half as long.
H: Pastures, poor turf. Calcifugous. Prefers sandy loose soils low in nutrients. Absent in limestone regions, otherwise local throughout.
AI: Differs from the similar *D. seguieri* which always has a glabrous (smooth) stem.

Cheddar Pink
Dianthus gratianopolitanus
Pink family
Caryophyllaceae

June–July   10–25 cm   D; ♃

IM: Solitary flowers at the end of a stem, 2–2.5 cm in diameter. Petals along the outer edge have fairly short teeth. Calyx often tinged with violet, surrounded below by 4–6 epicalyx scales barely ¼ as long as the calyx and which may be blunt or pointed. Leaves never have keel, bluish-green. Plant often forms small cushions.
H: Very rare. Nowadays only found on the limestone cliffs of Cheddar Gorge.

Dianthus seguieri
Pink family
Caryophyllaceae

June–Aug.   30–60 cm   D; ♃

IM: 1–8 flowers in loose head. They are deep pink in colour and often white-spotted near the base. The margins are bearded. Calyx cylindrical, glabrous, with 2–6 oval epicalyx scales at the base. Their pointed apices do not reach the edge of the calyx.
H: Not British. Poor mats, acid mountain meadows, chestnut thickets. Alpine plant. Found in south-western Europe and western central Europe. Very rare.

Dianthus superbus
Pink family
Caryophyllaceae

June–Sept.   30–90 cm   D; ♃

IM: Flowers solitary, on pedicels. Petals lilac-coloured to deep pink, often with a strong tendency towards lilac. Petals divided beyond the middle, often with dark spots, bearded. Flower spread out, generally over 2.5 cm in diameter. Short epicalyx scales at the base of the calyx, these reaching no more than 1/3 of calyx length. Flowers usually have strong smell.
H: Not British. Woodland thickets, mountain meadows, wet meadows. Scattered. Most of continental Europe.
AI: Similar: Pink (*D. plumarius*). Flower spread out, under 2.5 cm in diameter, pink to white. Calyx scales reach to approx 1/4 the length of the calyx. Not British. Eastern central Europe. Rare.

Moss Campion
Silene acaulis
Pink family
Caryophyllaceae

July–Aug.   1–10 cm   D; ♃

IM: Plant grows in dense cushions. Flowers solitary on the stems which are usually very short at first but lengthen later. Petals purple to pink. Leaves opposite, upper ones ovoid, lower ones narrow, 5–15 mm long.
H: Cliffs, ledges and screes in the mountains. Likes calcareous loose soils. North Wales, Lake District, Scotland.

Red Campion
Silene dioica
Pink family
Caryophyllaceae

May–June   30–90 cm   D; ♃

IM: Flowers numerous, in terminal dichasia. They are dull pink to purplish-red, rarely white. Plant is dioecious: male and female flowers are on separate plants. Female flowers have a calyx with 20 veins, male flowers have one with 10 veins, their flowers are usually smaller and duller. Entire plant covered with soft hairs. Leaves opposite, upper ones ovoid.
H: Damp meadows, hedgerows and woodland. Common in most areas. Wetness indicator.
AI: Red Campion has been placed with other species in the genus *Melandrium*; *M. dioicum, M. rubrum*.

Sticky Catchfly
Lychnis viscaria
Pink family
Caryophyllaceae

June–Aug. 30–60 cm D; ♃

IM: Flowers grow in a fairly loose panicle. They reach a diameter of 2 cm. The petals are purplish-red and slightly notched at the apex. The dark viscid rings below the upper nodes on the stem are striking. Leaves opposite. Plant glabrous or only with slight covering of short hairs.
H: Dry meadows, heaths, dry woodland. Prefers soil low in lime. Rare.
AI: The Sticky Catchfly can be easily recognized by its viscid rings. There is no proven knowledge regarding their importance but it is probably safe to assume that they ward off harmful insects.

Ragged-Robin
Lychnis flos-cuculi
Pink family
Caryophyllaceae

May–June 30–75 cm D; ♃

IM: The flowers grow in loose dichasia. They are either light pink or occasionally white. The petals are conspicuously deeply divided. Leaves opposite, spatulate to lanceolate.
H: Meadows. Wetness indicator. Common.
AI: The Ragged-Robin is one of the plants which is frequented particularly often by leaf hoppers when laying their eggs. These larvae take what they need to survive from the juice of the plant and the combination of the juice plus their breath forms a saliva-like froth which remains on the plant. In the past it was not possible to explain the occurrence of this froth. It was thought to be 'devil's work'.

Soapwort
Saponaria officinalis
Pink family
Caryophyllaceae

July–Sept.   30–90 cm   D; ♃

IM: Stem erect, often tinged with red; leaves on stem are sessile, opposite, broadly ovoid. Flowers in dense terminal corymbs on the main stem and its branches. Petals spread out flat from long cylindrical calyx, only slightly crenate at apex, each petal with two small scales in the throat of the corolla.
H: Hedgerows, waysides, almost always near habitation. Common in most areas.
Al: Perhaps native in the south west where it grows along streams. Elsewhere probably introduced as an old cottage-garden herb, hence its association with habitation.

Saponaria ocymoides
Pink family
Caryophyllaceae

April–Oct.   10–30 cm   D; ♃

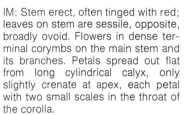

IM: The plant produces numerous prostrate or ascending stems which together form a dense turf or cushion. Flowers 1.5–2.5 cm in diameter, red. Calyx inflated-tubular, with short hairs. Leaves opposite.
H: Not British. Rubble heaps, stony mats and rocky thickets. Indicator of lime. South west and southern central Europe.
Al: The plant is occasionally planted in rockeries. This species is a popular rock-garden plant and very occasionally escapes.

Orpine
Sedum telephium
Stonecrop family
Crassulaceae

July–Sept.   20–60 cm   D; ♃

IM: Leaves ovoid, smooth, flat but thick and fleshy. Stem erect. Inflorescence has many flowers packed together, often spread out in almost umbellate arrangement.
H: In open woodland and hedgerows. Likes relatively dry stony ground rich in nutrients. Scattered throughout, in some parts local or rare; may also be found growing wild from gardens (old ornamental plant).

Water Avens
Geum rivale
Rose family
Rosaceae

May–Sept.   20–60 cm   D; ♃

IM: Several flowers in a lax cyme, drooping. The reddish-brown sepals are conspicuous. The petals are orange-red or yellowish. Leaves alternate, irregularly pinnate, upper ones trifoliate.
H: Wet meadows, flat moors, ditches, light wet woodland. Common in northern England, Wales and Scotland, local or rare in southern Scotland.
AI: The individual plants within the species vary very greatly, but so far it has not been possible to clearly define any further divisions. In larger groups one often finds 'anomalies': the bracts form an integral part of the flowers, the flower does not droop, etc.

Marsh Cinquefoil
Potentilla palustris
Rose family
Rosaceae

June–Sept.   10–50 cm   D; ⚃

IM: Flower deep purple, almost brown-ish-red — not only the shorter nar-rower petals but also the sepals which are a dull purplish-red on the inside (but usually conspicuously green on the outside). Leaves palmately lobed with 5–7 lobes. Stem prostrate or erect.
H: Fens, marshes and heaths. Usually found on acid soil which is flooded at least part of the year. Commoner in the north but widely distributed through-out Britain.
AI: Its classification in the genus *Potentilla* is sometimes disputed and it has been known as *Comarum palus-tre*. There are no known hybrids with other species of the genus.

Common Stork's-bill
Erodium cicutarium
Geranium family
Geraniaceae

April–Oct.   15–50 cm   D; ⊙ - ⊙

IM: Flowers approx. 1 cm in diameter, light purple to pink and often with lighter-coloured spots. Leaves pin-nate, leaflets deeply dissected. Beak of the fruit 3–4 cm long with a ring-shaped constriction below the tip.
H: Fields, sand dunes and waste land. Prefers a sandy soil. Scattered throughout Britain but commonest in coastal districts.
AI: The popular name refers to the beak-shaped fruit.

Cut-leaved Crane's-bill
Geranium dissectum
Geranium family
Geraniaceae

May–Oct.   10–50 cm   D; ☉ – ☉

IM: Flowers in pairs, small, 8–10 mm in diameter, light purplish-red. Stem of inflorescence shorter than its bract. All leaves petiolate. Stem branched, ascending or erect. Leaves cleft almost to the base and composed of 5–7 lobes.
H: Fields, gardens, wayside verges. Likes stony ground rich in nutrients, dry rather than moist. Scattered.
AI: Probably originates from the western Mediterranean area. From there it has been introduced and established itself not only in Europe but also in the temperate zones of both the northern and the southern hemisphere.

Long-stalked Crane's-bill
Geranium columbinum
Geranium family
Geraniaceae

May–Sept.   15–50 cm   D; ☉

IM: Flowers in pairs, small, 1.2–1.7 cm in diameter, light purple. Stems of inflorescence always longer than the bract. All leaves petiolate. Stem branched, erect or ascending. Leaves cleft almost to the base, 5–7 segments.
H: Fields, gardens, path verges. Likes sandy rather dry, chalky soil. Scattered, but nowhere common becoming rarer in the north.
AI: Probably originates from the eastern Mediterranean area. From there it has not only established itself in northern Europe but has spread across the entire northern hemisphere.

Hedgerow Crane's-bill
Geranium pyrenaicum
Geranium family
Geraniaceae

June–Sept.   15–50 cm   D; ♃

IM: Flowers in pairs, small, 10–15 mm in diameter, purplish-violet or violet in colour. Stem of inflorescence longer than bract. Leaves have short petioles. Stem little branched, ascending or erect. Leaves roundish, kidney-shaped at the base, 3–7 cm in diameter, slightly indented to form 7–9 lobes.
H: Field margins, pathways and hedgerows. Found in loamy soil. Scattered.
AI: Probably originates from the mountains around the Mediterranean. The plant has only been established in Britain for approximately 200 years.

Herb Robert
Geranium robertianum
Geranium family
Geraniaceae

June–Oct.   15–50 cm   D; ☉ – ☉

IM: Flowers in pairs, small, 1.4–1.8 cm in diameter, pink. Sometimes also very pale pink with darker veins. Stem of inflorescence much longer than the bract. Leaves cleft almost to the base in 3–5 leaflets, which are in turn divided almost to the central vein. Whole plant usually reddish tinged.
H: Woodland, hedgerows, shingle beaches, walls, waste land. Common.
AI: In coastal areas there is a subspecies found on sand. It is smaller and has a prostrate stem (ssp. *maritimum*). *G. purpureum* is similar, lacks reddish tinge, has smaller flowers.

Marsh Crane's-bill
Geranium palustre
Geranium family
Geraniaceae

June–Sept.   20–100 cm   D; ♃

IM: Flowers in pairs, flowers only 2.5–3 cm in diameter. Petals only slightly crenate, reddish-violet to pale purplish-red. No glandular hairs on the peduncles. Stem branched, ascending, with coarse hairs. Leaves have 7 palmate lobes.
H: Not British. River banks, ditches, damp meadows and damp open woodland areas. Requires permanently moist soil.
AI: Marsh Crane's-bill is predominantly found in eastern Europe, as far east as Siberia and west as far as the Rhine.

Bloody Crane's-bill
Geranium sanguineum
Geranium family
Geraniaceae

June–Aug.   10–50 cm   D; ♃

IM: Flowers solitary, 2.5–3 cm in diameter, carmine. Petals crenate. Stem and peduncles have projecting hairs. Leaves 5–7 palmate lobes. Leaf lobes linear, 1 or 2 segments at the apex.
H: Dry woodland, sand dunes, semi-dry turf. Likes sunny spots. Often found on limestone. Local but spread over most of Britain. Least common in the south. Usually in large numbers in localities where it occurs.

Wood Crane's-bill
Geranium sylvaticum
Geranium family
Geraniaceae

June–Sept.   30–60 cm   D; ♃

IM: Flowers in pairs, 2–3 cm in diameter, reddish- or bluish-violet. Leaves 7–12 cm wide, usually 5–7 lobes with segments which do not go right to the leaf base. Stem erect, usually branched with a dense covering of hairs, glandular above, bent downwards at the bottom of the stem. H: Woodland, meadows and roadsides (up to above 500 m in Scotland). Needs damp soil rich in nutrients and humus. Never common but widely distributed in suitable habitats.

Dusky Crane's-bill
Geranium phaeum
Geranium family
Geraniaceae

July–Oct.   20–50 cm   D; ♃

IM: Flowers in pairs, 2–3 cm in diameter, brownish-violet in colour. In contrast to the other European species the petals are spread out flat or reflexed. Leaves 5–10 cm wide, dissected into irregular lobes the deepest cut to 1/3 of the leaf width.
H: Roadsides and hedgebanks. Prefers moist loamy soil low in lime. Rare. AI: Native of southern Europe. North of the Alps it is only found growing wild as a garden escape but has established itself locally in England, Wales and southern Scotland.

227

Musk Mallow
Malva moschata
Mallow family
Malvaceae

July–Sept.　　30–60 cm　　D; ♃

IM: Flowers pale red, pink or almost white, 4–5 cm in diameter. Outer sepals 3–5 mm long and only about 1 mm wide. Upper leaves palmately lobed into 5–7 segments almost to the base of the leaf. Hairs on the stem unbranched (magnifying glass needed).
H: Dry grassland, hedgebanks. Requires soil rich in nutrients. Not uncommon, occurring throughout Britain though never in large numbers.
AI: A variable plant especially in the way the leaves are dissected. Similar: *M. alcea*: outer sepals oval, 4–8 mm long and 2–4 mm wide. Rarely found and not persisting.

Common Mallow
Malva sylvestris
Mallow family
Malvaceae

July–Sept.　　20–120 cm　　D; ♃

IM: 2–6 flowers in a raceme borne in the leaf axils, reddish-violet in colour, approx. 4 cm in diameter. Petals vary slightly in size, and have a notched margin. Upper leaves palmately dissected but not for more than 2/3 of their length. Stem erect. Leaf lobes crenate.
H: Roadsides, hedgerows and waste places. Nitrogen indicator. Widely distributed and common in southern England, rarer further north.
AI: Native of the Mediterranean region but has been known in Britain since Roman times and is usually considered native though its exact status is doubtful.

Dwarf Mallow
Malva neglecta
Mallow family
Malvaceae

June–Sept.   30–50 cm   D; ☉–♃

IM: Flowers in axillary clusters, pale pinkish-red to almost white. Flower does not open wide but is funnel-shaped. The flower diameter is therefore not relevant, only the length of the flower. This is between 8–15 mm. The flower is considerably longer than the calyx especially on those plants which remain small. The flower stalk is bent over. Upper leaves are palmately lobed but not for more than ²/₃ of their length. Stem usually prostrate.
H: Weedy areas along roadside and in waste places. Widespread in southern England but never common.
Al: Similar: Small-flowered Mallow (*M. pusilla*) with flowers only about 5 mm long and never longer than the sepals. Occasionally found in waste places.

Wild Angelica
Angelica sylvestris
Umbellifer family
Umbelliferae

July–Sept.   30–200 cm   D; ♃; (+)

IM: Flowers in double umbels, each with 20–40 rays, either without bracts or reduced to only a few and falling early. Secondary umbels with numerous bracteoles. Stem hollow, glaucous-blue to reddish, tinged with white. Leaves 2–3 pinnate, petiolate and with conspicuously inflated leaf sheaths.
H: Frequent in fens and marshes along the banks of rivers and ditches, in wet meadows as well as in wet woodlands.
Al: Wild Angelica was a popular medicinal plant and is one of the many Umbelliferae which have either white or reddish flowers (p. 69; p. 368).

Bird's-eye Primrose
Primula farinosa
Primrose family
Primulaceae

May–July   5–20 cm   D; ♃

IM: Rose-purple flowers, carried in umbels, approx. 1 cm in diameter. The 5 petals are spread out flat; flower stalks are mealy when young. The calyx is small. The leaf margins are crenulate and the undersides are covered with yellowish or white meal.
H: Needs peaty soil in calcareous areas. Found from Derbyshire to Scotland where it is sometimes abundant.
AI: Similar: Long-flowered Primrose (*P. halleri*), corolla tube usually 2–3 cm long (makes it easy to identify), calyx 1–1.5 cm long. Not known in Britain. South-eastern Alps, western Alps. Very rare.

Primula clusiana
Primrose family
Primulaceae

May–July   2–5 cm   D; ♃

IM: Usually only 2 flowers on each peduncle. 3 cm or more in diameter. Flower lobes not quite flat but partly bell-like in shape. They are divided to $\frac{1}{3}$–$\frac{1}{2}$ of their length. Leaves slightly sticky at most, light green above and grey-green below. The margin is frequently lighter in colour with a narrow scarious edge.
H: Not British. Needs stony ground rich in lime which is covered with snow for long periods.

Scarlet Pimpernel
Anagallis arvensis
Primrose family
Primulaceae

July–Oct.   8–15 cm   D; ⊙

IM: Flowers 5–7 mm in diameter, usually brick red. Petal margins usually slightly crenate. Flowers borne on slender stems from the leaf axils. Stem generally prostrate. Leaves opposite, occasionally in whorls of three, sessile, ovate.
H: Root crop fields, gardens, waste places. Indicator of light soils. Needs good supply of nutrients. Common.
AI: There is also a blue subspecies which should not be confused with *A. foemina*. The petals of all forms of the Scarlet Pimpernel are only slightly crenate.

Sea Milkwort
Galux maritima
Primrose family
Primulaceae

May–June   5–15 cm   D; ♃

IM: The flowers are stemless and solitary in the axils of the leaves. They reach a diameter of approx. 8 mm. Usually pale pink, somewhat darker towards the throat of the corolla. The leaves grow to 5 mm long and 3 mm wide. They are extremely fleshy and grow very close to the short stems. These are usually prostrate, spreading and rooting.
H: Needs salty, sandy or silty ground. A seashore plant found mostly at the edge of salt marshes or cliffs. Frequent around Britain.
AI: Sea Milkwort grows along virtually all coasts in the northern hemisphere, may be rarer in some locations, i.e. the Baltic coast.

231

Common Cyclamen
Cyclamen purpurascens
Primrose family
Primulaceae

June–Sept. 5–20 cm D; ⚄

   ▽

IM: Flowers solitary on their peduncles, their recurved petals very conspicuous. The long peduncles curl up like corkscrews while the fruit is forming. Strong scent. Leaves evergreen, reni- or cordiform. Leaf margin slightly crenate.
H: Not British. Needs somewhat damp soil containing humus and rich in nutrients. Forest in the Alpine foreland and in the Alps. Very rare.
AI: Occasionally Cyclamen may initially be confused with *Erythronium denscanis* which has 6 recurved petals. Not British.

Sea Pink
Armeria maritima
Sea Lavender family
Plumbaginaceae

May–Sept. 20–40 cm D; ⚄

    ▽

IM: Inflorescence 1.5–2.5 cm wide, borne in somewhat flattened compact globular heads, containing 10–30 flowers, usually pink but may also be purplish-red. Petal lobes crenate. Leaves approx. 1–2 mm wide and 5–10 cm long and are thick in texture.
H: Found on salt marshes and shingle banks. Tolerates high salt content. Common on cliffs and widely distributed around British coastline. Also found in peaty and rocky areas of some Scottish mountains to 1400 m.

Common Centaury
Centaurium erythraea
Gentian family
Gentianaceae

July–Oct. 10–50 cm D; ⊙

    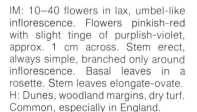

IM: 10–40 flowers in lax, umbel-like inflorescence. Flowers pinkish-red with slight tinge of purplish-violet, approx. 1 cm across. Stem erect, always simple, branched only around inflorescence. Basal leaves in a rosette. Stem leaves elongate-ovate.
H: Dunes, woodland margins, dry turf. Common, especially in England.
Al: Similar: *C. pulchellum*. Stem usually branched right from the base. No basal rosette leaves. Smaller (3–15 cm). Likes damp, even wet habitat in marshy meadows. Local, mostly near the sea in southern England and Ireland.

Lesser Bindweed
Convolvulus arvensis
Convolvulus family
Convolvulus

June–Oct. 30–100 cm D; ⨄

IM: Flowers usually solitary, rarely 2–3 in leaf axils; funnel-shaped, slight scent. Stem prostrate or twining to the left, glabrous. Leaves alternate, petiolate, sagittate or hastate at the base.
H: Fields, gardens, pathways, waste ground. Nitrogen indicator. Common.
Al: Roots, up to 2 m long, used to store nutrients and then provide for further growth if stems and leaves are destroyed.

Dodder
Cuscuta europaea
Dodder family
Cuscutaceae

June–Sept.   20–100 cm   D; ⊙

IM: The host plant (Nettle, Hedge Bindweed, Mugwort) is surrounded and penetrated by a network of thin thread-like stems. Flowers, pale red and sometimes almost white, in tangled clusters. Often only seen when the plant is closely inspected.
H: Wasteland, river banks. Rare.
AI: All species parasites. Similar: Common Dodder (*C. epithymum*): host plants: Thyme, Broom, Heather; sometimes found on heaths. *C. epilinum*: on flax. Only Common Dodder is likely to be seen in Britain.

Common Comfrey
Symphytum officinale
Borage family
Boraginaceae

May–June   30–120 cm   D; ♃; (+)

IM: Entire plant covered with rough hairs. Leaves narrowly ovoid, distinctly decurrent. Flowers small, campanulate, drooping, in scorpioidal cymes.
H: On damp to wet ground, always rich in nutrients. In wet meadows, on river banks and in ditches. Found throughout Britain but less so in the north.

Pulmonaria obscura
Borage family
Boraginaceae

March—April   15—40 cm   D; ♃

IM: Several flowers together in umbellate-like head. Peduncles of axillary inflorescences are as long as their bracts. Flowers like cowslips, opening red, becoming violet and finally blue as they fade. No narrowing of basal leaves. No spots on the leaves.
H: Not British. Woodland. Likes calcareous loamy soil. Scattered and local in northern Europe. Usually abundant where it occurs.
Al: Similar: Lungwort (*P. officinalis*): peduncles of axillary inflorescence shorter than the respective bract. Spotted leaves. Not British. Alps, Alpine foreland. Rare.

Vervain
Verbena officinalis
Verbena family
Verbenaceae

July—Oct.   30—60 cm   D; ⊙ - ♃

IM: Numerous small (3—5 mm long) reddish-violet or pale lilac flowers in a spike. Inflorescence conspicuously squarrosely branched. Leaves deeply divided, upper ones less so.
H: Roadsides and waste places. Nitrogen indicator. Local. In Britain commonest in the south.
Al: Vervain is thought to have originated from the Mediterranean area. Requires warmth.

Deadly Nightshade
Atropa bella-donna
Nightshade family
Solanaceae

June—July   5—150 cm   D; ♃; +

IM: Single flowers in axils of upper leaves. They have a greenish-red tinge, lobes are deep brownish-red, brownish-violet or purplish-violet. Stem erect, leaves ovate, decurrent. Usually a large leaf grows next to a small leaf. Fruit a berry, large and black.
H: Open woodland areas especially on chalky soils. Needs rather moist soil rich in nutrients. Rather rare.
AI: Deadly Nightshade is deadly poisonous. It contains hyoscyamine and smaller quantities of atropine.

Mountain Valerian
Valeriana montana
Valerian family
Valerianaceae

April—July   10—60 cm   D; ♃

IM: Entire inflorescence almost flat, umbellate with many individual flowers. Individual flowers up to 2.5 mm long, usually pale pink, rarely entirely white. Stem erect, hollow. Leaves on the non-flowering shoots narrow abruptly towards the stem. Only solitary leaves have 3 segments, normally they are ovate, lanceolate with 3—8 leaf pairs on one stem.
H: Not British. Stony places or scree; Alps, Alpine foreland. Scattered.
AI: Similar: Three-leaved Valerian (*V. tripteris*). Stem usually contains floury substance, not hollow. Scree and stony places. Not British. Alps, Alpine foreland and higher upland areas in southern central Europe. Rare.

Marsh Valerian
Valeriana dioica
Valerian family
Valerianaceae

May–July   10–30 cm   D; ♃

IM: Flowers in small clusters in rounded head at the end of the stem. Flowers dioecious: male and female flowers are found on separate plants. Male larger than the female, flowers pinkish. Basal leaves entire, stem leaves pinnately divided.
H: Banks of rivers, damp meadows, fens and boggy areas. Scattered throughout Britain in suitable habitats.
Al: Similar: Tuberous Valerian (*V. tuberosa*). Flowers usually bisexual. Basal leaves at least 1½ times as long as wide, usually 3 times longer than wide. Rhizome forms tubers. Only the southern Alps. Rare.

Common Valerian
Valeriana officinalis
Valerian family
Valerianaceae

July–Sept.   30–170 cm   D; ♃ ; (+)

IM: Flowers in terminal whorled panicle of considerable size. Flowers bisexual, flesh pink to very pale whitish-red, scented. All leaves opposite (6–9 pairs), pinnate (15–21 leaflets), glabrous.
H: Damp areas in woodland, in meadows and ditches. Also found on dry calcareous soils. Widely distributed though nowhere common.
Al: Similar: *V. pratensis*: stem has only 5–7 leaf pairs; leaves usually short with solitary hairs. Stem glabrous. Moors, meadows, marshy woodland. Likes the warmth. Very rare; not British.

Flowering Rush
Butomus umbellatus
Flowering Rush family
Butomaceae

June–Aug.   50–150 cm   M; ♃

Meadow Saffron
Colchicum autumnale
Lily family
Liliaceae

Aug–Oct.   5–20 cm   M; ♃; +

IM: 10–30 flowers in a lax umbellate inflorescence, up to 2–2.5 cm across. Outer petals shorter and narrower than inner ones. Inner petals usually have conspicuous dark red veins. Basal leaves reed-like, fluted, stiffly erect.
H: Reed beds in stagnant or slow-flowing water, mud ditches, canals and river margins. Local but scattered throughout Britain, except Scotland. Likes the warmth.
Al: Flowering Rush can be found almost everywhere but is not common anywhere; despite its extensive area of distribution virtually no variations within the species are known.

IM: Flowers on whitish 'stalk'. Free section of the petals 4–7 cm long. No leaves present during flowering time. Leaves, like tulip leaves, appear in the following spring.
H: Meadows, damp open woodland. Likes nitrogen. Rare but in abundance in a few places in England.
Al: Similar: *C. alpinum*: free section of the petals only 2–3 cm long. *C. bulbocodium*: flowers appear in the spring together with leaves which are hood shaped at the apex. Very rare. Not British. All species are very poisonous.

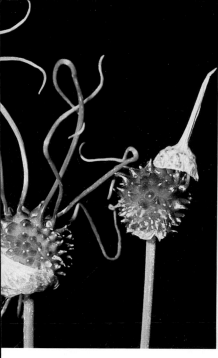

Crow Garlic
Allium vineale
Lily family
Liliaceae

June–Aug. 30–60 cm M; ♃

IM: Inflorescence a false umbel usually with bulbils instead of flowers. Where flowers form these have long peduncles and the leaves are like chives. Stem is covered with hairs to about half way up.
H: Roadsides, fields. Can be a serious weed in arable land. Common in England and Wales.
AI: Similar: Round-headed Leek (*A. sphaerocephalum*). Inflorescence rarely has bulbils, only flowers with very short peduncles. Dry turf. Rare. Only known in 2 sites in Britain.

Martagon Lily
Lilium martagon
Lily family
Liliaceae

June–Aug. 30–120 cm M; ♃

IM: 2–10 flowers, very rarely more, in a lax raceme. The flowers droop; 5–7 cm across. Petals have dark brown-red spots and when in full bloom petals are folded back. Leaves narrow ovoid, margin entire, in whorls.
H: Open woodland. Likes calcareous soil containing nutrients. Not native to Britain but naturalized in a few places.
AI: It is native to much of Europe eastwards to Siberia and Mongolia.

Pheasant's Eye
Adonis aestivalis
Buttercup family
Ranunculaceae

May—July   30—50 cm   D; ⊙ ; (+)

IM: Flowers solitary, scarlet, more rarely yellowish-red. Petals spread out. Sepals clinging. Small fruit without black spots. Leaves bi- or tripinnate.
H: Fields, waste ground. Likes dry calcareous soil. In Britain it has never been more than of casual occurrence. Al: Similar: *A. autumnalis* (*A. annua*): sepals horizontal or projecting backwards, flowers usually dark red. Garden plant originating from the Mediterranean region, occasionally a weed in cornfield. Now rarely seen.

Houseleek
Sempervivum tectorum
Stonecrop family
Crassulaceae

July—Sept.   10—60 cm   D; ♃

IM: The peduncle of the inflorescence rises from a dense rosette of basal leaves and is covered with scale-like leaves. It bears 10—25 flowers which are all closely compressed; 1—2 cm across, 10—20 petals.
H: Rocks and walls. Only grows wild in the Alps. Otherwise an ornamental plant which has become naturalized. Very rare.

Purple Loosestrife
Lythrum salicaria
Loosestrife family
Lythraceae

July–Sept. 60–160 cm D; ♃

IM: Flowers in whorls on a long spike; 1.2–1.8 cm across. Leaves opposite, decussate, occasionally 3 in a whorl, rounded at the base. Stem erect, quadrangular, also covered with short hairs like the leaves.
H: River banks, reed beds, fens, wet meadows, wet woodland. Common.
AI: Similar: Slender Loosestrife (*L. virgatum*): leaves not rounded, narrower at the base. Entire plant glabrous. Leaves long, slender and grow closer to the stem. Not British. Eastern Europe to Austria. Rare.

Dwarf Snowbell
Soldanella pusilla
Primrose family
Primulaceae

May–Aug. 2–10 cm D; ♃

IM: A single flower on each peduncle. Constantly drooping; pale pinkish-violet. Campanulate flower (approx. 1–1.5 cm long) is cut into a fringe of numerous segments to about ¼ of its length. Leaves are round to reniform, never wider than 1 cm, margin entire, never thick.
H: Not British. Often under late snow patches in the central mountain ranges, especially east of the Rhine in the Alps, scattered.
AI: The Snowbell species resemble each other. *S. minima* nearly always has numerous small glandular hairs on the peduncle. Not British.

Hemp Agrimony
Eupatorium cannabinum
Daisy family
Asteraceae (Compositae)

July–Sept.   40–150 cm   D; ⊙ – ♃; (+)

IM: Flowers in dense corymbs at the top of long stems. All flowers tubular in shape. Some leaves opposite having 3–5 segments. Leaflets lanceolate, coarsely serrate.
H: Moist woodland areas, banks of rivers, fens and marshes. Moisture indicator, somewhat calcicolous. Common, growing in colonies.
AI: Previously used as a medicinal plant. Its medicinal value is however disputed, although the plant does contain an unidentified bitter substance.

Adenostyles alliariae
Daisy family
Asteraceae (Compositae)

July–Aug.   50–150 cm   D; ♃

IM: Flower heads in umbel-like axillary inflorescences; these grow so closely together that they virtually form an overall umbrella-like inflorescence. The individual heads contain only 3–6 flowers. The uppermost stem leaf is usually sessile with diffuse base. Leaf undersides have felt-like covering of hairs which can be rubbed off.
H: Not native to Britain. Alps, occasionally also in the Black Forest and in the Vosges in open woodland and in high bushy areas. Scattered.
AI: Similar: *A. glabra*: all leaves petiolate. Capitula usually have 3 flowers. Alps. Scattered on limestone. Not native to Britain.

Butterbur
Petasites hybridus
Daisy family
Asteraceae (Compositae)

March—April   30–60 cm   D; ♃

IM: Flowers in racemose capitula. Flowers appear before the leaves. They are dioecious. Only leaf scales on peduncle. The very large leaves appear after flowering period. They are round and 60 cm across.
H: River banks, ditches, river meadows, forest margins. The male plant is common through the British Isles, the female limited to parts of northern England.
AI: Similar: Alpine Butterbur (*P. para-doxus*): leaves appear at the end of the flowering period but only grow to 20 cm across. Undersides constantly covered with white felt-like hairs. Conspicuously triangular in shape. Not British. Limestone scree slopes in the Alps. Rare.

Purple Coltsfoot
Homogyne alpina
Daisy family
Asteraceae (Compositae)

May—Aug.   10–30 cm   D; ♃

IM: Stems carry a single flower 2–3 cm across. The thread-like flowers are purplish-red. Basal leaves are round-reniform, petiolate, toothed, without any felty covering of hairs. Scale-like stem leaves found on the lower third of the stem. Plant often has runners.
H: Rare on 2 mountain ledges in Scotland. Usually considered an introduction.
AI: Similar: *H. discolor*: capitula around 1 cm across, basal leaves covered with thick felt. Scale-like stem leaves found in middle third of stem. No runners. Not British. Limestone Alps. Dolomites. Scattered.

243

Mountain Everlasting
Antennaria dioica
Daisy family
Asteraceae (Compositae)

May—June   8—25 cm   D; ♃

      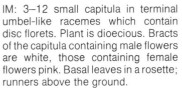

IM: 3—12 small capitula in terminal umbel-like racemes which contain disc florets. Plant is dioecious. Bracts of the capitula containing male flowers are white, those containing female flowers pink. Basal leaves in a rosette; runners above the ground.

H: Dry heaths and mountain slopes often in leached soil over limestone. Frequent in northern Britain.

AI: Similar: Carpathian Cat's-foot (*A. carpatica*): bracts of the male capitula white only at the tips and along the margin; on the female flowers they are translucent, brownish. No runners. Not British. Very stony Alpine turf. Rare.

Yarrow
Achillea millefolium
Daisy family
Asteraceae (Compositae)

June—Aug.   8—45 cm   D; ♃

IM: Stem erect, leaves alternate, bi- or tripinnate, leaflets divided into 2—5 parts. Flowers in capitula, arranged in loose corymbs: on the inside yellowish-white disc florets, on the outside usually only 4—5 white or rarely red ray florets.

H: Common in meadows, semi-dry turf, banks, pastures, arable fields and along waysides and hedgerows. Prefers loose loamy soils which are rich in nutrients and not too moist.

AI: The colour of the ray florets varies from white through pure white to reddish pink and deep red.

244

Alpine Thistle
Carduus defloratus
Daisy family
Asteraceae (Compositae)

June–Oct.   30–120 cm   D; ♃

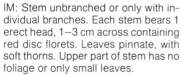

IM: Stem unbranched or only with individual branches. Each stem bears 1 erect head, 1–3 cm across containing red disc florets. Leaves pinnate, with soft thorns. Upper part of stem has no foliage or only small leaves.
H: Not British. Open woodland, thickets, mountain meadows, moderately hilly areas in southern Germany, Alps. Rare.

Musk Thistle
Carduus nutans
Daisy family
Asteraceae (Compositae)

July–Aug.   30–100 cm   D; ♃

IM: Little branched stem; at the end of each branch a single drooping head 3.5–7 cm across. It contains red disc florets only. Leaves pinnate, with long thorns each at least 4 mm long, sometimes even 6 mm.
H: Fields, waysides, waste ground, usually on chalky soils. Scattered throughout but frequent only in the south.
Al: Similar: *C. platylepis*: drooping flower heads only 3–4 cm across. Leaves pinnate, thorns less than 3 mm long. Not British. Paths, Alpine patures. Only southern and western Alps. Rare.

Spear Thistle
Cirsium vulgare
Daisy family
Asteraceae *(Compositae)*

June–Oct.   60–130 cm   D; ☉

IM: Stem little branched; at the end of each branch is a single head 2–4 cm across, containing red disc florets. The bract beneath each head has a light cobweb-like covering of hairs. Leaves are conspicuously decurrent, with a fine web-like covering on the undersides.
H: Roadsides, waste places. Likes calcareous soil rich in nitrogen. Common.
AI: A variety of the Spear Thistle (*C. hypoleucum*) has the undersides of its leaves covered with white felt.

Marsh Thistle
Cirsium palustre
Daisy family
Asteraceae *(Compositae)*

July–Sept.   90–200 cm   D; ☉

IM: Stem little branched; at the end of each branch there are several sessile or short stalked flower heads, about 1 cm across and 1.5 cm long. Leaves markedly decurrent; stem looks as though it has prickly wings. Leaves also have very long prickles.
H: Marshes, wet meadows and damp woodlands. Likes moisture and avoids very calcareous soil. Common.
AI: The Marsh Thistle can vary greatly, depending on the habitat, particularly in height, leaf shape and the number of prickles.

Stemless Thistle
Cirsium acaule
Daisy family
Asteraceae (Compositae)

July–Sept.   5–20 cm   D; ♃

IM: Inflorescence single, normally stalkless head, 2.5 cm long and almost equally wide. It contains only red disc florets. Leaves pinnatifid and spine tipped, the lobes ovoid.
H: Grasslands, particularly on chalk and limestone. Locally common in southern England.
AI: *C. caulescens* has flowers with stems to 20 cm high. The plant is found throughout southern and western Europe. Rare.

Saw-wort
Serratula tinctoria
Daisy family
Asteraceae (Compositae)

July–Sept.   30–100 cm   D; ♃

IM: Stem with few branches; flowers in a lax corymb of 10–40 small flowers. The stalked flowers barely reach 1 cm across but grow to a length of 1.5 cm. Purplish-red disc florets sometimes tend towards a violet colour. The leaves are undivided or pinnate and conspicuously sharply serrate.
H: Rather moist open woodland, and grassland especially on chalky soils. Local but never common throughout England and Wales. Rare in Scotland.

Common Knapweed
Centaurea nigra
Daisy family
Asteraceae *(Compositae)*

July–Sept.   20–80 cm   D; ♃

IM: Stem stout with few branches. Each branch bears one head which may reach 2–4 cm across. There are no enlarged florets around the margin of the flower. Below the flower head the stem is sometimes thickened. Leaves oval to lanceolate. Stem usually erect.
H: Grassland, roadsides and waste places.
AI: Within the species several sub-species are distinguished: ssp. *nemoralis*: height over 60 cm, relatively free branching with little swelling beneath the flowers. All the bract appendages on ssp. *nigra* are black.

Brown Knapwood
Centaurea jacea
Daisy family
Asteraceae *(Compositae)*

June–Oct.   30–100 cm   D; ♃

IM: Stem only branched at the top and not very freely. Branches with one head at the end up to 3–5 cm across. Head contains both disc florets and marginal florets which are conspicuously larger. Middle and lower leaves alternate, not divided. Lower leaves often notched to pinnately divided.
H: Grassland and waste places. Not native to Britain but established in a few places in southern England.

Greater Knapwood
Centaurea scabiosa
Daisy family
Asteraceae (Compositae)

July–Aug. 30–130 cm D; ♃

IM: Stem little branched. Single flower head at the end of each branch up to 3.5–6 cm across. The heads contain disc and marginal florets, the latter being conspicuously the larger. Bracts have a dark brown edge. All stem leaves pinnate.
H: Dry turf, meadows, cliffs, roadsides esp-
ecially on chalky soils. Common.
Al: Commonest in the south but occurs throughout Britain. In Europe it is found from Finland to the Caucasus and in western Asia.

Downy Burdock
Arctium tomentosum
Daisy family
Asteraceae (Compositae)

July–Aug. 50–150 cm D; ☉

IM: 5–50 flowers in a dense corymb at the end of the stem. Heads, covered with thick layer of web-like hairs, are up to 2–3 cm across. They contain only disc florets. The bracts are hooked (burs). Leaves very large, rounded or heart-shaped at the base.
H: Roadsides and waste places especially the banks of rivers. Likes calcareous loamy soil rich in nitrogen. Rare, casual.

Arctium nemorosum
Daisy family
Asteraceae (Compositae)

July–Aug.   100–250 cm   D; ☉

IM: 3–5 heads, 3–4.5 cm across, a cluster at the end of the stems. Stems may be covered by very fine layer of web-like hairs, usually glabrous. Bracts only slightly hooked. Leaves very large, those at the base slightly heart-shaped.
H: Woodland, usually in open areas or in clearings, roadside and waste places. Scattered.
AI: Easy to identify in typical habitats as most climbing species do not occur. Nevertheless hybrids have been recorded, mainly near to residential areas located in woodland.

Lesser Burdock
Arctium minus
Daisy family
Asteraceae (Compositae)

July–Sept.   50–130 cm   D; ☉

IM: 5–12 heads in a cluster at stem end; with light covering of web-like hairs, 1–2.5 cm across. They contain disc florets only. Bracts hooked. Branches erect and spreading. Stems leafy, the leaves being large and rounded or slightly heart-shaped at the base.
H: Paths, waste places. Likes loamy soil. Nitrogen indicator. Scattered.
AI: Similar: Greater Burdock (*A. lappa*): 5–12 heads in an umbel-like arrangement on the stem. Each head grows to 3–4 cm across. Pathways and waste places. Nitrogen indicator. Scattered.

Red Hare's Lettuce
Prenanthes purpurea
Daisy family
Cichoriaceae (Compositae)

July—Aug.   60—160 cm   D; ☉

IM: Numerous heads in a very lax panicle, each containing only 3—5 ray florets. The elegant heads 1.5—2 cm across. Stem erect, branching only at the very top. Leaves glabrous with heart-shaped amplexicaul base, undersides bluish-green. Lower leaves elongate-lanceolate, notched. Margin of upper leaves is usually entire.
H: Not British. Native to mainland Europe in woodland. Likes soil rich in humus but not containing too much lime.
Al: Those varieties where the leaf margin is always entire and the leaf narrow are classed as ssp. *angustifolia*, to distinguish them from the 'typical' forms.

Orange Hawkweed
Hieracium aurantiacum
Daisy family
Cichoriaceae (Compositae)

June—Aug.   20—50 cm   D; ♃

IM: 5—20 heads in a panicle on a branched stem. Heads have glandular hairs. Ray florets orange-yellow to brownish red, usually deep purplish-red when dried. Leaves in rosette arrangement, elongate and tongue-shaped, margin entire or slightly toothed, hairy.
H: Not British. Alpine mats and thickets. Frequent ornamental plant; away from the Alps growing wild on poor meadows and along paths. In the Alps scattered, otherwise rare.
Al: Similar: *H. caespitosum*: usually 15—30 capitula. Flowers only deep yellow, not clearly orange-yellow. Do not become purplish-red when dried. Not British. Scattered.

251

Marsh Gladiolus
Gladiolus palustris
Iris family
Iridaceae

June–July   30–70 cm   M; ♃

IM: 3–8 flowers in an unbranched spike. They grow to 2–3 cm long, are purplish-red and usually turn bluish when dried. Flowers incline downwards. Stem erect. Leaves 0.5–1 cm wide.
H: Moorland. Dislikes fertilizer. Very rare in northern Europe.
Al: Similar: *G. imbricatus*: 3–8 flowers in a lax unilateral spike. Flowers grow to 2 cm long. Leaves 1–2 cm wide. Moorland, thickets. Occasionally cultivated in Britain, but not native.

Red Helleborine
Cephalanthera rubra
Orchid family
Orchidaceae

May–July   20–80 cm   M; ♃

IM: 4–12 flowers in a lax spike. They are pinkish-red or purplish-red, occasionally with a tinge of violet. The lip does not have a spur. The upper leaves are erect, the lateral leaves are spread far apart when the flowers are in full bloom. Leaves ovoid-elongate, 6–12 cm long and 2–4 cm wide.
H: Woodland. Likes warmth. Needs well drained soil containing mull. Rare.
Al: Red Helleborine is undoubtedly one of the most beautiful orchids native to Britain.

Dark Red Helleborine
Epipactis atrorubens
Orchid family
Orchidaceae

June–Aug.   30–60 cm   M; ♃

IM: 10–30 flowers in a lax somewhat 1–sided spike. Flowers approx. 1 cm across, purplish-red with a tinge of brown or violet. Lip does not have spur. A lateral constriction divides it into a front and a rear section, giving it a 'folded' look. Outer petals form a wide bell. Leaves elongate-ovoid.
H: Woodland, rocks and screes. Likes calcareous soils. Rare.
AI: Similar: *E. purpurata*: 30–60 flowers in a compact cluster. Flowers approx. 1.5 cm across or wider, whitish to reddish in colour. Entire plant tinged with violet. Woodland. Rare.

Pyramidal Orchid
Anacamptis pyramidalis
Orchid family
Orchidaceae

June–July   20–50 cm   M; ♃

IM: Inflorescence initially decidedly pyramidal, then somewhat cylindrical (when the lower flowers have faded). Flowers have thread-like spur equalling the ovary in length. Flowers deep rose-purple in colour. Lip is paler, and wider than it is long, divided into 3. Leaves narrow-lanceolate.
H: Grassland on chalk and limestone; dry open woodland and thickets, more rarely on stable dunes. Locally frequent.
AI: When the Pyramidal Orchid occurs together with the Fragrant Orchid or with members of the *Orchis* species hybrids may well be found.

Round-headed Orchid
Traunsteinera globosa
Orchid family
Orchidaceae

June—July   20—50 cm   M; ♃

     ▽

IM: Inflorescence markedly globular or oval. It contains 80—120 flowers which barely reach a length of 1 cm. Flowers pale pink or purplish-red, often with a tendency towards violet. Lip elongate to trilobed, with dark spots. Spur slender. Outer petals drawn out into a conspicuously slender tip which is thickened at the front in the shape of a club.
H: Not British. Mountains and outskirts of relatively hilly areas. Grows on meadows or semi-dry turf which is rich in nutrients but unfertilized. Rare.
AI: Native to Poland southwards to Spain, north—central Italy and southern Bulgaria.

Green-winged Orchid
Orchis morio
Orchid family
Orchidaceae

May—June   8—40 cm   M; ♃

   ▽

IM: Inflorescence a lax spike containing 4—12 flowers. These are relatively large. Lip alone up to 1 cm or more. It is wider than it is long and divided into four lobes. Spur short, fat and projects horizontally. Remaining petals bend inwards to form a conspicuous helmet shape. Stem erect, leaves elongate-lanceolate.
H: Meadows and pastures, especially on limestone soils. Locally abundant, rarer in the north.
AI: First orchid to flower in the year. Has decreased over the last few decades owing to a lack of suitable habitats.

Burnt Orchid
Orchis ustulata
Orchid family
Orchidaceae

May–June   8–20 cm   M; ♃

IM: Dense globular to conical flower spike. Blossoms very small, about 5 mm long, initially brownish-red, later contrasted by the red-spotted white lip. The remaining petals are pressed together to form a helmet shape. Leaves are lanceolate.
H: Widespread but local in England, on grassy hills and dry meadows. Prefers calcareous soil, poor in nutrients but warm and loamy or loess.

Military Orchid
Orchis militaris
Orchid family
Orchidaceae

May–June   20–25 cm   M; ♃

IM: Inflorescence a lax spike 5–10 cm long containing 20–40 flowers. These are pale pink or pale purplish-red flushed with lilac. Lip is 1–1.5 cm long, divided into 4 narrow lobes. Spur is short, thick, pointing downwards. Outer petals bend inwards to form a helmet shape, bearing conspicuous dark red veins. Lip has red spots.
H: Semi-dry turf or meadows, also in dry thickets and dry open woodland on chalk and limestone.
AI: This is one of the rarest of British Orchids, being restricted to one site each in Suffolk and Buckinghamshire.

Lady Orchid
Orchis purpurea
Orchid family
Orchidaceae

May–June   30–80 cm   M; ♃

IM: Dense cylindrical spike 5–10 cm long containing more than 30 flowers. These are brownish–red, the lip is noticeably lighter, pink or almost white with numerous small red spots, 1.5–2 cm long and divided into 4 lobes, the front 2 being wider than the others. Spur is short, fat, pointing downwards. Outer petals bend inwards to form a helmet shape.

H: Woodland with calcareous moist soil. Likes the warmth. Rare. Now restricted to a few sites in Kent. Abroad, it ranges across Europe to western Asia, but is always very local.

Orchis laxiflora spp. palustris
Orchid family
Orchidaceae

May–July   20–50 cm   M; ♃

IM: Inflorescence a very lax spike with few flowers (5–15); spike grows to 5–10 cm long. Flowers dark purplish–red or light wine red. Outer petals spreading. Lip approx. 1.5 cm long and always wider than it is long, divided into 4 lobes. The 2 small inner lobes are somewhat longer than the lateral ones. Leaves narrow, 1.5–2 cm at the base, 10–20 cm long.

H: Open moorland, moorland meadows. Likes warmth. Very rare.

Al: Similar: Jersey Orchid (*O. laxiflora* sp. *laxiflora*): central lobes of lip shorter than the lateral ones. Western Europe including Channel Islands (but not mainland Britain), and the Mediterranean area. Rare.

Early Purple Orchid
Orchis mascula
Orchid family
Orchidaceae

May–June   20–50 cm   M; ♃

IM: Spike 8–15 cm long, usually composed of many flowers. These are purple, pink and usually flushed with violet. Lip has 4 lobes and dark spots, with cylindrical spur which spreads horizontally. Outer petals projecting. Leaves are widest only in the middle, with or without darker spots.
H: Semi-dry turf, poor unfertilized meadows and open thickets or deciduous woodland. Calcicolous. Scattered and locally common. Abroad, this species has a wide range through Europe and extends into north Africa and northern and western Asia.

Monkey Orchid
Orchis simia
Orchid family
Orchidaceae

May   20–40 cm   M; ♃

IM: Inflorescence short, cylindrical or globular; starts flowering at the top and progresses downwards (other species flower in the reverse order). Flowers purplish-red or almost white. Lip 1–1.5 cm long, divided into 2 lateral sections and a middle section which is wide and curved with 2 long lobes. Spur is short, thick, pointing downwards. Lip is covered with fine red spots.
H: Grassy slopes, and scrub in chalk hills of Kent and Oxford; rare. Occurs abroad in central and southern Europe, east to the Caucasus and south to north Africa.

Heath Spotted Orchid
Dactylorhiza maculata
Orchid family
Orchidaceae

June–July   20–60 cm   M; ♃

IM: Inflorescence a dense cylindrical to pyramid-shaped spike 4–8 cm long. Flowers light pink to almost white, with light purple patterns. Lip is trilobed, flat. Spur cylindrical, pointing downwards. Outer petals spreading, 5–7 mm long and thus smaller than the lip which grows to approx. 1 cm long.

H: Damp woodland, heaths, open moorland, in peaty or acid soils. Scattered; where the plant occurs there are frequently colonies full of individual variations.

AI: The examples which grow on calcareous soil are usually classified as a separate species of Spotted Orchid (*D. fuchsii*).

Elder-flowered Orchid
Dactylorhiza sambucina
Orchid family
Orchidaceae

April–June   15–25 cm   M; ♃

IM: Short spike. In *D. sambucina* ssp. *sambucina* the spike is dense flowered, in *D. sambucina* ssp. *insularis* the flowers are loosely arranged. Outer petals spreading. Spur longer than ovary. Bracts leafy (not membraneous). Leaves elongate-ovoid, unspotted.

H: Only cultivated in Britain. Widespread in Europe: meadows, scrub and light open woodland.

AI: The spike can vary from red through all the different shades to yellow. Yellow plants are usually more common.

Early Marsh Orchid
Dactylorhiza incarnata
Orchid family
Orchidaceae

May–July   20–60 cm   M; ♃

IM: Inflorescence dense cylindrical spike 4–15 cm long, the flowers flesh pink or light red. Lip is divided into 3 rather indistinct lobes. Spur cylindrical, pointing downwards. Outer petals spreading. 4–6 unspotted stem leaves. Lower and middle bracts of the inflorescence conspicuously longer than their respective flowers, upper ones usually as long as their flowers.
H: Marshes, wet meadows, open wet moorland. Widely distributed.
AI: The Meadow Orchid comes in many different forms and flower colours. Occasionally cream or yellow specimens have been found.

Irish Marsh Orchid
Dactylorhiza majalis
Orchid family
Orchidaceae

May–July   10–50 cm   M; ♃

IM: Inflorescence cylindrical-pyramidal, dense spike 5–10 cm long. Flowers lighter or darker shade of purplish red. Lip is trilobed. Spur cylindrical, pointing stiffly downwards. Outer petals spreading. Entire flower 1.5–2 cm long. 3–6 stem leaves always spotted. Bracts in inflorescence usually tinged with red, the lower ones longer than their flowers.
H: Marshes, fens, wet meadows, wet moorland, in Ireland and western Scotland, not in England or Wales.
AI: Widespread in Europe, extending to central Russia, Siberia and the Caucasus. There it varies in stature, leaf shape and flower colour.

Fragrant Orchid
Gymnadenia conopsea
Orchid family
Orchidaceae

May–Aug.　　15–60 cm　　M; ♃

IM: Inflorescence cylindrical-pyramidal, dense spike which grows to 5–10 cm long. Flowers pink or pale purple with a tinge of violet, strongly scented. Lip wide, trilobed. Marginal petals horizontal and projecting. Spur thin and thread-like, at least 1½ times as long as the ovary.
H: Grassland, especially chalk and limestone, fens, marshes, woodland. Locally abundant.
Al: *B. conopsea* var. *densiflora* has bright rose-red or magenta flowers which smell of cloves. It is found only in Anglesey and Isle of Wight.

Vanilla Orchid
Nigritella nigra
Orchid family
Orchidaceae

May–Sept.　　5–25 cm　　M; ♃

IM: Inflorescence a compact, rounded spike. Flowers blackish-purple, approx. 0.5 cm long. Lip petal-like but conspicuously larger than the true petals. Innermost petals at most only half as wide as outer ones. Flowers smell very distinctly of vanilla. Leaves narrow, like grass: foliage rises up stem.
H: Not British. Meadows in the Alps and Alpine foothills; also in the Pyrenees and Norway. Scattered.

Man Orchid
Aceras anthropophorum
Orchid family
Orchidaceae

May–June   20–30 cm   M; ♃

IM: Inflorescence is a narrow spike usually 5–15 cm long. Flowers do not have spur. Outer petals come together to form helmet shape. They are green, have red or violet veins and margin. Lip approx 1 cm long, divided into narrow lobes.
H: Grassland, scrub and woodland. Mainly on chalk and limestone. Thinly scattered though locally abundant in southern England.
AI: It is possible to see the deeply divided lip as the limbs of a hanging man (anthropophorum = carrying a man).

Lizard Orchid
Himantoglossum hircinum
Orchid family
Orchidaceae

April–June   20–80 cm   M; ♃

IM: Inflorescence a lax spike which grows 15–25 cm long. Outer petals light green, forming a helmet shape, often adhering along the margins. Conspicuous red veins. Lip trilobed: lateral lobes 5–7 mm long, usually brownish. Median lobe 5–7 cm long, 2-lobed at the apex.
H: Grassland, open thickets, wood margins, mainly on chalk or limestone; rare.
AI: The species cannot be mistaken. In the Balkans there is the larger *H. calcaratum* with a lip narrower and more deeply divided.

Corydalis cava
Fumitory family
Fumariaceae

March–April   10–20 cm   D; ♃; +

IM: Stem erect, unbranched, with alternative deciduous leaves. These are bi- to tripinnate, bluish-green, glabrous. Ultimate segments are ovoid, often repeatedly dissected. 10–20 flowers form a dense raceme, bracts have entire margins. Flowers may be white to purple.
H: A rare escape from gardens which may become established in a few places.
AI: Similar: Solid-tubered Fumitory (*C. solida*), (see right).

Solid-tubered Fumitory
Corydalis solida
Fumitory family
Fumariaceae

April–May   10–20 cm   D; ♃; +

  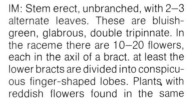

IM: Stem erect, unbranched, with 2–3 alternate leaves. These are bluish-green, glabrous, double tripinnate. In the raceme there are 10–20 flowers, each in the axil of a bract. at least the lower bracts are divided into conspicuous finger-shaped lobes. Plants with reddish flowers found in the same locality as those with white flowers.
H: Woodland, thickets. Local, often in colonies which have many different variations. A native of Europe, north and west Asia. Not native to Britain, but grown in gardens and naturalized locally.
AI: Similar: *C. intermedia*: only 1–5 flowers in a drooping inflorescence. Margin of bracts is entire.

Common Fumitory
Fumaria officinalis
Fumitory family
Fumariaceae

May–Oct.   10–40 cm   D; ⊙ ; (+)

IM: 10–50 flowers in a raceme 6–9 mm long. Flowers light purple, black-ish-red at the apex. Leaves double pinnate. Apices of leaflets approx. 2 mm wide.
H: Wasteland fields and gardens. Common.
AI: *F. vaillantii*: 6–12 flowers, 5–6 mm long, light pink. Calyx less than 1 mm long. Very local. *F. parviflora*: 10–20 flowers, 5–6 mm long. Flowers almost white, only red at the apex. Local.

Crown Vetch
Coronilla varia
Pea family
Fabaceae (Leguminosae)

June–Sept.   30–130 cm   D; ♃; +

IM: 10–20 flowers which grow to 1–1.5 cm long, sessile in a terminal umbel. They are purple, pink or white. The angular stems are prostrate or somewhat ascending. Leaves with long petioles, pinnate and have 11–25 leaflets. Each leaflet is on a very short petiole and is narrow-ovoid in shape.
H: Grassland, pathways, open scrub. Scattered in Europe, but only locally naturalized in Britain.
AI: Crown Vetch survives on the poorest of soils. It improves soil, because the bacteria in its root nodules make nitrogen.

Red Clover
Trifolium pratense
Pea family
Fabaceae (Leguminosae)

June–Oct. 15–45 cm D; ♃

IM: Usually 2 inflorescences at the end of each stem. They are rounded ovoid and are 2–3.5 cm long. Calyx half the length of the flower and has only 10 veins. Stem usually erect and hairy.

H: Meadows and roadsides. Often grown in fields. Very common.

AI: Red Clover comes in many different varieties. These differ from one another in, among other things, the hairs on the stem, the length of the flowers and the flower colour. The cultivated races are also not uniform and there is much evidence of hybridization between wild and cultivated races.

Zigzag Clover
Trifolium medium
Pea family
Fabaceae (Leguminosae)

June–Aug. 20–50 cm D; ♃

IM: Usually only 1 inflorescence at the end of each stem which is slightly rounded-ovoid and may become 2–4 cm long and 2–3 cm wide. Calyx glabrous, only the teeth of the calyx have conspicuous ciliate margin. Stem hairy, usually bent in a zigzag at each leaf node. Leaflets are 2–4 times longer than they are wide.

H: Grassland, scrub, roadsides. Likes loamy soil. Common.

AI: Similar: Alsike clover (*T. hybridum*); more vigorous, to 60 cm, flower head globular, pink, carried on a short stem well above the uppermost leaf.

Trifolium rubens
Pea family
Fabaceae (Leguminosae)

June–July   30–60 cm   D; ♃

IM: 1–2 cylindrical inflorescences, 3–7 cm long and 2 cm thick. Calyx usually glabrous on the outside or covered with short hairs. Calyx teeth have conspicuous ciliate margin. Stem glabrous. Leaflets up to 6 cm long and 3–8 times longer than wide.
H: Not British. Dry open woodland and scrub, central Europe.
AI: Similar: Crimson Clover (*T. incarnatum*): 1 inflorescence up to 3–5 cm long, 1.5–2.5 cm thick. Outside of calyx hairy. Leaflets max. 3 cm long and 1–1.5 cm wide. An annual native to southern and western Europe: much cultivated and locally naturalized.

Persian Clover
Trifolium resupinatum
Pea family
Fabaceae (Leguminosae)

April–Sept.   10–50 cm   D; ☉

IM: Inflorescence solitary on long peduncles in the axils of the upper leaves. Each head 1–1.5 cm across. Flowers look odd initially as individual flowers are twisted round 180° so that the keel is facing upwards; reddish-violet or pale red in colour, smelling distinctly of honey.
H: Not British. Path verges, roadsides, waste ground. Sometimes cultivated.
AI: The wild form is smaller and is occasionally considered a species in itself: *T. suaveolens*.

265

Common Sainfoin
Onobrychis viciifolia
Pea family
Fabaceae (Leguminosae)

May–June   30–60 cm   D; ♃

IM: Inflorescence a long lax raceme. Flowers 1–1.5 cm long, red or pink. Stem ascending or erect, with pinnate foliage. Leaves with 19–25 narrow leaflets.
H: Well-drained grassland, roadsides, waste ground. Well scattered and appearing as wild in chalk and limestone grassland. Formerly used as a fodder crop and still sometimes planted for garden ornament.

Common Vetch
Vicia sativa
Pea family
Fabaceae (Leguminosae)

May–July   30–80 cm   D; ☉

IM: 1–2 flowers growing individually on short peduncles in leaf axils, each one 2–2.5 cm long. The standard is light purple or pink; wings carmine and darker than the standard; keel is whitish-pink. Stem more or less ascending. 8–12 leaflets, approx. 4–5 mm wide. The pinnate leaves usually terminate in a branched tendril.
H: Roadsides, waste places, also planted as a fodder or green mature crop.
AI: Similar: *V. angustifolia*: smaller flowers and more prostrate, almost the same colour, only about 3 mm wide. Roadsides, dry grassland.

Narrow-leaved Everlasting Pea
Lathyrus sylvestris
Pea family
Fabaceae (Leguminosae)

July—Aug.   90—200 cm   D; ♃

IM: 3—10 flowers in a lax raceme, each 1.2—1.8 cm long, bright purplish-red. Stem prostrate, ascending or climbing, quadrangular, with 2 distinct wings. Leaves pinnate, composed of 2 leaflets and a branched tendril.
H: Open woodland, scrub, hedgerows. Scattered and local.
Al: 3 races are distinguished: typical subspecies (ssp. *sylvestris*) 3—6 flowers, leaflets 10—30 mm wide. Ssp. *angustifolius*: leaflets less than 5 mm wide. Scree slopes. Rare. Ssp. *platyphyllos*: leaflets 25—40 mm wide.

Sea Pea
Lathyrus japonicus
Pea family
Fabaceae (Leguminosae)

June—July   20—50 cm   D; ♃

IM: 3—10 flowers in a lax raceme. Keel is almost white, standard purple tending towards blue. Flowers approx. 1.5 cm long. Stem never winged, prostrate. 6—8 leaflets and branched tendril. Leaflets 2—4 cm long and half that width.
H: Seaside beaches and dunes. Very local, from Suffolk to Kent, then scattered to Cornwall and south Wales. Also one locality in western Ireland.

Tuberous Pea
Lathyrus tuberosus
Pea family
Fabaceae (Leguminosae)

June—Sept.   30—120 cm   D; ♃

IM: 1—5 flowers in a long-stalked raceme from the axils of the upper leaves. Flower 1.5—1.8 cm long, brilliant carmine or purplish-red, occasionally tending towards violet. Leaves made up of a pair of leaflets and a branched tendril. Subterranean stem with tubers.
H: Native to western Asia and Europe, in Britain only as a naturalized plant, occurring in hedgerows and very rarely in cornfields; rare.

Black Pea
Lathyrus niger
Pea family
Fabaceae (Leguminosae)

May—June   30—80 cm   D; ♃

IM: 3—10 flowers in a lax cluster on a stalk from upper leaf axil. Flowers 1—1.5 cm long, purple to violet in colour, the actual petals often paler than the veins. Stem erect, branched, without wings, angular. Leaves comprise 8—12 leaflets. When dried the entire plant goes black.
H: Rocky woods on mountain slopes in Scotland, rare, maybe extinct. Also naturalized in one site in Sussex.

Lathyris liniifolius
Pea family
Fabaceae (Leguminosae)

April–June   15–40 cm   D; ♃

IM: 3–6 flowers in a lax cluster which is situated in the leaf axil and may reach 7 cm in length. Flowers initially red, then dirty blue, 11–22 mm long. Stamens tubular in shape. Tube has a straight edge. Leaves comprise 4–6 leaflets whose undersides are usually distinctly bluish-green. Short point at leaf apex. Stem conspicuously winged even if this is normally only narrow.
H: Not British. In Europe found in woodland, heaths, and mountain meadows.
AI: This plant is occasionally mistaken for Spring Pea (see p. 333). It is however easy to recognize thanks to its winged stem.

Spring Pea
Lathyrus vernus
Pea family
Fabaceae (Leguminosae)

April–June   20–60 cm   D; ♃

IM: 2–7 flowers in a lax cluster situated in a leaf axil; can grow to 6 cm long. Flowers initially red, then dirty blue, 1.5–2 cm long. Leaves made up of 4–6 leaflets approx. 1/2 as wide as long. Short point at leaf apex. Stem quadrangular and clearly without any wings.
H: Not British. In Europe found in woodland, preferably deciduous. Prefers calcareous soil. Scattered, common locally.
AI: Spring Pea is occasionally confused with *Lathyrus liniifolius* (see p. 333). It is however easy to recognize because the stem is not winged.

Alpine Sainfoin
Hedysarum hedysaroides
Pea family
Fabaceae (Leguminosae)

July–Aug.   15–50 cm   D; ♃

IM: 10–40 flowers in a somewhat 1-sided axillary raceme, up to 5–10 cm long. Each flower is 1.5–2 cm long, drooping. They are usually purple-red, more rarely creamy-coloured. Stem erect, unbranched, angular. Leaves pinnate, 9–19 leaflets. These grow to 1.5–3 cm in length and are lanceolate, sessile.
H: Not British. Grassland, screes, stony slopes in the limestone Alps, more rarely in the central Alps and Pyrenees; uncommon. Sometimes cultivated in gardens.

Tufted Milkwort
Polygala comosa
Milkwort family
Polygalaceae

May–June   5–25 cm   D; ♃

IM: 10–30 flowers in a racemose inflorescence which is initially pyramidal in shape. The bracts beneath the flowers about as large as the newly-opened flowers (approx. 4 mm) and form a 'tuft' at the top of the relatively dense inflorescence shortly before opening. Flowers usually red, very rarely blue, occasionally lilac. Stem ascending or erect. Leaves alternate, spatulate to invert-ovoid.
H: Not British. In Europe found in dry turf and poor meadows.
Al: Similar: Common Milkwort (*P. vulgaris*): bracts max. 2 mm long, and therefore not tufted. Native to chalk and limestone grassland in Britain, usually blue.

White Dittany, Burning Bush

Dictamnus albus
Rue family
Rutaceae

May–June   40–120 cm   D; ♃; +

IM: 5–25 flowers in an erect terminal raceme, 2–3 cm across. Petals of unequal length. Basic colour pale pink. Veins deep red or reddish-violet. Stem erect. Leaves unpaired pinnate. 7–11 leaflets, short hairs, finely toothed and translucently spotted.
H: Open scrub, forest margins. Prefers stony loose calcareous or loess ground. Native to southern Europe only. Cultivated in Britain.
AI: The plant contains ethereal oils. On hot days they evaporate so strongly that they can be ignited, hence the popular name 'Burning Bush'.

Indian Balsam

Impatiens glandulifera
Balsam family
Balsaminaceae

July–Oct   50–200 cm   D; ☉

IM: 5–20 flowers in an erect axillary cluster; up to 2.5–4 cm long with short conspicuous spur pointing downwards. Stem is erect and usually unbranched. Leaves 10–25 cm long, sharply serrate.
H: Wet woodland, river and lake banks. Originally a garden plant from the Himalayas, nowadays established widely.
AI: Similar: *I. balfourii*: 3–10 flowers per axillary raceme. Flowers are 2-coloured, white at the top, pink at the bottom. Plant rarely grows over 1 m high.

271

Wall Germander
Teucrium chamaedrys
Mint family
Lamiaceae (Labiatae)

July—Sept.   15—30 cm   D; ♃

IM: 2—6 flowers in the axis of the upper leaves all facing one way. Flower 1—1.5 cm long, fairly light reddish-violet in colour; no upper lip. Lower lip has 5 lobes. Stem ascending or erect, lower section woody. Leaves elongate-cuneate, deeply toothed, rounded.
H: Grassland, scrub, usually on calcareous soil. Central and southern Europe, not in the British Isles, but cultivated and locally naturalized.
AI: Similar: Water Germander (*T. scordium*): only 1—4 flowers (usually 3—4) in the axils of the upper leaves. Flowers 1-sided, less than 1 cm long, light purple, without upper lip. Stem not woody based; only in moist to wet places; very rare in Britain.

Bastard Balm
Melittis melissophyllum
Mint family
Lamiaceae (Labiatae)

May—July   20—50 cm   D; ♃

IM: Stem quadrangular, erect, little branching. Broad leaves opposite and decussate, stalked, ovoid, conspicuously wrinkled, coarsely round-toothed margin. Entire plant has dense covering of soft hairs. Flowers few in number in axils of upper leaves, often all favouring one side; smells of honey.
H: Light deciduous forests, woods and hedgerows. Prefers loose calcareous soils, warm but not too dry. Local to rare in Wales and southern parts of England.
AI: The flowers are usually white spotted with pink but may sometimes be more or less completely pink.

Common Hempnettle
Galeopsis tetrahit
Mint family
Lamiaceae (Labiatae)

Galeopsis pubescens
Mint family
Lamiaceae (Labiatae)

July–Oct.   10–80 cm   D;☉–☉

June–Oct.   20–60 cm   D;☉–☉

IM: 10–16 flowers in whorled sessile inflorescence terminating each stem. Flowers 1.5–2 cm long, their upper lip helmet-shaped. Lower lip has hollow tooth on each side. These are conical in shape and facing forwards. Central section of lower lip is more or less square.
H: Weedy places on fields and wastelands, also in light open woodland areas. Common.
Al: Similar: *G. pubescens*: see right. Large-flowered Hempnettle (*G. speciosa*): flowers 2.5–3 cm long. Lower lip usually has bright violet spot on it (see p. 191).

IM: 10–16 flowers in whorled sessile inflorescence terminating each stem. Flowers 2–2.5 cm long, their upper lip helmet-shaped. Lower lip has a hollow tooth on each side, approx. 5 mm long pointing slightly forwards. Lower lip cropped at the front or slightly crenate, with dark violet and yellow spots. Stem slightly swollen at the nodes and clad with a mixture of long and short hairs.
H: Not British. Light open woodland, fields. Scattered.
Al: Similar: Common Hempnettle (*G. tetrahit*): see left. Large-flowered Hempnettle (*G. speciosa*): flowers 2.5–3 cm long. Lower lip usually has bright violet spot (see p. 191).

Black Horehound
Ballota nigra
Mint family
Lamiaceae (Labiatae)

June–Aug.   60–130 cm   D; ♃

IM: 4–10 flowers 1–1.5 cm long, on short peduncles in the axils of the upper and middle leaves; they are purplish-violet with white veins. Stem erect or ascending, hairy, branched, angular. Leaves in opposite pairs, heart-shaped to ovoid. Whole plant rank smelling.
H: Waste places, roadsides, hedgerows and walls. Nitrogen indicator. Common.
AI: 2 subspecies: that with leaves wider than 3 cm and calyx teeth which are over 4 mm is regarded as the typical subspecies and referred to as ssp. *nigra*. The leaves of the ssp. *foetida* are narrower than 3 cm.

Spotted Deadnettle
Lamium maculatum
Mint family
Lamiaceae (Labiatae)

March–Oct.   30–80 cm   D; ♃

IM: Plant resembles nettle, but without stinging hairs. Many flowers in axils of middle and upper leaves, 2–3 cm long. Lower lip has large middle lobe, divided into 2 parts, and 2 small lateral lobes. Stem erect or ascending. Leaves opposite alternate, petiolate, ovate, 3–5 cm long, green or with a central white stripe.
H: Woodland, scrub, roadsides, river banks. Likes damp soil rich in nutrients. Native to Europe; only naturalized locally in Britain, though much grown in gardens.
AI: Within the species many variations have been reported. The variations are to be found in virtually all the characteristics of the plant, especially size, leaf margin, hair covering.

Henbit
Lamium amplexicaule
Mint family
Lamiaceae (Labiatae)

March–Oct. 15–25 cm D; ⊙

IM: Plant resembles stinging nettle but without stinging hairs. 6–10 flowers in axillary whorls in upper leaf axils; up to 1–1.5 cm long; red, tending towards violet. The uppermost leaves are amplexicaul. The lower ones have long petioles and are opposite alternate. The stem is usually branched from the base.
H: Fields, gardens, waste places, hedgerows, roadsides. Common.
AI: Some of the flowers of the Henbit do not open. The closed flowers can often be identified by their outstandingly bright red colour. Seed forms through self-pollination.

Red Deadnettle
Lamium purpureum
Mint family
Lamiaceae (Labiatae)

March–Oct. 10–40 cm D; ⊙

IM: Plant resembles stinging nettle but without the stinging hairs. 3–5 flowers in whorls in the upper leaf axils. Flowers 1–2 cm long; purple, usually with a strong shade of violet. Tip of the stem and the uppermost leaves usually also tinged with violet. Stem normally erect. All leaves are petiolate, opposite, alternate, ovate, wrinkled, crenate-toothed.
H: Waste places, fields, roadsides and gardens. Very common.
AI: Cut-leaved Deadnettle (*L. hybridum*) has the appearance of a hybrid between Red Deadnettle and Henbit but is a true breeding species.

Betony
Betonica officinalis
Mint family
Lamiaceae (Labiatae)

June—Aug. 30—60 cm D; ♃

IM: Flowers are in a head-like terminal spike and in whorls in the axils of the uppermost leaves. Each flower is 1—1.5 cm long, pink or light purple, with a white spot towards the throat of the corolla. Basal leaves tufted with long petioles (stalk considerably longer than the leaf blade). Stem quadrangular, covered with coarse hairs like the leaves. Stem leaves petiolate, alternate, opposite, ovate, rounded-toothed.
H: Grassland, often woodland, hedgebanks and heaths; common.
AI: Within the species one distinguishes the following groups: *B. hirsuta*: leaves have woolly layer on both sides. Rare. *B. stricta*: calyx has bearded teeth. Rare.

Limestone Woundwort
Stachys alpina
Mint family
Lamiaceae (Labiatae)

June—Aug. 50—100 cm D; ♃

IM: 6—18 flowers in whorl-like clusters in the axils of terminal leaves. Stems erect. Flowers around 1.5 cm long or slightly longer, rather light flesh pink and a little dull. Margin of upper lip entire. Lower lip approx. twice as long as upper lip. Lower lip without markings. Leaves 5—20 cm long, pronouncedly serrate.
H: Light woodland areas on calcareous soil rich in mull. Very rare. Absent in lowland areas.
AI: Limestone Woundwort is rare anywhere but in the Alps.

Hedge Woundwort
Stachys sylvatica
Mint family
Lamiaceae (Labiatae)

June–Aug.   60–120 cm   D; ♃

IM: 6–16 flowers in whorl-like inflorescences in upper leaf axils, forming terminal spikes with long bracts. The flowers are usually 1.2–1.5 cm long, purplish-red. The upper lip is shorter than the lower lip with distinct white markings.
H: Woodland hedgebanks, field margins, waste ground; common.
AI: The pale forms may be taken for Limestone Woundwort. They are easily told apart: the lower lip of Hedge Woundwort always has white markings.

Marsh Woundwort
Stachys palustris
Mint family
Lamiaceae (Labiatae)

June–Aug.   10–60 cm   D; ♃

  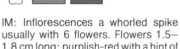

IM: Inflorescences a whorled spike usually with 6 flowers. Flowers 1.5–1.8 cm long; purplish-red with a hint of violet. Upper lip is approx. 1/2 as long as the lower lip, which has light spots. Leaves 3–5 times longer than wide, oblong, lanceolate, crenate-toothed, 5–12 cm long.
H: Wet to damp grassland, fens and swamps; locally common.
AI: Abroad it has a wide range, Europe, temperate Asia east to Japan and North America.

Marjoram
Origanum vulgare
Mint family
Lamiaceae (Labiatae)

July–Oct.   30–60 cm   D; ♃

IM: Numerous flowers in the upper leaf axils and at the end of the branches in head-like clusters in a compound panicle, approx. 5–6 mm long; pinkish-red to purplish-red. The bracts also have a reddish tinge. Leaves ovate, the margin often somewhat wavy or indistinctly toothed.
H: Grassland, roadsides, scrub and forest margins. Prefers calcareous soil. Locally common on chalk and limestone formations.
AI: The species has many variations, these differing according to the number of flowers, their colour and the shape of the inflorescence.

Breckland Thyme
Thymus serpyllum (sensu lato)
Mint family
Lamiaceae (Labiatae)

June–Oct.   10–25 cm   D; ♃

IM: Plant forms quite lax cushions. Flowers in head-like terminal inflorescence or sessile in whorls in upper leaf axils. Stem rounded, quadrangular or indistinctly so, with hairs all round or with just 2 ribs of hairs.
H: Sandy areas, short grassland, roadsides, heaths and screes; common.
AI: The most common Thyme species in Britain is *T. articus* ssp. *praecox* (syn. *T. drucei*). True *T. serpyllum* is only in East Anglia.

Field Cow Wheat
Melampyrum arvense
Figwort family
Scrophulariaceae

June–July   10–30 cm   D; ⊙ ; (+)

IM: Bracts pink, the flowers in their axils forming a dense terminal spike; purple, with a whitish tube and yellow throat, 2–2.5 cm long. Stem erect and usually branched; hairy.

H: Weedy areas in corn fields in southern England, usually where the soil is limy. Very rare.

AI: 20 years ago Cow Wheat was invariably present, though never common. As a result of the use of weedkillers it has virtually disappeared. Semiparasite.

Red Bartsia
Odontites verna (syn. *rubra*) ssp. *serotina*
Figwort family
Scrophulariaceae

Aug–Oct.   10–40 cm   D; ⊙

IM: Numerous flowers in upper leaf axils forming a rather one-sided spike; purplish pink; 1 cm long; hairy. Stem usually erect and begins branching at its base. The leaves are opposite, lanceolate and are widest in the basal half.

H: Grassland, fields, waste places, especially where the soil is limy. Common.

AI: *O. v.* ssp. *verna*: usually approx. 20 cm high. Branches of the erect stem go off at conspicuously sharp angles. Flowering time June–July. All species of *Odontites* are semi-parasites.

Foxglove
Digitalis purpurea
Figwort family
Scrophulariaceae

June–Aug.   60–180 cm   D; ☉; +

IM: Inflorescence a long, wand-like, one-sided raceme. Flowers bell-shaped, somewhat lopsided, pendant, each one 3–5 cm long and almost 2 cm in diameter at the mouth. The throat is spotted. Basal leaves form a rosette. Leaves ovate, toothed and have grey, felt-like covering on the underside.
H: Light woodland, heaths, roadsides and rocky slopes, mainly on acid soils. Locally common.
AI: Important medicinal plant. Contains numerous glycosides, the main one digitalin. Much grown in gardens and sometimes escaping to waste ground and pathsides.

Whorled Lousewort
Pedicularis verticillata
Figwort family
Scrophulariaceae

July   5–20 cm   D; ♃; (+)

IM: Numerous purplish-red flowers in a dense, clustered or head-shaped inflorescence approx. 1.5 cm long. Upper lip of each flower cropped at the apex; no teeth. Lower lip glabrous along the margin and projecting; it is half as long as the upper lip. Stem with 4 rows of hairs. Stem leaves in whorls of 3–4.
H: Not British. Usually in limestone country between 1300–2000 m in damp grassland on screes. Widely spread in Europe, north to sub-Arctic Russia.
AI: Can be picked out immediately among the red-flowering species in this genus because of the whorled leaves. Semi-parasite.

Lousewort
Pedicularis sylvatica
Figwort family
Scrophulariaceae

May–June   5–15 cm   D; ☉-24; (+)

IM: 5–15 flowers in a usually elongate terminal inflorescence. Flowers grow to 2–2.5 cm long, light pinkish-red. Upper lip rounded at the apex, with a tooth approx. 1 mm long on both sides. Lower lip shorter than upper lip. Stem prostrate, usually ascending at the tips. Leaves approx. 3 cm long, pinnate, glabrous, alternate.
H: Needs damp, acid soil, usually on moorland and wet heaths. Widespread but local; commonest in Scotland.
AI: Stunted plants of the Marsh Lousewort (*P. palustris*) can occasionally resemble the Lousewort. It can be recognized by its branched, erect stems.

Toothwort
Lathraea squamaria
Figwort family
Scrophulariaceae

March–May   10–25 cm   D; 24

IM: The entire plant is without chlorophyll. It is either white, pink or flesh-coloured. Numerous flowers, 1–1.5 cm long, in a dense 1-sided raceme, nodding at the tip when young. Fleshy stem base carries pale-coloured scale-like leaves.
H: In woodland and scrub; uncommon.
AI: A complete parasite, drawing nourishment from the roots of deciduous trees. Frequently found on Alder, Hazel or Poplar. In the right habitat Toothwort appears to live for many years.

Mezereon
Daphne mezereum
Daphne family
Thymelaeaceae

Feb.–April   50–150 cm   D; ♄; +

IM: At flowering time plant has no leaves or leaf buds are just beginning to show green at tips. Flowers are pinkish-red to reddish-violet or rarely white; strong scent. Stem erect and fairly well branched, often with a strikingly wrinkled bark. When rubbed the bark has an unpleasant smell. The fruit ripens in midsummer and is a bright red drupe.
H: Found in woodland, usually on chalk and limestone formations; rare.
AI: The plant contains the poisonous substance mezerine. On mucous membranes it can lead to unpleasant irritations.

Striped Daphne
Daphne striata
Daphne family
Thymelaeaceae

May–July   5–35 cm   D; ♄; +

IM: An evergreen species, bearing 8–12 flowers in terminal clusters on branch tips. They are glabrous on the outside, pinkish-red and smell like lilac. The leathery, oblanceolate, glabrous leaves tend to be clustered at ends of branches, 1–2.5 cm long.
H: Found wild only in the Alps (limestone Alps) on stony slopes and heaths where the soil is well drained. Sometimes cultivated in other parts of Europe, including Britain.
AI: Similar: *D. ptraea*: usually only 2–7 flowers in the terminal flower clusters. Flowers usually deeper shade of red. Only southern limestone Alps.

Rosemary Daphne
Daphne cneorum
Daphne family
Thymelaeaceae

May–June   10–30 cm   D; ♄; +

IM: An evergreen species forming wide mats. 6–10 flowers in terminal clusters, with external thick layer of clinging hairs; deep pinkish-red; smell similar to carnations. Leathery leaves narrowly ablanceate and distributed evenly along the stem. Young stems covered with fine downy hairs.
H: Found in grassland, among rocks and in open woodland, usually in limy soil in central Europe. Not native in Britain but widely cultivated.
AI: Cannot be confused outside the Alps, where it is easily distinguished from Striped Daphne by hairs on the branches and flower size and colour.

Cranberry
Vaccinium oxycoccos
Heath family
Ericaceae

June–Aug.   10–80 cm   D; ♄

IM: Flowers solitary or in small groups up to 4 close to branch ends. Flowers small (approx. 5 mm across), their 4 or 5 petals reflexed, reddish-white to pink or deep pink. Peduncles conspicuously long and thin. Prostrate stems usually creep quite a distance across moss. Leaves normally evergreen, rolled up at the edges.
H: Restricted to acid peat bogs, but there sometimes in abundance.
AI: Fruits contain large amount of vitamin C. They only taste pleasant after they have been subjected to frost.

Cross-leaved Heath
Erica tetralix
Heath family
Ericaceae

June–Sept.　　15–50 cm　　D; ♄

IM: 5–15 flowers in a terminal head which nods. Urn-shaped flowers approx. 6–8 mm long and flesh pink, with 4 small lobes at the apex. Branches erect, covered with white hairs. 3–4 evergreen leaves in a whorl; covered with stiff hairs.
H: Bogs, wet heath and moorland; also in open woodland where the soil is moist and acid.
Al: Abroad it is widely spread in western and northern Europe, extending northwards to central Finland.

Erica carnea (syn. *E. herbacea*)
Heath family
Ericaceae

Jan.–Aug.　　15–40 cm　　D; ♄

IM: Usually more than 30 flowers in a conspicuous 1-sided terminal inflorescence; flesh pink; approx. 5–7 mm long, 4 small lobes at the apex. Needle-shaped, glabrous leaves usually in whorls of 4 along the stem.
H: Not British. Native to the Alps, southern and central Europe and adjacent regions, on heaths and in light sub-Alpine woodland, usually between 1500 and 2200 m.
Al: Many cultivated varieties widely grown as ornamental plants.

Small-leaved Elm
Ulmus minor (syn. *U. carpinifolia*)
Elm family
Ulmaceae

March–April   5–35 m   D; ♄

IM: Flowers borne in dense clusters, appearing before the leaves, greenish-red with virtually no pedicel. The winged nutlet (samara) is glabrous. Wing obovate, with nutlet set off-centre. Seeds ripen and fall as the leaves expand. Leaves 4–10 cm long. Leaf blades obovate to oblanceolate, toothed and set very obliquely on the petiole.
H: Widespread, but local, in Europe in lowland forest, but also much planted.
Al: Less common since the onset of Dutch elm disease. Similar: English Elm (*U. procera*), commonest Elm in Britain pre Dutch elm disease. Still found in some areas. Leaves similar to *U. minor* but rough.

Wych Elm
Ulmus glabra
Elm family
Ulmaceae

March–April   20–40 m   D; ♄

IM: Flowers borne in dense clusters appearing before the leaves; greenish-red, virtually no pedicel. The winged fruit is glabrous; wing broadly elliptical, with nutlet set in the centre. Seeds ripen and fall as the leaves expand. Leaves 8–16 cm long. Leaf blades ovate, toothed and very harsh textured; borne obliquely on the stem. The 2 halves of each leaf are therefore very different from one another.
H: Throughout Europe but local, often in hill or mountain woods. The only truly wild elm in Britain, but also much planted in the past. Susceptible, but less prone to Dutch Elm disease than *U. minor.*
Al: Similar: Small-leaved Elm and English Elm, see left.

Crab Apple
Malus sylvestris
Rose family
Rosaceae

April–May   2–10 m   D; ♄

IM: Twigs sometimes thorny. Leaves petiolate, broadly to almost round, often with off-centre apex. Leaf smooth, rarely more than 4 cm long, underside glabrous. Corymbs with few flowers. Anthers yellow, petals white or pink, 1–3 cm long. Fruit a small apple 2–3 cm across, dry and sour, somewhat woody.
H: Deciduous woodland and light thickets, hedgerows. Likes calcareous, well-moistened soils rich in nutrients. Common in England and Wales, becoming rarer in Scotland.
AI: Very similar to the Apple and partially a hybrid of this is the cultivated apple (*M. domestica*) with its many different varieties.

Wild Cotoneaster
Cotoneaster integerrimus
Rose family
Rosaceae

May   1–2 m   D; ♄

IM: 2–4 somewhat bell-shaped flowers carried in nodding clusters of 2–4 in leaf axils. Flowers whitish, pink or purplish tinted, each one 5–8 mm long. Leaves alternate, margin entire, rounded to ovoid. 2–5 cm long, undersides covered with thick white felt, uppersides glabrous. Fruit pea-sized becoming blood red when ripe.
H: In Wales only, very rare. Scattered through Europe on limestone hills among rocks.
AI: Similar: *C. tomentosus*. Usually only 1–2 flowers in leaf axils. Leaf undersides, sepals and fruit covered with felt-like hairs. Stony thickets on limestone. Very rare. Not British.

Dog Rose
Rosa canina
Rose family
Rosaceae

June   1.3–3 m   D; ♄

 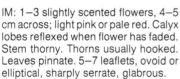

IM: 1–3 slightly scented flowers, 4–5 cm across; light pink or pale red. Calyx lobes reflexed when flower has faded. Stem thorny. Thorns usually hooked. Leaves pinnate. 5–7 leaflets, ovoid or elliptical, sharply serrate, glabrous.
H: Deciduous woodland, thickets. Common.
AI: Within the genus there are several species hard to distinguish from one another (e.g. *R. squarrosa*). *R. obtusifolia*: leaf undersides glandular-hairy; thickets; rare. *R. dumetorum*: leaves hairy on the underside along the veins; thickets; scattered.

Rosa gallica
Rose family
Rosaceae

June   30–150 cm   D; ♄

IM: Flowers usually solitary, 6–7 cm across, bright red to dark purplish-red, inside at the base normally whitish. Peduncle stems covered with glands. Leaf margin glandular, often 5 leaflets only on flowering branches. Leaves smell slightly of vinegar.
H: Not British. Forest margins, roadsides; scattered in Europe. Grown in gardens in Britain.
AI: Many suckers grow from the plant's roots so that in one habitat usually whole colonies grow up which, above the surface, seem to be independent.

Crowberry
Empetrum nigrum
Crowberry family
Empetraceae

May–July   30–50 cm   D; ♄; (+)

IM: Flowers barely 3 mm long, inconspicuous, solitary in the axils of the
upper leaves. Leaves needle-shaped,
alternate or almost in whorls, very
short petioles, glossy, undersides
white, with rolled-under edges.
H: Moors, heaths, dunes, alpine rocks.
Needs acid soil. Usually abundant in
those localities where it occurs.
AI: Two different races within the
species: one has male and female
plants. The male flowers pink, the
female purple. The other race is
hermaphrodite.

Bog Rosemary
Andromeda polifolia
Heath family
Ericaceae

May–Oct.   15–30 cm   D; ♄; +

IM: 1–5 flowers in a terminal inflorescence. Flowers globular to ovoid,
campanulate, pink, 5–8 mm long. At
the front tip of the bell are 5 small
lobes. Narrow leaves, 3–5 mm wide,
with rolled-under margins; uppersides dark green with conspicuous
veins, undersides light bluish-green.
Stem erect or ascending.
H: Bogs and wet heaths; scattered,
local and decreasing, mainly in central
Ireland and northern England to mid-
Wales.
AI: The plant is losing habitats as bogs
are drained and turned into farmland;
contains poison, andrometoxin, just in
its leaves or, more probably, in all its
organs.

Cowberry
Vaccinium vitis-idaea
Heath family
Ericaceae

June–Aug.　　10–30 cm　　D; ♄

Bilberry
Vaccinium myrtillus
Heath family
Ericaceae

May–June　　15–40 cm　　D; ♄

IM: Leaves leathery, evergreen; rolled up at the edge. Several flowers in terminal racemes, pink or pure white, slightly drooping. Flowers campanulate, usually 5, rarely 4 fused petals. Fruit: a berry, first white, then shining red when ripe, in dense clusters, usually unilateral.
H: In mixed and coniferous woodland, high moorland, heaths with stunted bushy growth. Common in the mountains and sometimes becoming dominant. Requires acid, meagre soil saturated at intervals and containing coarse humus.
AI: Similar: Bearberry (*Arctostaphylos uva-ursi*), especially when this is not in flower. The leaf edges are flat (p. 114).

IM: Axillary flowers solitary; globular-campanulate, greenish and usually tinged with red. As a rule they have 5, occasionally 4 petal-lobes. Leaves deciduous, ovate, pointed, margin slightly rounded-toothed, green on both sides. Stem angular, green. Berries blue-black.
H: Moors, heaths, acid woods, usually on hills or mountains. Usually abundant in the localities where it occurs. Common, except for eastern England from the Humber to the Thames.
AI: Similar: Bog Bilberry (*V. uliginosum*); leaves obovate to oval, without teeth, the undersides bluish-green. Stems brown. Moors and peaty forests. Scattered in west Scotland; rare in extreme north of England.　289

Hairy Alpenrose
Rhododendron hirsutum
Heath family
Ericaceae

May–Aug.　　50–120 cm　　D; ♄

IM: Flowers in a terminal umbel, funnel-shaped to campanulate, approx. 1.5 cm long, with 5 lobes, light red, hairy on the inside. Leaves elliptic evergreen, leathery, light green and glossy on the upperside, matt on the underside and spotted initially with yellow, then with brown glandular scales. The entire leaf margin covered with conspicuous layer of ciliate hairs.
H: Only cultivated in Britain. In central and eastern Alps. 2400 m. Scattered and locally abundant where it occurs.
Al: Similar: Rusty Alpenrose (*R. ferrugineum*): see right.

Rusty Alpenrose
Rhododendron ferrugineum
Heath family
Ericaceae

May–Aug.　　50–200 cm　　D; ♄

IM: Flowers in a terminal umbel, funnel-shaped to campanulate, approx. 1.5 cm long, with 5 lobes, dark red, hairy on the inside. The narrowly oblong to elliptic leaves evergreen, leathery, dark green on the top, the undersides covered with a dense layer of rusty yellow glandular scales. Leaf margin rolled under and never has cilitate hairs.
H: Cultivated in Britain. Alps, Pyrenees and the Jura in peaty acid soils.
Al: Similar: Hairy Alpenrose (*R. hirsutum*): leaves have conspicuous ciliate hairs, limestone Alps.

Heather
Calluna vulgaris
Heath family
Ericaceae

July–Sept.　　20–50 cm　　D; ♄

IM: Flowers in terminal racemes, sometimes branched. Each flower 2–4 mm long and deeply cleft in 4 lobes; pink to purplish-red, shorter than the petal-like 4-lobed calyx of the same colour. Leaves in 4 rows on the stem, scale-like.
H: Found on heaths, moors, bogs and in open woods where the soil is acid; common.
AI: Heather does not decay easily. Crude humus is formed from its dead remains.

Spiny Restharrow
Ononis spinosa
Pea family
Fabaceae (Leguminosae)

June–Sept.　　30–60 cm　　D; ♄

IM: Flowers axillary in a loose raceme on the upper part of the stem. Stem with 2 lines of hairs only, erect or ascending, often thorny. Leaves made up of 3 finely toothed leaflets.
H: Dry pastures, roadsides and waste ground; scattered and local.
AI: 2 groups within the species: Spiny Restharrow and Creeping Restharrow (often listed as *O. repens*). Creeping Restharrow has no thorns; is not rhizomatous, and its stem is evenly covered with hairs.

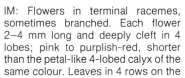

Columbine-leaved Meadow Rue
Thalictrum aquilegifolium
Buttercup family
Ranunculaceae

May–June   50–150 cm   D; ♃

IM: Lilac to purple or white flowers consist of virtually only the bushy projecting stamens which are arranged in a rather dense panicle. Leaves alternate on the stem, bi- or tripinnate with rounded leaflets which are crenate at the apex.
H: Damp woodland, river banks, mountainsides, eastern and central Europe.
AI: Only cultivated in Britain. In the past the plant was used to dye cloth; leaves contain a yellow dye.

Round-leaved Penny-cress
Thlaspi rotundifolium
Mustard family
Brassicaceae (Cruciferae)

July–Sept.   5–15 cm   D; ♃

IM: Stem creeping, producing erect or ascending flowering shoots which bear many leaves. Leaves glaucous, ovoid, margin entire or serrate. Flowers in compressed corymbs. Fruit oval, somewhat flattened, approx. twice as long as wide.
H: Not British. Only in Alpine areas over 1000–1500 m.
AI: Prevalent form is distinguished by its blue-tinged corolla with darker veins. White-flowered form is rare.

Dame's Violet
Hesperis matronalis
Mustard family
Brassicaceae (Cruciferae)

May—July   40—100 cm   D; ☉-♃

IM: Numerous flowers in erect open racemes; violet or white; up to 2 cm across. The ripe pods measure up to 9 cm. Basal leaves ovoid, usually wither during later part of flowering period; up to 15 cm long. The stem leaves hairy.
H: Cultivated in Britain. Forest margins, roadsides and waste places, usually on somewhat moist soil. Native to Europe, western and central Asia locally.

Perennial Honesty
Lunaria rediviva
Mustard family
Brassicaceae (Cruciferae)

May—July   30—150 cm   D; ♃

IM: 10—30 flowers; approx. 1.5 cm across; usually pale violet, sometimes whitish-violet. Ripe fruits are particularly conspicuous: 3—5 cm long, in rare cases to even 9 cm and approx. ⅓ as wide as they are long. Leaves petiolate with deep heart-shaped lobes, toothed.
H: Cultivated in Britain. Woodland on humus, stony and damp ground. Throughout Europe.
AI: Grown in borders of perennial flowers but not frequently seen. Common Honesty (*L. annua*) is more frequently seen, both in gardens and naturalized by roadsides and on waste ground.

293

Cuckoo Flower
Cardamine pratensis
Mustard family
Brassicaceae (Cruciferae)

April–June   15–60 cm   D; ♃

Im: Basal leaves form rosette, pinnate. Leaflets rounded, terminal leaflet usually larger. Stem leaves pinnate with narrow tips. Hollow stem. Inflorescence a raceme. Flowers large (approx. 1–1.5 cm across), petals longer than sepals. Fruit much longer than wide. Flower colour depends on habitat: white (shady), pink, mauve or deep puple (dry).
H: Mainly in damp meadows and pastures on loamy soil. Indicator of rich ground and ground water. Common.
Al: Similar: Narrow-Leaved Bittercress (C. *impatiens*), flowers only 0.5 cm across, petals as long as sepals, whitish; fruit bursts if touched; woods.

Coralroot
Cardamine bulbifera
Mustard family
Brassicaceae (Cruciferae)

April–May   30–70 cm   D; ♃

IM: Flowers usually violet, sometimes pink or white. No basal rosette of leaves. Leaves at least partially pinnate. Upper leaves narrow and entire. Dark brownish-purple bulbils in leaf axils.
H: Deciduous and mixed woodland in hilly areas on soil rich in nutrients and usually calcareous. Local in southern England, Midlands to southern Scotland.
Al: Coralroot reproduces mainly by means of its bulbils as seeds are rarely formed. Ants carry off the bulbils, so often only small numbers in each locality. Synonym: *Dentaria bulbifera*.

Cross Gentian
Gentiana cruciata
Gentian family
Gentianaceae

July–Oct.　　10–40 cm　　D; ♃

IM: Flowers have short peduncles or none at all, arising in the upper leaf axils and sometimes lower down, either solitary or up to 3 in a group. Flowers 2–2.5 cm long, campanulate and erect, with 4, more rarely 5 blunt lobes, cleft to approx. ⅓ of their length. Leaves opposite and lanceolate with leathery appearance.
H: Not British. Mainly in southern, central and eastern Europe, north to Holland. Thickets, forest margins and grassland. Very rare.
AI: Species very much reduced by fertilizers on grassland where it used to be found.

Fringed Gentian
Gentianella ciliata
Gentian family
Gentianaceae

Aug.–Oct.　　10–25 cm　　D; ☉–♃

IM: Stem usually with one terminal flower, more rarely 2–10. Flowers 2–5 cm long, cleft to about ½ into 4 lobes. Lobes have long fringe particularly at the base. Flower deep blue, more rarely pale blue. Margin of petal lobes often slightly rolled. Leaves linear-elongate with a single vein.
H: Not British. Grows in light open woodland and grassland on limestone formations.
AI: Easiest Gentian to recognize in Europe; not common anywhere, nevertheless widely distributed. No subspecies known.

Corn Mint
Mentha arvensis
Mint family
Lamiaceae (Labiatae)

June—Oct.　　15—50 cm　　D; ♃

IM: All flowers in axillary whorls in upper 6—10 leaf pairs. Stem tip leafy. Leaves elongate, more rarely rounded, always toothed and hairy, opposite, alternate. Stem quadrangular.
H: River banks, ditches, wet areas in fields, meadows, woodland. Common in the south, less so in the north and Scotland.
AI: It is difficult to differentiate clearly between the subspecies. Also hybrids of the Corn Mint and other species within the genus are by no means rare.

Spearmint
Mentha spicata
Mint family
Lamiaceae (Labiatae)

July—Aug.　　30—90 cm　　D; ♃

IM: Inflorescence a slender, whorled spike, often branched. Floral bracts very narrow, almost like bristles. Flowers blue-lilac, 3 mm wide. Leaves 6—10 cm long, 2—3 cm wide, almost sessile, never wrinkled.
H: River banks, ditches, damp meadows, roadsides, waste ground. Native to central Europe only, but widely naturalized elsewhere, including the British Isles. Much cultivated as a herb for flavouring.
AI: Similar: Water Mint (*M. aquatica*): terminal inflorescence dense, rounded; beneath it 1—2 axillary flower whorls. River, stream and pond banks, marshes and fens. Common.

Brooklime
Veronica beccabunga
Figwort family
Scrophulariaceae

May–Aug. 20–60 cm D; ♃; (+)

IM: Usually 10 flowers (occasionally more) in a lax axillary raceme. Flowers 6–8 mm across, divided into 4 blue petal lobes. Leaves opposite, glabrous, glossy, petiolate and notched, oval to rounded.
H: Ponds, streams, rivers, marshes and wet grassland; common.
AI: Plants within this species may vary considerably. Submerged plants look very different. Water Speedwell (see right) always has leaves more than twice as long as wide.

Blue Water Speedwell
Veronica anagallis-aquatica
Figwort family
Scrophulariaceae

June–Oct. 15–50 cm D; ♃

IM: Usually 20–50 flowers in a dense axillary raceme, 4–6 mm across and divided into 4 pale blue petal lobes. Leaves opposite, usually glabrous, sessile or with short petioles, semi-amlexicaul, lanceolate, up to 2 cm long.
H: Rivers, streams, ponds and wet meadows; fairly common.
AI: In Europe this species has many varieties, but in Britain, the regional populations are fairly uniform.

Ivy-leaved Speedwell
Veronica hederifolia
Figwort family
Scrophulariaceae

March–May   5–30 cm   D; ⊙

IM: Flowers solitary in leaf axils, 2–5 mm across, blue or bluish-violet, more rarely white. Stem prostrate or ascending, branched. Leaves 3–7 lobed, ciliate and slightly hairy.
H: Hedgerows, waste ground, fields and gardens, occasionally. in forest clearings. Very common.
AI: Similar: *V. hederifolia*, ssp. *sublobata* has fruit stems longer than 4 times the length of the calyx. Ssp. *hederifolia* has fruit stems twice as long as the calyx.

Grey Field Speedwell
Veronica polita
Figwort family
Scrophulariaceae

March–Sept.   5–20 cm   D; ⊙

IM: Flowers solitary in leaf axils. 4–8 mm across, dark blue. Stem prostrate (but not rooting), ascendiig or erect. Leaves 0.5–1.2 cm long, rounded, dark green, somewhat glossy. Fruit stem at maturity as long as the leaves or shorter.
H: Gardens. Common.
AI: Similar: Field Speedwell (*V. agrestis*): leaves conspicuously longer than they are wide. Fruit stem at least 1½ times as long as the leaves. Flowers pale blue and white. Weedy areas, cultivated ground. Local in the south, common in the north.

Common Field Speedwell
Veronica persica
Figwort family
Scrophulariaceae

March—Dec.   10—40 cm   D; ☉-☉

IM: Flowers solitary in leaf axils, 8—12 mm in diameter, sky blue with whitish or yellowish spot in the throat. Stem prostrate or ascending. Leaves heart-shaped or ovate, coarsely toothed, minutely ciliate and hairy on the veins beneath.
H: Waste ground, fields and in gardens. Common.
AI: Plant is a native of western Asia. It must have spread via Turkey to the Balkans around 1800 and from there to the south-eastern part of central Europe. First recorded in Britain 1825.

Fingered Speedwell
Veronica triphyllos
Figwort family
Scrophulariaceae

March—May   5—15 cm   D; ☉

IM: Flowers in a short, open raceme; 5—7 mm across, dark blue. Flower stems longer than the calyx. Stem erect, lower part branched. Middle and upper leaves 3—5 lobed, lower ones ovoid.
H: Sandy fields in East Anglia, very rare.
AI: Similar: *V. praecox*: flowers barely over 5 mm across. Leaves undivided. Sandy fields in East Anglia. Rare. *V. acinifolia*: flowers only 3—5 mm across, light blue. Middle and upper leaves undivided. Damp muddy fields. Very rare.

Wall Speedwell
Veronica arvensis
Figwort family
Scrophulariaceae

March—Sept. 5—20 cm D; ⊙

IM: Flowers in erect racemes. They are light blue, with very short petioles and only grow to 4—5 mm in diameter. Leaves toothed, lower ones heart-shaped to ovate, upper ones narrower usually with margin entire.
H: Waste ground, fields, gardens, heaths and grassland; common.
AI: *V. verna*: flowers rich blue, 3—4 mm in diameter. Middle leaves pinnate, lower ones ovate and barely toothed. Plant 5—10 cm high. Sandy fields in East Anglia; rare. *V. dillenii*: flowers dark blue, 5—7 mm in diameter. Middle leaves pinnate, lower ones ovate. Sandy ground, but not in Britain.

Heath Speedwell
Veronica officinalis
Figwort family
Scrophulariaceae

June—Aug. 15—30 cm D; ⁒; (+)

IM: 15—25 flowers in fairly axillary racemes, approx. 6 mm across usually lilac, sometimes very pale or almost white. Stem creeping, with ascending flowering stems. Leaves opposite, hairy, leathery, toothed, with short petioles.
H: Open woodland, heaths and grassland, usually on somewhat acid ground. Common.
AI: The species is very evenly distributed. Nevertheless there are virtually no reports of any varieties other than the occasional occurrence of white or pink flowered specimens.

Germander Speedwell
Veronica chamaedrys
Figwort family
Scrophulariaceae

April–June   15–30 cm   D; ♃; (+)

IM: 10–30 flowers in racemes in axils of upper leaf pairs. Flowers 10 mm across bright blue with darker veins. Stem with normally 2 conspicuous rows of hairs. Leaves opposite, short petioles or sessile, up to 3.5 cm long, almost twice as long as wide, ovate, toothed and hairy.
H: Grassland, open woodland, hedgerows and roadsides. Common.
AI: Similar: *V. urticifolia*: usually only 4 lax clusters. Flowers 6–8 mm across. Stem evenly covered with hairs or glabrous. Leaves up to 10 cm long. Woodland. Scattered. Not British.

Veronica austriaca
Figwort family
Scrophulariaceae

May–Aug.   15–50 cm   D; ♃

IM: Flowers in dense axillary racemes at the top of the stems. Flowers 1–1.5 cm across, dark blue. Stem ascending or erect, covered with curly hairs. Leaves ovate to oblong-lanceolate, sessile, or lower ones with short petioles.
H: Scrub, woodland and grassland. Scattered throughout Europe. Much cultivated.
AI: The species currently comprises various groups. The one described above is most common, once classified as *V. teucrium*.

Hoary Plaintain
Plantago media
Plaintain family
Plantaginaceae

May–June   15–30 cm   D; ♃

IM: Stem 2–5 times as long as flower spike. Spike up to 8 cm long, dense. Flowers inconspicuous. Stamens lilac, on long purple filaments. Leaves in a rosette, margins slightly toothed. Leaf blade at least 4 times as long as petiole.
H: Dry grassland, meadows, roadsides, usually on limy soils; widespread but local, less common in the north.
AI: Similar: *P. intermedia*: stem twice as long as flower spike. Spike slender. Stamens short and only initially pale lilac. Leaf blade max. twice as long as petiole. Leaves normally flat on the ground. Damp fields and roadsides. Not British.

Field Madder
Sherardia arvensis
Madder family
Rubiaceae

May–Oct.   5–30 cm   D; ☉

IM: Flowers in a terminal, rounded, false umbel of few flowers, each 3–4 mm across. Prostrate or ascending stem conspicuously quadrangular. Leaves arranged in whorls of 5–6 on the upper parts of the stem, but only in 4s at the base. Leaves have single vein, rough along the margins.
AI: Fields, grassland, roadsides, waste ground; widely spread but local.
AI: Field Madder never very common, but until the advent of chemical herbicides it was never absent in any area where the soil conditions were suitable.

Teasel
Dipsacus fullonum
Scabious family
Dipsacaceae

July–Aug.   90–200 cm   D; ☉

IM: Flowers in a dense thimble-shaped head with protruding, bristle-like bracts. Flowers lilac, opening in rings from the middle upwards and downwards. Bracts of the capitulum bearing small spines and facing upwards. Margin of stem leaves entire or toothed. Stems erect, ribbed and prickly.
H: Roadsides, hedgerows, waste ground and grassland. Widespread but local, commoner in the south.
Al: Similar: *D. laciniatus*: bracts of the capitulum project horizontally or downwards, without thorns. Stem leaves irregularly pinnate. Not native in Britain.

Devil's-bit Scabious
Succisa pratensis
Scabious family
Dipsacaceae

July–Aug.   90–200.cm   D; ☉

IM: Flowers in dense hemispherical heads, 1.5–2.5 cm across; mauve to violet-blue. Marginal flowers no larger than inner ones. Between flowers conspicuous black bristles (pull out flowers to see). Stem below capitulum covered with clinging hairs. Leaves opposite, ovoid-lanceolate, undivided.
H: Damp meadows, open moorland, damp open woodland. Scattered.
Al: Similar: *S. inflexa*: flowers lilac. There are no black bristles between the flowers. Very rare in open moorland. Not British; predominantly in eastern Europe.

Dianthus superbus
Pink family
Caryophyllaceae

June–Sept.   30–90 cm   D; ♃

IM: Flowers solitary, on pedicels. Petals lilac to deep pink, often with strong tendency towards lilac. Petals arching, fringed, divided beyond the middle, often with dark spots. Flower generally over 2.5 cm across. Short epicalyx scales at base of calyx no more than ⅓ of calyx length. Stem leaves opposite, often somewhat bluish-green, 3–10 mm wide. Flowers usually have strong scent.
H: Cultivated in Britain. Open woodland, scrub, mountain and wet meadows in much of Europe.
Al: Similar: Pink (*D. plumarius*): flower opening to 2.5 cm across, pink to white. Not British. Eastern central Europe.

304

Columbine
Aquilegia vulgaris
Buttercup family
Ranunculaceae

June–July   30–60 cm   D; ♃; +

IM: 3–12 flowers, each 3.5–5 cm across in very open panicle. 5 petals with spurs. Spur erect, bent into a hook at the end. Leaves doubly divided into 3.
H: Damp woodland, fens, wet meadows; native and naturalized; local and rare.
Al: Similar: Purple Columbine (*A. atrata*): flowers brownish-violet in colour. Stamens extend 1 cm beyond unfolded flower. Woodland, meadows. *A. einseleana*: flower 2–4 cm across. Often only 1 flower, max. 6. Spur barely curved: eastern limestone Alps. Rare. Alpine Columbine (*A. alpina*): flower diameter 5–8 cm. Spur barely curved at tip. 1–3 flowers. Alps. Rare. None native to Britain.

Meadow Crane's-bill
Geranium pratense
Geranium family
Geraniaceae

June–Sept.　　30–60 cm　　D; ♃

IM: Inflorescence several axillary peduncles from top of erect stems each having 2 flowers. Flowers 2.5–4 cm across, blue, sometimes with violet undertone. Peduncles bend downwards after flowering. Leaves large, palmate, with 7 toothed lobes.
H: Meadows, roadsides. Scattered, common locally, but not in northern Scotland.
AI: The Meadow Crane's-bill is distributed predominantly in eastern Europe. In meadows with rich soil, it can occur in such abundance that its blue flowers dominate the scene. It is rarely so abundant in Britain.

Wood Crane's-bill
Geranium sylvaticus
Geranium family
Geraniaceae

June–Sept.　　30–60 cm　　D; ♃

IM: Inflorescence several axillary peduncles from tops of erect stems each having 2 flowers. Flowers 2–3 cm across, reddish or bluish-violet. Leaves palmate 7–12 cm wide, usually divided into 7 segments, divisions never as deep as the stem.
H: Open woodland, meadows, hedgebanks, mountain rocks. Well distributed in northern England and Scotland, rare or absent elsewhere. Where it occurs it can be in large numbers.
AI: Some Wood Crane's-bill vary in petal colour.

Sea Holly
Eryngium maritimum
Umbellifer family
Apiaceae (Umbelliferae)

June–Oct.　　10–40 cm　　D; ♃

  ▽

IM: Inflorescence a compact hemispherical terminal umbel which elongates after flowers have withered. Flowers small, blue, tending towards violet. Involucral bracts spread out like stars, 2–4 cm long, wavy and with spiny teeth. Basal leaves rounded or reniform, also with teeth with long, spiny tip. Stem richly branched. Plants often form semi-spherical 'bush'. Whole plant is tinged with blue-grey.
H: Dunes, shingle beaches, always near the sea, around whole of Britain.

Blue Pimpernel
Anagallis foemina
Primrose family
Primulaceae

June–Sept.　　10–20 cm　　D; ☉

IM: Single axillary flowers approx. 5 mm across; bluish-violet inside, blue outside. Petals do not overlap, front margin conspicuously toothed. Stem prostrate. Leaves opposite, 0.5–2 cm long, narrow ovoid.
H: Fields and waste ground; rare.
AI: Syn: *A. arvensis* spp. *foemina.* Similar: Scarlet Pimpernel *A. arvensis*: flowers red, rarely mauve or blue. Petals touch each other or overlap, never toothed at the apex. Fields, gardens, waste places, roadsides. Common.

Sea Lavender
Limonium vulgare
Sea Lavender family
Plumbaginaceae

July–Sept.   20–50 cm   D; ♃

IM: Numerous violet flowers in dense cymes, in stiff, panicle-like inflorescence. Each flower 6–8 mm long, with 5 petal lobes spread out in semicampanulate fashion; usually conspicuously crenate. All leaves in a basal rosette; 5–20 cm long, 1.5–3 cm wide.
H: Salt marshes, scattered around the coasts of England and Wales but not Scotland.
AI: Varieties growing on beaches of the Mediterranean, Atlantic, North Sea and Baltic differ somewhat from one another.

Lesser Periwinkle
Vinca minor
Dogbane family
Apocynaceae

April–May   10–20 cm   D; ♃

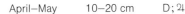

IM: Flowers solitary, light blue-puple, and occasionally white, 2–3 cm across. Petal lobes spread out flat. Stem trailing, woody at the base. Flowering stems ascending. Leaves opposite, lanceolate, leathery, evergreen, glabrous, up to 4 cm long.
H: Woodland, hedgebanks and roadsides. Scattered. Not considered native to Britain.
AI: Frequently cultivated as is Greater Periwinkle (*V. major*): flower 4–5 cm across. Plant grows to 50 cm. Leaves have ciliate margin, up to 10 cm long. Less hardy than *V. minor*.

Marsh Gentian
Gentiana pneumonanthe
Gentian family
Gentianaceae

July–Sept.   10–40 cm   D; ♃

IM: Usually 1–3 flowers at stem end, occasionally up to 7; 3.5–5 cm long; 5 green lines on outside. Stem erect, unbranched. Leaves opposite, narrow and blunt.

H: Wet heathland in England and Wales. Local and decreasing with loss of suitable habitats.

Al: Similar: Milkweed Gentian (*G. asclepiadea*): numerous flowers either single or in 2s and 3s usually in upper leaf axils.

Milkweed Gentian
Gentian asclepiadea
Gentian family
Gentianaceae

June–Sept.   40–70 cm   D; ♃

IM: Flowers terminal, in the axils of middle and upper leaves, forming a somewhat 1-sided spike; each flower is 3–5 cm long, dark blue with reddish-violet spots on the inside, erect and narrowly campanulate. There are 5 narrow pointed petal lobes, between which is a wide triangular 'tooth'. Leaves are ovoid-lanceolate, opposite, alternate, often in one plane when the stem is arching over.

H: Cultivated in Britain. Damp meadows and woods on calcareous soils.

Al: Similar: Marsh Gentian (*G. pneumonanthe*) (see left): flowers usually solitary at stem end; green spotted stripes inside.

Stemless Gentian
Gentiana acaulis
Gentian family
Gentianaceae

May–Aug.   5–10 cm   D; ♃

IM: Single, erect flower at stem end, 3–6 cm long. Peduncle very short. Only 1–2 pairs of stem leaves on the stalk, often no stem leaves at all. Remaining leaves in a basal tuft or rosette forming clumps.
H: Cultivated in Britain. Mountains of Europe.
AI: 2 groups within the species *G. acaulis*. *G. acaulis*: leaves approx. 8 cm long; flowers with conspicuous olive green longitudinal stripe inside. On acid soils. *G. clusii*: leaves approx. 2.5 cm long, rarely up to 6 cm. No olive green stripe on flower inside. On limy soils.

Spring Gentian
Gentiana verna
Gentian family
Gentianaceae

April–Aug.   3–15 cm   D; ♃

IM: Single or, more rarely, 2–3 terminal flowers on erect stems each bearing 1–3 leaf pairs. Flowers deep blue, 2.5–3 cm long. Basal leaves in a tuft or a rosette, 1–3 cm long and approx. ½ as wide; blunt.
H: Mountain meadows, open moorland, usually on limestone formations. Rare, but often in large numbers where it occurs.
AI: Does not tolerate fertilizers which explains the reduction in its numbers over recent years. In the Alps several similar species grow which are not easily differentiated. They usually have smaller leaves.

Phacelia tanacetifolia
Waterleaf family
Hydrophyllaceae

June–Oct.   15–50 cm   D; ☉

IM: Numerous flowers in compact cymes forming panicle-like inflorescence; lavender-coloured; campanulate to funnel-shaped; 4–6 mm across; the 5 stamens conspicuous — approx. twice as long as corolla, extending far beyond it. Stem erect, often branched, covered with coarse hairs. Leaves alternate, simple or bipinnately lobed.
H: Waste ground; occasional.
AI: Originates in California. Introduced into Europe (including Britain) as an ornamental and as a bee plant.

Common Comfrey
Symphytum officinale
Borage family
Boraginaceae

May–June   30–120 cm   D; ♃; (+)

IM: Entire plant covered with rough hairs. Leaves rather narrowly ovoid, distinctly decurrent. Flowers small, campanulate, drooping, in scorpioidal cymes.
H: On damp to wet ground, always rich in nutrients. In wet meadows, on river banks and in ditches. Found throughout Britain but less so in the north.

Soft Lungwort
Pulmonaria mollis
Borage family
Boraginaceae

April–May   10–30 cm   D; ♃

IM: Several flowers in cymes from the upper leaf axils. Flowers cowslip-like, with violet corollas which become lilac-coloured on fading. Basal leaves are narrower close to the stem; up to 45 cm long or more and approx. ⅓ of that in width. Leaves in the middle of the stem shorter. Whole plant softly hairy.
H: Deciduous woodland on calcareous soil in central and south-eastern Europe. Scattered and local.
AI: Similar: *P. angustifolia*: basal leaves narrower towards the stem. Flowers bright blue. Local.

Pulmonaria obscura
Borage family
Boraginaceae

March–April   15–40 cm   D; ♃

IM: Several flowers in cymes from the upper leaf axils. Flowers cowslip-like, with red blossoms becoming violet then blue on fading. Basal leaves ovate-cordate, not or only very faintly spotted.
H: Not British. Woodland, on calcareous formations. Scattered and local in northern Europe. Abundant in localities where it occurs.
AI: Similar: Lungwort (*P. officinalis*): peduncles of axillary inflorescences shorter than respective bract. Spotted leaves. Not British. Alps, Alpine foreland. Rare.

Field Forget-me-not
Myosotis arvensis
Borage family
Boraginaceae

May—Aug.   10—30 cm   D; ☉ - ☉

IM: Numerous flowers in a relatively dense inflorescence each 3—4 mm across. Peduncles stand erect. During flowering they are 1—2 mm long. They spread as the fruit develops. Stem of fruit is 2—3 times as long as the calyx (which distinguishes it from small-flowered forms of Wood Forget-me-not). Basal leaves roundish ovate, petiolate, in rosettes, greyish-green. Stem leaves oblong-lanceolate, sessile.
H: Roadsides, cultivated places and sandy dunes.
Al: Similar: Wood Forget-me-not (*M. sylvatica*): flowers 5—7 mm across, rarely smaller.

Water Forget-me-not
Myosotis scorpioides
Borage family
Boraginaceae

May—Oct.   15—40 cm   D; ♃

IM: 10—20 flowers in a relatively lax raceme; flowers 4—10 mm across. Calyx has adpressed hairs (unlike Wood Forget-me-not where some individual hairs stand out on the calyx). Stem angular. Leaves elongate-lanceolate, sessile, hairy.
H: Wet places, streamsides.
Al: There are closely related forms classed as species by some authorities. *M. caespitosa*: stem round or indistinctly angular, branched from below the middle; scattered. *M. secunda* with fruiting pedicels 3—5 times the length of the calyx. Commonest in hilly districts.

Wood Forget-me-not
Myosotis sylvatica
Borage family
Boraginaceae

May–July   15–50 cm   D; ♃

!M: 10–25 flowers in a lax raceme; each 5–10 mm across. Calyx has many individual hairs which stand out; occasionally there are only a few. Leaves in a rosette. Stem leaves becoming narrower, twice as long as they are wide.
H: Woodland. Locally abundant.
Al: Sometimes confused with garden escapes which are often hybrids with *M. alpestris* an alpine species from Europe.

Purple Gromwell
Buglossoides purpurocaeruleum
Borage family
Boraginaceae

April–June   15–50 cm   D; ♃

IM: Flowers in terminal cluster; buds brownish-red, young flowers reddish, then turning blue. Flowers 1–1.5 cm across. Stem erect, unbranched. Leaves lanceolate, up to 8 cm long, 1.5–2 cm wide.
H: Dry deciduous woodland and thickets. Grows best in calcareous soil rich in humus. Rather rare, usually occurs in small numbers.
Al: In Britain it is confined to southern counties. In Europe it extends to the Mediterranean and eastwards to Asia Minor.

Bugloss
Anchusa arvensis
Borage family
Boraginaceae

May–Oct.   15–45 cm   D; ⊙

IM: Numerous flowers in several simple or branched axillary cymes or clustered at the end. Flowers light blue, 5–7 mm across approx. 1 cm long. Corolla tube S-shaped and facing upwards. Stem angular. Leaves undulate with stiff hairs.
H: Weedy places in fields, sandy heaths and near the sea. Prefers loose sandy ground. Rare.
Al: Used to be classed as *Lycopsis arvensis*. Its numbers have been greatly reduced by chemical pesticides; can still be found in field margins.

Vervain
Verbena officinalis
Verbena family
Verbenaceae

July–Oct.   30–60 cm   D; ⊙-♃

IM: Numerous small (3–5 mm long) reddish-violet or pale lilac flowers in a spike-like inflorescence; conspicuously squarrosely branched. Leaves deeply divided, upper ones less so.
H: Roadsides and waste places. Nitrogen indicator. Local. In Britain, commonest in the south.
Al: Probably originates from the Mediterranean. Requires warmth.

Bittersweet
Solanum dulcamara
Nightshade family
Solanaceae

June–Aug.   30–300 cm   D; ♄; +

IM: Flowers in umbellate clusters in leaf axils and at the stem end. Flowers violet, approx. 1 cm across; with 5 lobes usually folded back. Stem becomes woody; is erect or ascending. Leaves long-ovate glabrous, often deeply lobed.
H: Grows in damp soil rich in nutrients. Woodland, fen carr, shingle beaches and waste ground. Common.
AI: Contains a poisonous alkaloid. The fruits are bright red berries which, if eaten, lead to severe poisoning.

Common Cornsalad
Valerianella locusta
Valerian family
Valerianaceae

April–May   5–40 cm   D; ☉

IM: Several small, inconspicuous flowers in terminal groups of small clustered inflorescences. Flowers pale lilac blue. Stem erect and much branched. Lower stem leaves spatulate, upper ones lanceolate.
H: Weedy areas in root crop fields, hedgebanks and dunes. Locally frequent.
AI: Several similar species can only be accurately identified by means of distinguishing features on the fruit wall. Grown as salad plants in numerous different varieties. Available when other salad plants virtually non-existent.

Alpine Bellflower
Campanula alpina
Bellflower family
Campanulaceae

July–Aug.   5–15 cm   D; ☉ - ♃

IM: Usually 2–8 flowers (rarely only 1 or 2) in a short cluster. Flowers 3–4 cm long, light bluish-violet. The style divided into 3. Between each sepal, a short recurved tooth. Stem erect, with loose woolly hairs. Basal leaves and lower stem leaves narrow spatulate, slightly crenate at the apex, becoming gradually narrower towards the stem, with loose woolly covering of hairs.
H: Not British or mainland European. Needs moist soil low in lime. Eastern Alps and mountains of the Balkan peninsula.
Al: May be confused with small examples of the Bearded Bellflower.

Bearded Bellflower
Campanula barbata
Bellflower family
Campanulaceae

June–Aug.   10–30 cm   D; ♃

IM: 2–12 flowers in a substantial cluster often 10 cm long or longer. Initially it is erect, later drooping. Flowers 1.5–3 cm long, light blue or pale lilac, with hairs along the veins and along both sides of the lobes. Narrow basal leaves.
H: Not British. Prefers somewhat stony moist ground low in lime. Scattered in the mountains of central Alps, Europe, also in Norway.
Al: White-flowered forms are not infrequent.

Harebell
Campanula rotundifolia
Bellflower family
Campanulaceae

June–Sept.   5–50 cm   D; ♃

IM: Up to 8 flowers in a lax panicle. Buds are erect but the flowers are pendent. Flowers 1.5–2 cm long, divided to no more than ⅓ their length. Leaves evenly distributed along the stem which has downy hairs at the base (check with magnifying glass). Stem leaves narrow lanceolate, margin entire, longer than 2 cm. Basal leaves have often withered by flowering time.
H: Meadows, dry grassland. Very common.
AI: The Latin name indicates the first basal leaves which are orbicular in shape.

Spreading Bellflower
Campanula patula
Bellflower family
Campanulaceae

May–Sept.   15–70 cm   D; ☉ - ☉

IM: Few flowers in freely branched panicles. Flowers erect on 2–5 cm, slender stalks; lobes conspicuously spread out, divided to approx. ½ the flower length. Erect branched stem has short hairs at the base.
H: Hedgebanks, light woodland. Local.
AI: Easy to identify from other species because flowers are well spread out. Within the species there are virtually no varying forms.

317

Nettle-leaved Bellflower
Campanula trachelium
Bellflower family
Campanulaceae

May—Sept.   50—100 cm   D; ♃

IM: Flowers in a semi-erect cluster; 3.5—4.5 cm long; petal lobes have conspicuous hairs. Sepals have stiff hairs. Stem erect, sharply angled, hairy. Upper leaves sessile, lower stem leaves deeply heart-shaped with long stem. Petioles never winged.

H: Semi-shade or shade and loamy soil, woodland. Scattered but widespread.

AI: Similar: Large Bellflower (*C. latifolia*): flowers 4—5 cm. Sepals glabrous. Stem bluntly angled. Petioles conspicuously winged. Woodland especially in the hilly areas of northern England and Scotland. Local.

Creeping Bellflower
Campanula rapunculoides
Bellflower family
Campanulaceae

June—Aug.   30—60 cm   D; ♃

IM: Flowers in a 1-sided raceme containing many flowers. They are nodding, 2—3 cm long, glabrous or have sparse long hairs along lobe edges; light violet. Stem round or slightly obtuse-angled. Stem leaves heart-shaped, ovate or ovate-elongate. Basal leaves usually withered by flowering time.

H: Fields and waste grassland, a weed in many old gardens.

AI: Creeping Bellflower has been introduced into Britain from Europe where it grows as far east as Asia Minor and the Caucasus.

Peach-leaved Bellflower
Campanula persicifolia
Bellflower family
Campanulaceae

June—July   70—120 cm   D; ⑴

IM: Few flowers in a semi-erect and 1-sided inflorescence. Flowers 2.5—4 cm across; usually equally long. No hairs on flower or calyx. Stem simple. Linear stem leaves are at most 1 cm wide, lower ones normally have small sharp saw-like teeth.
H: Needs loamy woodland soil rich in nutrients. Scattered. Introduced to Britain from Europe or Asia where it is native. Established in several places but the colonies always start as garden escapes.

Clustered Bellflower
Campanula glomerata
Bellflower family
Campanulaceae

May—Sept.   15—70 cm   D; ⑴

IM: Flowers stalkless in terminal heads, sometimes with a few axillary branches. They are virtually erect; 1.5—2.5 cm long, bluish-violet. Lower leaves rounded or heart-shaped. Entire plant covered with soft hairs.
H: Grassy places on calcareous soils, occasionally in woods and on cliffs. Locally common.
Al: Similar: *C. cervicaria*: flowers 1—2 cm long, light bluish-violet. Style conspicuously longer than the flower. Lower leaves narrower towards the stem, never rounded. Leaves and stem covered with prickly stiff hairs. Not British. Thickets and meadows in Europe. Very rare.

Venus' Looking-glass
Legousia speculum-veneris
Bellflower family
Campanulaceae

June–Aug.　　10–20 cm　　D; ☉

IM: Few flowers in a loose panicle; 1.5–2 cm across. Flower dark violet inside, somewhat lighter outside. Branched stem usually prostrate or turning upwards, more rarely erect; glabrous. Upper leaves lanceolate, sessile; lower ones lanceolate; petiolate.
H: Not British. Needs calcereous soil rich in nutrients and a mild warm climate. Commonest in southern Europe.
AI: Similar: *L. hybrida*: flowers at the end of the stem clustered as on spike, otherwise racemose, only 0.8–1.5 cm across, purplish-red and lilac. Arable fields. Rare.

Phyteuma nigrum
Bellflower family
Campanulaceae

May–July　　20–70 cm　　D; ♃

IM: Flowers in a dense conical spike which is curved before opening, dark violet-blue. Bracts at base of spike usually shorter than spike. Basal leaves twice as long as wide.
H: Not British. Needs loamy soil rich in nutrients and rather low in lime. Woodland, mountain meadows of the higher hilly regions of Europe.
AI: Similar: Blue-spiked Rampion (*P. betonicifolium*): flowers almost erect before opening; basal leaves approx. 3 times as long as wide; woodland; central Alps; scattered. Dark Rampion (*P. ovatum*): flowers bent upwards before opening; Alps; scattered.

Round-headed Rampion
Phyteuma orbiculare
Bellflower family
Campanulaceae

May—Sept.   10—50 cm   D; ♃

IM: 10—30 flowers in a globular head 1—2 cm across. Flowers bluish-violet, bent conspicuously inwards before opening. Basal leaves elongate-ovate, petiolate. Stem leaves elongate.
H: Locally abundant in chalk grassland in the south.
AI: Abundant in central Europe, the Rampions reach their northerly limit in Britain.

Sheep's Bit
Jasione montana
Bellflower family
Campanulaceae

June—Aug.   10—50 cm   D; ☉

IM: Numerous flowers in a globular head 1.2—2.5 cm across. Individual blossoms aprox. 1 cm long, light bluish-violet. Occasionally, white flowers are found. Stem branched. Leaves lanceolate-ovate, glabrous or with stiff hairs, usually conspicuously undulate along the edges and often bluntly toothed.
H: Sandy turf, rough grassland, heaths and cliffs. Locally abundant throughout Britain and Europe except for Mediterranean regions. In Britain it is commonest in Cornwall and in the Shetland Isles but can be found occasionally in most districts.

Lesser Grape Hyacinth
Muscari botryoides
Lily family
Liliaceae

April–May   10–25 cm   M; ♃

Muscari racemosum
Lily family
Liliaceae

April   10–40 cm   M; ♃

IM: Numerous flowers in a dense rac-emose inflorescence up to 2–5 cm long. Flowers approx. the same width as length; sky blue, drooping with white fringe around the apex. 2–3 basal leaves, almost flat.
H: Not British. Mountain meadows, light open woodland on calcareous loamy soil. Virtually only higher hilly areas of mainland Europe and Alps.
AI: Similar: Tassel Hyacinth (*M. como-sum*): flower cluster over 10 cm long when open; at the tip of the spike a crop of sterile blossoms face upwards. Gardens and waste ground.

IM: Numerous flowers in dense rac-emose spikes. Flower approx. twice as long as wide; sky blue, drooping, with white fringe around the mouth. Pedun-cle leafless. 4–6 basal leaves, grooved, appearing in autumn, approx. 3 mm wide.
H: Sunny, sandy turf. Rare.
AI: Similar: *M. neglectum*: flowers approx. 2½ times as long as they are wide. Inflorescence 2–4 cm long. Basal leaves approx. 5 mm wide, always longer than the stem. Frequent throughout Europe from the Mediter-ranean to southern Britain, but not in the north. Only native to sandy areas of East Anglian brickland.

Alpine Squill
Scilla bifolia
Lily family
Liliaceae

March—April   10—20 cm   M; ♃; +

IM: 2—8 flowers erect in a lax raceme; blue with a violet-colored flush. Stem has no leaves. Usually 2 basal leaves, approx. 1 cm across, usually as long as the stem; hood-shaped at the apex.
H: Not British. Occurs throughout mainland Europe in light woodland and somewhat moist soil rich in lime. Commonest in the Mediterranean region.
AI: *Scilla verna*, Spring Squill, which flowers in April and May and *S. autumnalis*, Autumn Squill, flowering in August and September; native to coastal areas of southern England.

Iris sibirica
Iris family
Iridaceae

May—July   30—90 cm   M; ♃; (+

IM: Flowers large, blue or bluish-violet, 6 petals: 3 outer petals wide, 3 inner ones narrow. Deciduous leaves approx. 5 mm wide, shorter than stem, in 3-rowed arrangement overlapping at the base.
H: Not British. Light woodland, wet meadows on ground rich in lime, and temporarily moist. Mainland Europe; never abundant.
AI: This plant does not survive either fertilizer or being cut down, which is why it dies out on grassy areas which are improved for grazing.

Spring Crocus
Crocus vernus
Iris family
Iridaceae

March–April   5–15 cm   M; ⚁

IM: Leaves grass-like, with white central stripe, appearing shortly after the flowers. Flowers have narrow petals, at least 4 times longer than wide (2–3 cm long). Virtually no hairs in the flower throat.
H: Native to Italy and the Balkan countries. In Britain it has become naturalized in meadows and pastures. Local in England and a few places in Scotland and Wales.
AI: The violet-flowering forms rarer than the white.

Purple Crocus
Crocus vernus ssp. *vernus*
Iris family
Iridaceae

March–April   10–30 cm   M; ⚁

IM: Petals 2.5–4 cm long, 8–15 mm wide. Stigma longer than stamens. Virtually no hairs in the flower throat. Flowers deep violet. Leaves grass-like, with white central stripe, appearing shortly after flowers.
H: In Britain only in gardens and occasionally naturalized.
AI: Originates around the Mediterranean. Brought to central Europe in the Middle Ages as an ornamental plant and has become naturalized in certain areas.

Pasque Flower
Pulsatilla vulgaris
Buttercup family
Ranunculaceae

March—May   5—40 cm   D; ♃; +

IM: 1 flower on each short peduncle; flower may reach 2—4 cm in length, lilac to dark violet. Petals have external covering of hairs. Funnel-shaped involucral bract below the flower, also densely covered with woolly hairs. Leaves dissected into many lobes, usually less than 5 mm wide.
H: Needs calcareous soil and short grassland. Local in south-eastern England.
AI: A number of colour forms grown in gardens; pure white, red and occasionally pink flowers occur.

Hepatica
Hepatica nobilis
Buttercup family
Ranunculaceae

March—May   8—25 cm   D; ♃; +

IM: Several stems arise from a leaf rosette, each stem bearing 1 flower. Flowers 2—3 cm across, normally blue, light bluish-violet or more rarely reddish-violet. Flowers have 6—10 petals. Leaves evergreen, trilobed, margin entire, often marbled with silver veining.
H: Native to mainland Europe where it likes loamy soil rich in mull. Scattered, usually in large numbers where it occurs.
AI: Occasionally listed under Anemones (*Anemone hepatica*)

Alpine Snowbell
Soldanella alpina
Primrose family
Primulaceae

April–June   5-15 cm   D; ⧾

IM: 2–3 flowers on a peduncle; usually pendent, or partially erect; campanulate to funnel-shaped, violet to blue. Flower divided to ½ its length in a fringe of segments, 1–1.5 cm long. Leaves rounded, 1–3 cm wide, margin entire.
H: Not British. Alps; snowy valleys and thickets alongside streams. Scattered.
AI: Soldanellas cultivated in rock gardens in Britain.

Mountain Aster
Aster amellus
Daisy family
Asteraceae (Compositae)

Aug.–Oct.   15–50 cm   D; ⧾

IM: 5–15 capitula in branched inflorescence; each capitulum 2–3 cm across. Individual flowers lilac or bluish-violet. 20–40 ray florets surround yellow disc florets. Bracts of capitula spread out. Stem erect, leaves lanceolate, hairy on the underside like the stem.
H: Not British. In Europe found in light woodland, thickets, especially in the higher hilly areas where the sub-soil is limy. Rare.
AI: Similar: Sea Aster (*A. tripolium*: 20–80 capitula in 1 inflorescence. Bracts or capitula pressed close together. Plant glabrous. Only found on salty ground.

Cornflower
Centaurea cyanus
Daisy family
Asteraceae (Compositae)

July—Oct.　　30—90 cm　　D; ☉

IM: Capitula solitary; stem usually branched; flowers spread out, 3–5 cm across. Disc florets red purple, ray florets bright blue, and large. Stem erect. Leaves not decurrent, alternate, rarely exceeding 5 mm in width.
H: Weedy places in cornfields, more rarely on waste ground. Rare, almost extinct.
Al: Cornflower is now absent from whole areas of the countryside, because of the use of chemical herbicides. Some forms still planted in the garden, often pink as well as blue.

Mountain Knapweed
Centaurea montana
Daisy family
Asteraceae (Compositae)

May—Oct.　　30—60 cm　　D; ♃

IM: Flower head 4–6.5 cm across at the end of each unbranched stem. Outer florets larger, deep blue; inner florets blue/red/violet. The involucre of the head is made up of bracts with blackish-brown edges with 5–9 fringe segments on either side. Leaf margin entire, decurrent, fluffy.
H: Not British. Native to mainland Europe. Needs calcareous loamy soil. Light woodland, mountain meadows. Higher hilly areas, Alps; scattered.
Al: Of the 400 species of Centaurea only *C. scabiosa* and *C. nigra* are frequently seen in Britain.

Creeping Thistle
Cirsium arvense
Daisy family
Asteraceae (Compositae)

July–Sept.   60–150 cm   D; ⌷

IM: Individual flowers in branched clusters. Each head 1–1.5 cm wide, with disc florets; usually a strong shade of lilac. Stem freely branched with mainly non-flowering branches. Leaves spiny, not decurrent, coarsely pinnate, usually with undulate margin.
H: Weedy places in fields, gardens and waste places. Very common.
AI: The Creeping Thistle very variable; very dry habitats — conspicuously hairy; shady areas and on damp subsoil — usually quite glabrous. White-flowered plants occur.

Chicory
Cichorium intybus
Daisy family
Cichoriaceae (Compositae)

July–Aug.   30–130 cm   D; ⌷

IM: Compound inflorescence: numerous heads in a cluster on upper ⅔ of stem. Heads, 4–7 cm across, containing only ray florets; bright blue, occasionally pink or white. Stem branched. Lower leaves coarsely toothed, upper ones undivided, amplexicaul.
H: Roadsides, dry grassland. Probably native in England and Wales but frequently a garden escape.
AI: Grown in 2 cultivated forms: one has rape-like roots (ssp. *sativa*) and provides the raw material for succory; the other form has a full leaf rosette (ssp. *foliosum*) and is grown as the salad plant.

Blue Lettuce
Lactuca perennis
Daisy family
Cichoriaceae (Compositae)

May–June   30–60 cm   D; ♃

IM: Several heads 3.5–4.5 cm across, in a paniculate, almost umbellate inflorescence. The heads contain 14–18 ray florets, normally pure blue, perhaps also bluish-violet or reddish-violet. Leaf margins entire, more often pinnate.
H: Not British. Native to Europe where it is found in calcareous, stony, loamy ground, dry turf and thickets.
AI: Flower heads close close in the afternoon and in dull weather. Rare nowadays because of the disappearance of suitable habitats. Once common locally and used for making salads.

Alpine Sow-thistle
Cicerbita alpina
Daisy family
Cichoriaceae (Compositae)

July–Sept.   50–200 cm   D; ♃

IM: Numerous heads in spike-like clusters at the end of the stems. These heads contain only bluish-violet ray florets. The stems of the inflorescence covered with reddish glandular hairs. Leaves divided into coarse toothed lobes, the lower more so than the upper. The terminal lobe spear-shaped.
H: Needs damp soil rich in nitrogen and low in lime. Found on meadows in the hilly regions in the Alps. In Britain only known on alpine rocks in eastern Scotland.
AI: The exact status of this plant in Britain is doubtful, many botanists believing it an introduction.

Limodore
Limodorum abortivum
Orchid family
Orchidaceae

May–July   10–50 cm   M; ♃

  ▽

IM: Entire plant leafless, usually tinged with blue or violet. Flowers 1.5–2.5 cm across; yellow, with violet tinge; lip usually violet with yellowish shading. Not all flowers open fully.
H: Not British. Loamy or loess soil with sufficient humus. Prefers semi-shade. Thickets. Native to Europe. It grows in the Upper Rhine area as far north as the Eiger Mountains in Germany and in the warmest Alpine valleys.
Al: The main area of distribution is the Mediterranean. Limodore does not flower every year even in suitable habitats.

Forking Larkspur
Consolida regalis
Buttercup family
Ranunculaceae

May–Sept.   10–50 cm   D; ⊙ ; (+)

IM: 3–7 flowers in a sparse forking cluster; flowers 1.5–2.5 cm wide, the spur up to 2.5 cm long. Usually dark blue, occasionally dark violet. Leaves deeply divided, double trilobed.
H: Not British (only found in Britain as a casual). Weedy places in cornfields or on dry waste ground. Mainland Europe.
Al: Forking Larkspur has disappeared from many parts because of chemical herbicides. Similar: *C. ajacis*: with usually more than 7 flowers in a dense cluster, blue and sometimes pink and white. Leaves never double trilobed but double pinnate, the pinnae themselves dissected. Rare in a few places.

Monk's-hood
Aconitum napellus
Buttercup family
Ranunculaceae

June–July   60–150 cm   D; ♃; +

IM: Flowers in terminal racemes; uppermost petal of each flower forms a wide helmet. Stem erect. Leaves petiolate and palmately lobed, 5–7 segments. Leaf sections are divided into narrow lobes.
H: Needs damp soil. In mainland Europe it is found in mountain meadows and in the highest hilly regions, and in the Alps. In Britain it is by steams, usually under light tree cover.
AI: Many variations of this species; frequently subdivided into subspecies.

Lupinus polyphyllus
Pea family
Fabaceae (Leguminosae)

June–Sept.   50–150 cm   D; ♃;

IM: Numerous flowers in an erect cluster, 15–60 cm long. Flowers 1.2–1.5 cm long, usually blue, more rarely violet or even red or white. Leaves palmately divided into 9–17 leaflets, up to 15 cm long 3 cm wide.
H: Not British. Rare in Europe but usually where it does occur it is in conspicuous abundance.
AI: The roots contain nitrogen-forming bacteria which helps to improve the soil. For this reason it is planted in some regions as an agricultural crop.

331

Lucerne
Medicago sativa
Pea family
Fabaceae (Leguminosae)

June–Sept.   20–80 cm   D; ♃

IM: Numerous flowers in small, head-like clusters, 2–3 cm long and not quite as wide; lilac, violet or reddish-violet. Stem branched. Leaves tri-lobed with ovate lanceolate leaflets. Terminal leaflet has distinctly longer petiole, up to 3 cm.
H: Roadsides, grassland, forest rides. Naturalized in light soils.
Al: Lucerne is widely grown as a fodder plant; escapes from cultivation not uncommon. Where it grows near the native Sickle Medick (*M. falcata*) it gives rise to hybrids with green and even black flowers.

Oxytropis montana
Pea family
Fabaceae (Leguminosae)

July–Aug.   5–15 cm   D; ♃

IM: Flowers drooping, initially in dense clusters, the stalks lengthening later so they become lax; bluish-violet. Keel pointed. Calyx teeth ¼–⅓ as long as calyx tube. Leaves have petiole tinged with red, pinnate, with 25–41 leaflets, almost glabrous.
H: Not British. Native to the Alps.
Al: Similar: *O. campestris*, dull yellow, and *O. halleri*, pale purple; both native to upland areas of Scotland.

Lathyrus liniifolius
Pea family
Fabaceae (Leguminosae)

April—June   15—40 cm   D; ♃

IM: 3—6 flowers in lax axillary cluster, up to 7 cm long. Flowers initiallly red, then dirty blue, 11—22 cm long. Stamens tubular, tube has straight edge. 4—6 leaflets per leaf, normally distinctly bluish-green on the underside. Short point at end of leaf. Stem narrowly but conspicuously winged.
H: Not British. In Europe found in woodland, heaths, mountain meadows.
AI: Occasionally confused with the Spring Pea (right). Its winged stem is easily recognizable, however.

Spring Pea
Lathyrus vernus
Pea family
Fabaceae (Leguminosae)

April—June   20—60 cm   D; ♃

IM: 2—7 flowers in lax axillary cluster, up to 6 cm long. Flowers initially red, then dirty blue, 1.5—2 cm long. Stamens tubular, tube has straight edge. 4—6 leaflets per leaf, each ½ as wide as long. Short point at leaf end. Stem quadrangular and quite definitely not winged.
H: Not British. In Europe found in woodland, preferably deciduous. Prefers calcareous soil. Scattered, but locally common.
AI: Occasionally confused with *Lathyrus liniifolius* (left). Stem not winged, therefore easy to recognize.

Smooth Tare
Vicia tetrasperma
Pea family
Fabaceae (Leguminosae)

June–July   20–60 cm   D; ⊙

IM: 1–3 flowers in a cluster with long stem. Flowers pale violet to lilac, approx. 5 mm long. Fruit usually has 4 seeds, rarely 5. Pinnate leaves have 6–10 leaflets and a tendril at the leaf apex.
H: Weedy areas of cornfields, grassland and waste places. Scattered.
Al: Similar: Hairy Tare (*V. hirsuta*): usually only 1 flower, pale blue, almost white, 5 mm long; fruit has 2 seeds; 12–20 leaflets per leaf; weedy areas; scattered. *V. tenuissima*: 1–3 flowers, pale blue, 8 mm long; fruit 5–6 seeds; 4–8 leaflets per leaf; weedy places; rare in southern England.

Bush Vetch
Vivia sepium
Pea family
Fabaceae (Leguminosae)

May–Aug.   30–60 cm   D; ♃

IM: 2–6 flowers in very short-stemmed clusters, spread out or drooping in axils of upper leaves. Stamens tubular, tube has crooked edge. Leaves pinnate, 8–16 leaflets, with pinnate tendril at the end. Stem climbs with leaf tendrils.
H: Grassland, hedgebanks and light woodland. Common.
Al: Some botanists recognize many variations within this species. The groups are distinguished on the basis of the variations in hair covering on the calyx and the differing width of the leaflets. The differences are however not always easy to spot and not always constant.

Tufted Vetch
Vicia cracca
Pea family
Fabaceae (Leguminosae)

June–Aug.   30–150 cm   D; ♃

IM: 20–40 flowers in a long-stemmed cluster. Flowers around 1 cm long, bluish-violet. Stamens tubular, tube has crooked edge. 12–20 leaflets. Instead of terminal leaf, a tendril usually with 2 lateral tendrils. Leaflets almost glabrous on the uppersides. Peduncle approx. 3/4 of leaf length out of whose axil it grows.
H: Grassland, light woodland. Scattered.
Al: Similar: *V. dasycarpa*: only 5–15 flowers in a cluster. Peduncle approx. 3/4 of leaf length out of whose axil it is growing. 12–20 leaflets with conspicuous hairs.

Fine-leaved Vetch
Vicia tenuifolia
Pea family
Fabaceae (Leguminosae)

June–July   50–100 cm   D; ♃

IM: 20–40 flowers in a long-stemmed cluster. Peduncle as long or longer than leaf out of whose axil it grows. Leaves 18–28 leaflets and a tendril at the end. Leaflets almost glabrous on uppersides, sparse clinging hairs on undersides.
H: A casual from Europe found on waste ground in a few localities. Rare.
Al: Similar: *V. villosa*: 10–30 flowers in a long-stemmed cluster. Peduncle approx. as long or longer than the leaf out of whose axil it is growing. 10–20 leaflets with projecting hairs. An occasional casual.

Dwarf Milkwort
Polygala amarella
Milkwort family
Polygalaceae

May–June   5–15 cm   D; ♃

IM: 10–40 flowers in a cluster; usually blue, more rarely reddish, each 2–4 mm long. Stem prostrate at the base, then ascending to erect. Leaves form a basal rosette, otherwise alternate, leaves taste bitter if chewed.
H: Needs moist soil rich in lime. Found in chalk grassland in southern England. Rare.
Al: Similar: Bitter Milkwort (*P. amara*): flowers larger (3–7 mm). inflorescence more lax. Moist hillside pastures on limestone in northern England. These species resemble each other closely, classed together under the name *P. amara*.

Common Milkwort
Polygala vulgaris
Milkwort family
Polygalaceae

May–Aug.   15–25 cm   D; ♃

IM: 5–30 flowers in a cluster; usually blue, lilac, more rarely red; each approx. 8 mm long. Bracts of the inflorescence 2 mm and therefore not projecting beyond flowers before blossoming. Stem erect or ascending. Leaves alternate, never in a rosette.
H: Meadows. Found also on heaths and dunes throughout Britain.
Al: In Britain can only be confused with *P. serpyllifolia*; alternate leaves; at least the lowest leaves opposite.

Heath Milkwort
Polygala serpyllifolia
Milkwort family
Polygalaceae

May–July   5–20 cm   D; ♃

IM: 3–10 flowers in a cluster; usually blue, occasionally almost white, approx. 5 mm long. Bracts approx. 1 mm long. Stem prostrate at base, then curved upwards and erect. Lower leaves opposite, but never in a rosette.
H: Grassland which is low in nutrients and lime. Widespread throughout Britain.
AI: Since the plant needs both a humid climate as well as soil low in lime it is found most frequently in north-western Europe, not extending as far south as *P. amara*.

Bog Violet
Viola palustris
Violet family
Violaceae

May–July   8–15 cm   D; ♃

IM: 2–6 flowers in a basal rosette. Peduncles solitary, growing out of the axils of the rosette leaves; approx. as long as the petioles and glabrous. Sepals blunt, glabrous. Flowers pale lilac, with dark brownish-violet veins. Flowers about 1.5 cm across.
H: Needs wet soil low in nutrients. Common except in the drier parts of eastern England.
AI: Similar: *V. stagnina* (Fen Violet) which occurs only in calcareous fens in eastern England and in Ireland. It has bluish-white flowers and a short spur.

Heath Dog Violet
Viola canina
Violet family
Violaceae

April—June   5—15 cm   D; ♃

IM: No rosette. All leaves borne along the stem, usually considerably longer than 2 cm and often longer than they are wide. Petal spur approx. 1.5 cm long. Flower barely longer than it is wide; bluish-violet.
H: Needs soil low in lime. Prefers sandy ground. Frequent throughout Britain.
AI: As well as the ssp. *canina* there are at least 2 more, one of which is rare in eastern England: Ssp. *montana*: petal distinctly longer than it is wide. Damp areas on heathland; rare.

Early Dog Violet
Viola reichenbachiana
Violet family
Violaceae

April—May   3—20 cm   D; ♃

IM: Basal leaves present, stem has foliage. Single axillary flowers; petal spur approx. 2 cm long or longer. Stem prostrate or ascending. Leaves crenate. Stipules have long fringes. Plant glabrous.
H: Woodland where ground is rich in humus.
AI: The Early Dog Violet is close to *V. riviniana*, Common Dog Violet. They are most easily distinguished by their spurs. *V. reichenbachiana* can be identified mainly by its slender violet-coloured spur. *V. riviniana* has a blunter spur which is white in colour.

Sweet Violet
Viola odorata
Violet family
Violaceae

Feb.–April   3–10 cm   D; ♃

IM: All leaves are basal, the stems being leafless. Flowers dark violet, scented. Petal with a spur approx. 15 mm long, the same colour as the petals. Leaves wide ovate to reniform, crenate. There is often a second flowering in autumn.
H: Dry thickets, hedgerows. Likes ground rich in nitrogen. Scattered.
AI: Sweet Violet is frequently planted, but many of its habitats close to houses may be the remains of wild populations. In cultivation there are forms with different flower colours (white, also found in the wild, pink and pale yellow).

Hairy Violet
Viola hirta
Violet family
Violaceae

April–May   5–15 cm   D; ♃

IM: All leaves basal. Peduncles grow singly or in small numbers from the leaf axils. Leaves usually more triangular in shape, always with at least a sparse covering of hairs. Petal spur approx. 17 mm long. Stipules (press the rosette apart to see them) are wide lanceolate, glabrous, with few fringes.
H: Needs calcereous soil. Meadows, woodland. Local.
AI: Because of its preference for calcareous grassland, this species is often found on prehistoric banks and earthworks in southern England.

Viper's Bugloss
Echium vulgare
Borage family
Boraginaceae

June–Sept.   30–120 cm   D; ♃

IM: Flowers single or in small groups in leaf axils on the upper ½ of stem. Flowers are red in bud, turning blue when open. Stem erect. Leaves lanceolate. Entire plant covered with bristles which are conspicuously thickened at their base.
H: Roadsides, waste places. Once a serious weed of arable fields. Common, especially on the south.
Al: Occasionally occurring as a casual: Pale Bugloss (*E. italicum*): flowers light violet, lilac or white, approx. 1 cm long. Calyx only covered with dense bristles. Probably originates in the eastern Mediterranean.

Ground Ivy
Glechoma hederacea
Mint family
Lamiaceae (Labiatae)

May–June   15–60 cm   D; ♃

IM: 2–3 flowers in leaf axils of the upper ½ of the stem; 1–2 cm long, bluish-violet. The upper lip is flat and thus inconspicuous. Stem creeping, ascending or erect. Leaves petiolate, reniform or cordiform, crenate.
H: Woodland, meadows, waste places. Common.
Al: This species is very varied. The size of the plants is usually determined by environmental conditions. It is remarkably tolerant of soil moisture, growing on dry road banks and also in pathways in marshland and woods.

Bugle
Ajuga reptans
Mint family
Lamiaceae (Labiatae)

May–June   15–30 cm   D; ♃

IM: Flowers without upper lip and with trilobed lower lip, 6–12 in false whorls in upper leaf axils, spike-like at the end of the stem. Bracts undivided. Basal leaves in a rosette, spathulate, slightly crenate. Plant spreads by runners along the ground.
H: Woodland, damp meadows, on loamy somewhat moist soil rich in nutrients. Very common in suitable habitats.
AI: Considerable variation in size and hair covering, depending on habitat. Occasionally also plants with pink or white flowers. In this case the chromoplast formation, which is controlled by several genes, has not been functioning properly.

Ajuga genevensis
Mint family
Lamiaceae (Labiatae)

April–June   5–30 cm   D; ♃

IM: Flowers without upper lip and with trilobed lower lip, 6–12 in false whorls in upper leaf axils, spike-like at the end of the stem. Bracts deeply cleft into 3 lobes, rarely just toothed. Plant has no runners.
H: Grows on dry ground. Occasionally naturalized but not wild in Britain.
AI: Similar: Pyramidal Bugle (*A. pyramidalis*): no rubbers. Leaves grow close to the stem. Basal leaves up to 10 cm long and 5 cm wide. Stem leaves smaller, margin entire or slightly crenate, often tinged with violet. Found in rock crevices in higher hilly areas in the north. Rare.

Skullcap
Scutellaria galericulata
Mint family
Lamiaceae (Labiatae)

June—Sept.   10—50 cm   D; ♃

IM: In the upper third of the stem there are 1—4 pairs of flowers in the leaf axils forming a 1-sided spike. Flowers bluish-violet in colour, 10—20 mm long. Lower lip usually lighter. Stem usually erect.

H: Needs wet ground. Reed beds, wet woodland areas, water meadows. Common in suitable habitats.

AI: The commonest of the 13 species which occur in Europe, being found in all mainland parts of the continent except the extreme north and south.

Lesser Skullcap
Scutellaria minor
Mint family
Lamiaceae (Labiatae)

July—Oct.   10—15 cm   D; ♃

IM: 1—3 pairs of flowers in the leaf axils of the upper third of the stem making a 1-sided spike. Flowers light pinkish-purple, occasionally with a touch of red, only 0.5—0.8 cm long. Stem ascending or erect.

H: Needs wet acid ground, usually found on wet heaths. Throughout Britain except the far north east.

AI: Similar: Spear-leaved Skullcap (*S. hastifolia*): in the upper fifth of the stem there are 2—5 pairs of flowers borne in a terminal raceme. Flowers blue, 1.8—2.5 cm long. Middle leaves have conspicuous spear-shaped lobes. Very rare, one site where it is a certain introduction.

Self-heal
Prunella vulgaris
Mint family
Lamiaceae (Labiatae)

May—Oct.   10—20 cm   D; ♃

IM: Flowers in a rounded cluster at the stem end; 1–1.5 cm long; upper lip helmet-shaped and flat. The calyx approx. ²/₃ the flower length. Directly below inflorescence is a pair of opposite leaves.
H: Needs loamy nitrogenous soil. Meadows and woodland. Very common.
AI: A plant of wide tolerances being found in damp woods, in all sorts of grassland. In gardens it is a common weed of damp lawns.

Large Self-heal
Prunella grandiflora
Mint family
Lamiaceae (Labiatae)

June—Aug.   5—25 cm   D; ♃

IM: Flowers dark violet, in rounded clusters at stem ends, 2–2.5 cm long. Upper lip helmet-shaped; calyx approx. ¹/₂ flower length. First pair of stem leaves a conspicuous distance from the inflorescence. Leaf margin crenate or entire.
H: Not native in Britain. Needs calcareous soil which is warm in the summer. Dry turf.
AI: Becoming more common as an ornamental rock plant; occasionally also with white or red flowers.

Meadow Sage
Salvia pratensis
Mint family
Lamiaceae (Labiatae)

May—July   20—60 cm   D; ♃

IM: 4—8 flowers in whorl-like inflorescences in the stem in terminal spikes, sometimes branched; hairy. Flowers usually bluish-violet, more rarely light blue, pink or white, 2—2.5 cm long, with very inflated upper lip. Leaves in a loose rosette with few stem leaves; leaves wrinkled, coarsely toothed-crenate.
H: Needs calcareous soil rich in nutrients. Rare in chalk grassland in southern England.
AI: Similar: *S. verbenaca*: flowers only 0.8—1.5 cm long. Lowest bract in the inflorescence always longer than the respective petals. In Britain grows only in Guernsey.

Whorled Clary
Salvia verticillata
Mint family
Lamiaceae (Labiatae)

June—Sept.   30—60 cm   D; ♃

IM: 12—24 flowers in whorls in the upper ⅓ of the stem in a loose spike; flowers 1—1.5 cm long; dark violet. Stem erect and hairy. Basal leaves usually withered by flowering time. Stem leaves ovate, heart-shaped at the base and usually with projecting lobes.
H: A rare plant occasionally found in waste places.
AI: Probably originates in south-east Europe. From there it has gradually spread northwards. It has established itself particularly in warmer regions.

Basil Thyme
Acinos arvensis
Mint family
Lamiaceae (Labiatae)

June–Aug.   10–30 cm   D; ☉ – ♃

IM: 2–3 flowers in whorls above one another on the upper part of the stem and also from leaf axis. Flowers 0.7–1 cm long; bluish-violet. Stem prostrate, ascending or erect, usually branched from the base and sparsely hairy. Leaves opposite, with short petioles, barely 2 cm long, ovoid.
H: Dry turf, scree along path verges. Likes warmth. Scattered.
AI: Basil Thyme is very varied. Over the last few decades it has been classified under various names: *Calamintha acinos*, *Satureja acinos*, *Satureja calamintha*.

Alpine Bartsia
Bartsia alpina
Figwort family
Scrophulariaceae

June–Aug.   5–20 cm   D; ♃

IM: Single flowers in upper leaf axils; 1.5–2.5 cm long; very dark violet; frequently indistinguishable from the bracts which are also tinged with dark violet. Upper lip of the flower inflated, the lower lip flat and trilobed. Leaves ovoidly crenate, opposite, hairy and bluntly toothed.
H: Needs damp ground rich in nutrients. Moorland in hilly regions of northern England and Scotland.
AI: Semi-parasite; uses sucker roots to draw nutritive salts and water from the plants whose roots it taps.

Alpine Toadflax
Linaria alpina
Figwort family
Scrophulariaceae

June–July   5–10 cm   D; ♃

IM: 2–8 flowers in a dense terminal cluster; reddish or bluish-violet, except throat which is almost always reddish-orange. Very rarely the flowers are entirely yellow. Flowers 1–1.5 cm long; upper lip bifid. Stem prostrate and only curved upwards at the tips. 3–4 leaves in a whorl; lanceolate margin entire.
AI: Not British. Alps and Alpine foothills, on scree and stony turf. Scattered, but occurs locally in strikingly large numbers.

Ivy-leaved Toadflax
Cymbalaria muralis
Figwort family
Scrophulariaceae

June–Aug.   30–60 cm   D; ♃

IM: Single axillary flowers on long stems. Flowers approx. 7 mm long, light violet with yellow palate. Spur blunt, short and only about ½ flower length. The often purplish stem is very thin and grows prostrate or hanging rooted along walls or rocks. Leaves widely heart-shaped, with 5–7 shallow palmate lobes, glabrous, undersides usually reddish.
H: Common on walls. It has established itself in Britain from gardens but is not found in wild habitats.
AI: Originates from the northern Mediterranean.

Small Toadflax
Chaenorhinum minus
Figwort family
Scrophulariaceae

June–Sept.   5–20 cm   D; ⊙

IM: Single axillary flowers on relatively long peduncles on the upper ½ of the stems. Flowers approx. 7 mm long, violet, the lower lip almost white. Spur short (2–3 mm), straight and somewhat pointed. Ripe capsules often tinged with red and from a distance resemble flowers. Usually few open flowers on the plant. Stem erect, leaves narrow-lanceolate, lower ones opposite.
H: Arable fields, railway ballast, roadsides and waste places. Scattered, especially in southern England.
AI: Also known under the name of *Linaria minor*; regarded as a typical railway weed. Originates from the Mediterranean.

Common Butterwort
Pinguicula vulgaris
Butterwort family
Lentibulariaceae

May–June   5–15 cm   D; ♃

IM: Flowers solitary, bluish-violet, somewhat lighter in the throat, with spur. Upper lip only slightly curved upwards. Lobes of the lower lip do not overlap each other or only a little. Leaves in basal rosette, yellowish, sticky, curled up around the edges.
H: Bogs and seepage areas between rocks. Rare, often in decreasing numbers.
AI: Similar: *P. grandiflora*; much larger with flowers to 20 mm; native to western Ireland. *P. lusitanica*; pale lilac and white flowers; found in the west of Britain.

Globularia punctata
Globularia family
Globulariaceae

May—July   5—30 cm   D; ⑭; +

IM: Numerous flowers in a rounded head; not surrounded by bracts; may reach 1—1.5 cm across. Flowers approx. 7 mm long and bluish-violet. Basal leaves in a loose rosette, round to ovoid, narrower towards the stem. Stem leaves much smaller, ovate, sessile.
H: Dry chalky turf. Cultivated in Britain.
Al: Similar: *G. nudicaulis*: capitula 1.5—2.5 cm across. Alps. Not in Britain though both are grown in gardens.

Small Scabious
Scabiosa columbaria
Scabious family
Dipsacaceae

June—Oct.   30—60 cm   D; ⊙ - ⑭

IM: Flowers in a head surrounded by bracts. Marginal florets larger than the inner ones. Flowers lilac to violet. Basal leaves and lowest pair of stem leaves usually undivided. Stem leaves pinnate, sparsely hairy.
H: Dry chalky grassland, rocks, cliffs. Frequent in suitable habitats.
Al: Similar: Shiny Scabious (*S. lucida*): flowers reddish or bluish-violet. Basal leaves and lowest pair of stem leaves have short hairs along the margin and the veins only, otherwise glabrous and somewhat glossy. Only in the Alps.

Field Scabious
Knautia arvensis
Scabious family
Dipsacaceae

June–Sept.   30–70 cm   D; ♃

IM: Flowers in a head surrounded by bracts. Marginal florets larger than the inner ones. Flowers lilac, violet or reddish-violet. Stem beneath the flower head covered with conspicuously projecting hairs. Leaves opposite, greyish-green. At least the upper stem leaves pinnately divided.
H: Meadows, roadsides, weedy communities on fallow land. Very common.
AI: Very varied. Might be confused with others in the genus. However it is the most common of all similar plants in Britain and over most of Europe.

Knautia dipsacifolia
Scabious family
Dipsacaceae

June–Sept.   30–100 cm   D; ♃

IM: Flowers in a head surrounded by bracts. Bracts almost as long as the flowers or longer. Marginal florets larger than inner ones. Flowers lilac or light bluish-violet. Stem almost completely covered with hairs, especially lower down. All leaves undivided, opposite, usually conspicuously hairy.
H: Not British. Mountain forests in Europe which are not too dry, Alpine pastures.
AI: In Europe there are similar species which are hard to distinguish from one another. In Britain only *K. arvensis* (left) is similar.

Greater Reedmace
Typha latifolia
Reedmace family
Typhaceae

June–Aug.   90–250 cm   M; ♃

  ▽

IM: Male spadix almost directly above the female which is more or less the same length. The female part of the spike is velvety and blackish-brown. Leaves are grass-like, slightly twisted, 1–2 cm wide. Plant forms creeping shoots and usually grows in dense clumps.

H: Reedbeds in stagnant or slow-flowing waters, ditches, ponds, canals. Frequent in suitable habitats.

AI: Similar: Lesser Reedmace (*T. angustifolia*): male and female have a spadix 3–8 cm length of stem between them. Leaves only 0.5–1 cm wide. Reedbeds. Widely distributed.

Branched Bur-reed
Sparganium erectum
Bur-reed family
Sparganiaceae

June–Aug.   50–150 cm   M; ♃

  ▽

IM: Leaves grass-like, stiff. Stem branched. Male and female flowers in separate round heads at end of branches, upper ones being male, lower ones female; of bur-like appearance when fruit is ripe.

H: Frequently found in reedbeds of stagnant or slow-flowing waters, in ditches and marshes. Likes nutrients. Common in almost all areas.

AI: Similar: rare species which do not however have a branched stem: Unbranched Bur-reed (*S. emersum*), Floating Bur-reed (*S. angustifolium*) with floating leaves, Least Bur-reed (*S. minimum*) with 2–5 capitula.

Broad-leaved Pondweed
Potamogeton natans
Pondweed family
Potamogetonaceae

June–Aug.   50–150 cm   M; ♃

IM: Flowers in a spike up to 8 cm long held several centimetres above water by 10 cm long stem. Individual flowers inconspicuous. Leaves ovate floating on the water, twice as long as they are wide, borne on long stems.
H: In shallow water (under 1 m in depth) in ponds, ditches and slow rivers. Common usually in large numbers in those localities where it occurs.
AI: Similar: *P. polygonifolius*: submerged leaves present all year round, lanceolate, transparent. Floating leaves barely longer than they are wide. Bog pools with acid water. Common.

Common Duckweed
Lemna minor
Duckweed family
Lemnaceae

June–Aug.   50–150 cm   M; ♃

IM: Plant composed of leaf-like structures (thalli) which float. Thalli grow 1.5–2 times as long as they are wide, 2–6 mm in length; flat (not inflated on the underside). Their roots hang free in the water.
H: Stagnant and slow-flowing waters.
AI: Similar: Ivy Duckweed (*L. trisulca*); leaf-like structures lanceolate, pointed, in opposite pairs, many together in a group, 4–10 mm long. Stagnant waters. Scattered. Gibbous Duckweed (*L. gibba*): leaf-like structures 2–5 mm long, inflated on the underside. Stagnant waters. Rare.

Lords and Ladies
Arum maculatum
Arum family
Araceae

April—May   30—45 cm   M; ♃; +

    ▽

IM: Greenish-white spathe encloses the spadix, male flowers above the female. The upper part of the spadix stalked and club-shaped, club emitting a smell of carrion. This serves as a fly-trap for the purposes of pollination. Basal deciduous leaves sagittate; sometimes black-spotted.
H: England and Wales, rarer in Scotland. On loose soil rich in nutrients in deciduous and mixed woodland, in thickets, also along hedgerows. Prefers habitats where the soil is loamy and rich in mull; likes warm situations.
AI: No possibility of confusion. The club can vary from white to violet. Other common names: Cuckoo-pint, Jack-in-the-pulpit.

Sweet Flag
Acorus calamus
Arum family
Araceae

April—June   15—50 cm   M; ♃; +

IM: Inconspicuous flowers in a lateral spadix, 4—10 cm long. Below spadix is a bract which can be 2—10 times longer than the spadix. Stem triangular in section; leaves linear, reed-like, margin entire, often wrinkled on one side.
H: Reedbeds of stagnant or slow-flowing waters. Rare. Found locally throughout Britain usually in shallow water.
AI: Cultivated since the 16th century for strewing on floors and since then has escaped from gardens and become naturalized.

Hop
Humulus lupulus
Hemp family
Cannabaceae

July—Aug. 1—7 m D; ♃

IM: Climbing plant. Plant dioecious; male and female flowers on different plants. Female flowers in yellowish-green cone-like catkins, 2—5 cm long. Leaves opposite, palmately lobed, 3—7 segments (apart from uppermost leaves of female plant which are not divided).
H: Lowland forests, damp thickets. Likes warm situations. Widely naturalized.
Al: Hops are extensively cultivated, probably grown since the 8th century. It contains a bitter substance which is important for the flavour of beer.

Asarabacca
Asarum europaeum
Birthwort family
Aristolochiaceae

April—May 5—10 cm D; ♃; (+)

IM: Single axillary flowers, lying on the ground or only slightly raised; occasionally also hidden under foliage, 1.5—2 cm long, brownish-green on the outside, reddish-brown on the inside. Leaves petiolate, reniform, glossy, winter-green, basal.
H: Needs calcareous soil containing humus, predominantly in deciduous, or more rarely mixed, woodland or coniferous forests. Possibly native in a few places in southern England. Rare.
Al: Contains a burning ethereal oil which is at least slightly poisonous.

Common Nettle
Urtica dioica
Nettle family
Urticaceae

June–Oct.   60–150 cm   D; ♃; (+)

IM: Male and female flowers on separate plants. Flower panicles long, pendulous. Plant has stinging hairs. Leaves opposite, longer than their petioles, usually over 5 cm, and 2–3 cm longer than they are wide.
H: Waste places, roadsides, woodland. Nitrogen and wetness indicator. Very common.
AI: Similar: Small Nettle (*Urtica urens*): male and female flowers on the same inflorescence, usually more female than male. Leaves normally less than 5 cm in length and max. 1½ times as long as they are wide. Waste places and cultivated ground. Common in south-east England. A non-stinging form rarely occurs.
354

Wood Dock
Rumex sanguineus
Dock family
Polygonaceae

June–Sept.   30–70 cm   D; ♃

IM: Flowers inconspicuous, in whorls on the upper ½ of the stem. Inflorescence has no leaves or at most only a lanceolate bract on each of lower flower whorls. Petals round-ovoid; very raised swellings. Often entire inflorescence tinged red, usually just the petals have a reddish tinge.
H: Woodland paths, light woodland areas, watersides. Always in ground at least occasionally damp. More common in southern Britain.
AI: Similar: Clustered Dock (*R. conglomeratus*): inflorescence has lanceolate bracts almost to apex of each of the whorls. River banks and light woodland areas.

Curled Dock
Rumex crispus
Dock family
Polygonaceae

July–Aug.　　30–100 cm　　D; ♃

IM: Flowers carried above the leaves in loose, sometimes branched spikes made up of whorls. Individual flowers inconspicuous. Leaves tongue-shaped and pronouncedly curled at the edges. Lowest leaves up to 30 cm long.
H: Weedy communities in waste ground and roadsides. Likes nitrogen. Common.
AI: Similar: Great Water Dock (*R. hydrolapathum*): leaves not curled at the edges, broadly lanceolate and much larger than those of *R. crispus*. Lowest leaves 30–80 cm long. Reedbeds of stagnant or slow-flowing water, also on waste ground which is temporarily flooded. Widespread.

Broad-leaved Dock
Rumex obtusifolius
Dock family
Polygonaceae

June–Aug.　　50–120 cm　　D; ♃

IM: Branched panicles made up of dense flower whorls. Lateral branches of inflorescence erect, not branched, brownish-red when plant bears fruit. Basal leaves large, with heart-shaped base and slightly undulating edges. There are bracts on lower ½ of the inflorescence.
H: Weedy communities on waste ground and roadsides.
AI: Similar: Golden Dock (*R. maritimus*): basal leaves usually less than 20 cm long, never have heart-shaped base but narrow down towards the stem. Inflorescence has bracts right to apex, yellow when bearing fruit, never reddish-brown. Local. In muddy places by ponds, reservoirs and lakes.

355

Monk's Rhubarb
Rumex alpinus
Dock family
Polygonaceae

July–Aug.   50–200 cm   D; ♃; (+)

IM: Inflorescence freely branched. Lateral branches erect and curved towards the main stem, making inflorescence noticeably dense. Often rust-brown as petals of the inconspicuous flowers are frequently tinged red. Basal leaves up to 60 cm long, ovate to round, almost as on Butterburs. Stem has longitudinal grooves.

H: Native to mainland Europe but introduced into Britain where it occurs locally.

AI: Monk's Rhubarb contains a great deal of oxalic acid and is therefore avoided by most grazing cattle.

Glasswort
Salicornia europaea
Goosefoot family
Chenopodiaceae

Aug.–Nov.   5–45 cm   D; ☉ - ☉

IM: Flowers inconspicuous, hidden behind small scales at the ends of the branches which are thickened and club-shaped. Stems fleshy, articulated, freely branched especially at the base. Branches curved upwards. Occasionally prostrate, more usually ascending or erect and green, greenish-yellow or dirt red.

H: Silted mudflats. Often planted along flat, heavily silted littorals to help reclaim the land. Frequent along coast and usually in large numbers.

AI: Glasswort is one of the native plants which needs salt. Many closely related species are recognized.

Fat Hen
Chenopodium album
Goosefoot family
Chenopodiaceae

July—Sept.   20—150 cm   D; ⊙

IM: Flowers inconspicuous, in small cymes which form a freely branched inflorescence. Clustered spikelets in the leaf axils, or compressed to form a compound inflorescence. Flower clusters mealy. Stem angular. Leaves lanceolate-rhomboid, also mealy.
H: Prefers ground rich in nitrogen. Wasteland, rubbish dumps, gardens, manure heaps. Very common.
AI: Very varied in appearance. The species can be divided into several races but it is not easy to differentiate clearly between them.

Good King Henry
Chenopodium bonus-henricus
Goosefoot family
Chenopodiaceae

May—Aug.   10—60 cm   D; ♃

IM: Flowers inconspicuous, in greenish-yellow dense cymes forming narrow cylindrical terminal panicle. All leaves sagittate, margin entire, covered with mealy powder on the undersides at least when plant is young. Plant dull green. Leaves often have undulate margins. Stem also slightly mealy beneath the inflorescence.
H: Frequently found in weedy communities close to farms and cottages and on waste ground. Frequent. Not truly native.
AI: Used to be eaten as a vegetable prepared like spinach, and is still cultivated though not so frequently as in the past.

357

Spear-leaved Orache
Atriplex hastata
Goosefoot family
Chenopodiaceae

July–Oct.   30–100 cm   D; ☉

IM: Flowers inconspicuous, in green-ish clusters arranged in spike-like inflorescences borne in the leaf axils or at the end of the branches. The female flowers have 2 spear-shaped bracts conspicuous when the plant is fruiting. Male flowers are on the same plant (monoecious). Leaves opposite or alternate, margin entire or toothed, glabrous or mealy. Lower leaves trian-gular to spear-shaped.
H: Weedy communities in fields, along paths, on waste ground and along the coast.
AI: Similar: Grass-leaved Orache (*A. littoralis*): all leaves narrowly lanceo-late, the lower ones also never hast-ate. Frequent along coastal banks.
358

Common Orache
Atriplex patula
Goosefoot family
Chenopodiaceae

July–Oct.   30–100 cm   D; ☉

IM: Flowers inconspicuous, in spike-like inflorescences tinged with green or red, in the leaf axils and at the ends of the branches. The female flowers have two triangular bracts which are 3–6 mm long which are conspicuous in fruit. Male flowers are on the same plant (monoecious), usually not in large numbers. All leaves alternate, rhomboid in shape, often hastate at the base.
H: Weedy communities on wasteland, along paths and on fields. Common.
AI: The only species most commonly found inland. *A. glabriuscula*, Bab-ington's Orache and *A. laciniata*, Frosted Orache, are found on the shore line. Both are silvery mealy.

Common Amaranthus
Amaranthus retroflexus
Cockscomb family
Amaranthaceae

July–Sept. 10–80 cm D; ⊙

IM: Numerous inconspicuous flowers in dense spikes in axils of upper leaves and at ends of stems. Flower bracts narrow into a spiny thorn. Petals have prominent central rib (check with magnifying glass). Stem erect, covered with downy hairs. Leaves rhomboid, up to 12 cm long, more than twice as long as they are wide.
H: Weedy communities. Rare.
AI: *A. hybridus*: stem glabrous, flower bracts twice as long as the leaves which are pointed and where the central rib does not project (check with magnifying glass). Waste ground. Not in Britain.

White Pigweed
Amaranthus albus
Cockscomb family
Amaranthaceae

Aug.–Oct. 20–50 cm D; ⊙

IM: Few inconspicuous flowers in simple spikes in axils of upper leaves. No spike at end of stem. Spikes light green. Flower bracts twice as long as petals, gradually narrowing down to form a spiny thorn. Stem prostrate to erect, light green, glabrous. Leaves ovate only approx. 2 cm long, with cartilaginous undulating margin, leafy to top of stem.
H: Weedy communities on rubbish tips, railway tracks, and waste ground. Rare.
AI: No species of *Amaranthus* is native to Britain; occurs only as a casual.

Parsley Piert
Aphanes arvensis
Rose family
Rosaceae

May–Oct.   5–10 cm   D; ⊙

IM: 10–20 flowers in dense clusters borne opposite the leaves. Stipules below flower heads all partly fused together with the petiole to form a cup. Flower approx. 1.5–2 mm long and made up only of calyx which is spread out. Leaves have 3–5 lobes. Plant is prostrate or slightly ascending.
H: Weedy areas especially in cornfields and dry sandy soils. Common.
AI: Similar: *A. microcarpa*: flowers not even 1 mm long. Sepals never spread out. Cornfields and on sandy soils. Less common.

Lady's Mantle
Alchemilla vulgaris
Rose family
Rosaceae

May–June   20–70 cm   D; ♃

IM: Flowers in a terminal panicle which is glabrous at the top. Flowers small and comprise only sepals. Rounded-reniform leaves have 7–11 lobes and are toothed. Between teeth are pores which secrete drops of water on damp nights.
H: Meadows, woodland paths, roadsides. Common.
AI: Species is normally divided into many micro-species. The reason lies in the method of propagation of the plant. Ovaries are not pollinated, in fact fertile pollen is not normally formed. Instead, vegetative embryos grow out of embryo-sac.

Salad Burnet
Sangusorba minor
Rose family
Rosaceae

May–June   20–70 cm   D; ♃

IM: Flowers in a tight globular head 1–1.5 cm across. Flowers green, sepals (petals absent) are tinged with red or brown along the edge. The styles are purple-red giving their colour to the flower. Leaves pinnate with 5–17 round and toothed leaflets. They are 10–20 cm long.
H: Dry grassland, chalky banks. Likes warmth. Widespread and common except in Scotland.
AI: A good indicator plant of chalky soils usually found with Rock Rose and Dropwort.

Great Burnet
Sanguisorba officinalis
Rose family
Rosaceae

June–Sept.   30–180 cm   D; ♃

IM: Dense terminal heads of deep purplish-red or brownish-red flowers. Stem erect and branched in the upper part. Leaves large, pinnate. Leaflets petiolate, ovoid, margin crenate.
H: Moist meadows. Grows on very damp, often peaty soil but also loamy. Does not form very large numbers. Common, locally, mainly in western parts of Britain.
AI: The inconspicuous flowers are generally bisexual, i.e. they have both stamens and ovaries. Ocasionally however you may find unisexual flowers. The very light seeds of the Great Burnet are dispersed by the wind.

Petty Spurge
Euphorbia peplis
Spurge family
Euphorbiaceae

June–Nov.   5–35 cm   D; ⊙ ; +

IM: Inflorescence umbellate usually with 3 main rays which are in turn branched. Glands in bracts are crescent-shaped (check with magnifying glass). Stem erect. Leaves on stem are alternate, soon falling. If present they are generally on a conspicuous petiole from the stem. Plant contains white milky juice.
H: Weedy areas in gardens, root-crop fields, waste places, roadsides. Common.
AI: At first glance *E. helioscopa*, Sun Spurge, may be confused with this species. However, the former usually has 5 main branches in its umbellate inflorescence.

Sweet Spurge
Euphorbia dulcis
Spurge family
Euphorbiaceae

May–June   10–50 cm   D;♃; +

IM: Umbellate inflorescence with 3–5 main rays which are not further branched or only forked once. Glands in bract are oval; in young plants they are yellow, then green, and finally reddish-yellow to purplish-red. Stem erect. Leaves 2.5–6 cm long and 1–2 cm wide, invert ovoid.
H: Introduced and naturalized in a few places, mainly in Scotland.
AI: Similar: *E. cyparissias*, Cypress Spurge, 9–15 rayed umbels; spreads with great rapidity in sandy soils; naturalized in southern England.

Dog's Mercury
Mercurialis perennis
Spurge family
Euphorbiaceae

April—May   15—30 cm   D; ♃; +

IM: Male and female flowers on separate plants. Dioecious. Male flowers in clusters on long-stalked spikes, female 1—3 on long stalks. Stem erect, with leaves in upper ½ only, unbranched. Leaves petiolate, ovate-lanceolate, dark green, 3 times as long as wide. Plant smells slightly unpleasant when rubbed.
H: Woodland, hedgerows. Very common and often in abundance in its habitats.
AI: An indicator of ancient woodland, it is rarely found where woodland has not occurred in the past.

Annual Mercury
Mercurialis annua
Spurge family
Euphorbiaceae

June—Oct.   25—50 cm   D; ☉ ; +

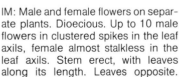

IM: Male and female flowers on separate plants. Dioecious. Up to 10 male flowers in clustered spikes in the leaf axils, female almost stalkless in the leaf axils. Stem erect, with leaves along its length. Leaves opposite. Stem has lateral branches and is quadrangular. Leaves petiolate, ovate-lanceolate, crenate. Plant smells unpleasant when rubbed.
H: Weedy areas. Scattered.
AI: Widespread throughout lowland Britain, often as a weed in parks and gardens. In some places plants of only one sex occur. On such occasions one plant spreads vegetatively.

Water-starwort
Callitriche palustris
Starwort family
Callitrichaceae

June–Oct.   2–20 cm   D; ♃

IM: Plant comprises a floating leaf rosette. Leaves up to 2 cm long, fairly narrow, tongue-shaped in appearance. Floating leaf rosette attached to a very thin, thread-like, submerged stem. Plant monoecious. Flowers very inconspicuous.
H: Slow-flowing or stagnant water. Land forms are occasionally found on dried up mud. Scattered.
AI: There are several very closely related species and subspecies characterized by fruit structure and also partly by fine details in leaf shape.

Mare's-tail
Hippuris vulgaris
Mare's-tail family
Hippuridaceae

May–July   10–150 cm   D; ♃

IM: Flowers small, inconspicuous in axils of upper leaves, comprising only a stamen and ovary. Stem is thick, up to 1 cm across bearing 4–20 linear leaves in each whorl. Whorls fairly compressed. Leaves needle-like or tongue-shaped. Submerged leaves limp.
H: Stagnant and slow-flowing water. Local. Usually occurs in large numbers.
AI: The Mare's-tail spreads by its runners and by shoots which break off and form roots.

Great Plantain
Plantago major
Plantain family
Plantaginaceae

June–Oct.　　15–30 cm　　D; ♃

IM: Individual flowers inconspicuous, in a long spike on a stem which is shorter than the leaves. Stamens yellowish-white, pollen sacs reddish-violet. Leaves in a basal rosette ascending or erect at an angle.
H: Weedy communities along paths, roadsides, waste places, meadows and pastures. Likes nitrogen, resistant to trampling. Very common.
AI: The growth point and flower spikes arise from below the leaves which protect them from injury.

Ribwort Plantain
Plantago lanceolata
Plantain family
Plantaginaceae

May–Oct.　　5–60 cm　　D; ♃

IM: Individual flowers inconspicuous, carried in a short cylindrical spike. Stamens white, later brown. Petals barely 2 mm long; brown. Stem erect, grooved. Leaves in a rosette, at least partly erect, 3–10 times as long as wide, with 3–7 conspicuous veins, hence its common name.
H: Meadows, pastures, roadsides, waste ground. Very common.
AI: Similar: *P. media*, Hoary Plaintain, finely hairy all over; cylindrical flower spikes have pinky-white anthers. Common on limy soils.

Pale Persicaria
Polygonum lapathifolium
Dock family
Polygonaceae

June–Oct.   25–75 cm   D; ☉

IM: Stem erect or ascending in bends, usually richly branched, with thickened nodes. Leaves oval, broadest over the basal ⅓, often with dark spots. Leaf sheath (ochra) membraneous, cornet-shaped, the uppermost with short cilia. Flower spikes at ends of branches, many-flowered, white or greenish or rarely pink.
H: Weedy places in fields, on banks of rivers and ponds, less common along paths or in water. Likes moisture and plenty of nutrients. Common.
Al: Similar: Redshank (*P. persicaria*, p. 214), all leaf sheaths have fringe of cilia, often grow together in similar habitats. Flowers also white or red but usually pink.
366

Annual Knawel
Scleranthus annuus
Pink family
Caryophyllaceae

May–Oct.   8–20 cm   D; ☉

IM: Flowers inconspicuous, in dense clusters in leaf axils or at ends of branches. No petals, 5 sepals 2 mm long, 2–5 stamens barely 1 mm long. Sepals ovoid, pointed, with very narrow dry membraneous white margins. Stem erect. Leaves opposite or clustered, linear or awl-shaped.
H: Weedy areas in fields and gardens. Prefers sandy ground which is at least slightly acid. Scattered.
Al: Divided into several subspecies. The differences between them lie in characteristics of fruit and sepals.

Stinking Hellebore
Helleborus foetidus
Buttercup family
Ranunculaceae

March–April 30–50 cm D; ♃; +

IM: Paniculate pendulous inflorescence made up of several nodding, bell-shaped flowers. Sepals overlap one another, often with red margin at the apex. The stem is leafy to the base. Leaves are palmately lobed; becoming less dissected to the top of the stem where they merge into bracts. No actual basal leaves present. Lower stem leaves evergreen.
H: Grows in calcareous soil. Dry woodland, more rarely scree. Scattered and probably native in southern England.
AI: In Europe a plant of western, more maritime regions.

Green Hellebore
Helleborus viridus
Buttercup family
Ranunculaceae

March–May 30–50 cm D; ♃; +

IM: The 2 basal leaves are deciduous. 1–4 flowers somewhat bent over but not totally pendent. No petals. Sepals wide ovoid, spread out, overlapping at the edges. Leaves divided into 7–11 lobes, outer lobes further divided. Segments doubly serrate.
H: Needs moist calcareous ground containing humus. Deciduous woodland. Local in England.
AI: Several Hellebores are widely cultivated but none have become naturalized, so there is unlikely to be any confusion over identification.

Water Avens
Geum rivale
Rose family
Rosaceae

May–Sept.　　20–60 cm　　D; ♃

IM: Several flowers in a lax cyme, drooping. Reddish-brown sepals conspicuous. Petals dull orange-pink. Leaves alternate, irregularly pinnate, upper ones trifoliate.
H: Wet meadows, flat moors, ditches, wet woodland and rock ledges. Common in northern England, Wales and Scotland, local or rare in southern England.
AI: The individual plants within the species vary very greatly, but so far it has not been possible to clearly define any further divisions. In larger groups one often finds 'anomalies': the bracts form an integral part of the flowers, the flower does not droop, etc.

Garden Angelica
Angelica archangelica
Umbellifer family
Apiaceae (Umbelliferae)

June–July　　50–250 cm　　D; ☉; (+)

IM: Flowers in compound umbels. Main umbel has 20–30 rays (branches). Stem is floury round the umbel, round, hollow, branched at the top, green and as broad as a human arm at the base. Leaf sheaths inflated.
H: Weedy communities at watersides, in reedbeds. Rare. Not native in Britain though locally naturalized.
AI: Similar: Giant Hogweed (*Heracleum mantegazzianum*): marginal florets in the umbels conspicuously enlarged. Leaves are coarsely trifoliate, often over 1 m long. Entire plant up to 3 m high and more. Ornamental plant, cultivated and also growing wild in meadows along streams. Both species can cause blisters when sap gets on skin later exposed to sun.

Deadly Nightshade
Atropa bella-donna
Nightshade family
Solanaceae

June–July   5–150 cm   D; ♃; +

IM: Single flowers in axils of upper leaves. They have a greenish-red tinge; lobes are deep brownish-red, brownish-violet or purplish-violet. Stem erect, leaves ovate, decurrent. Usually a large leaf grows next to a small leaf. Fruit a berry, large and black.
H: Woodland and thickets on limy soils. Rare.
AI: Deadly Nightshade is deadly poisonous. It contains hyoscyamine and smaller quantities of atropine.

Moschatel
Adoxa moschatellina
Moschatel family
Adoxaceae

March–April   5–10 cm   D; ♃

IM: The flowers are in 5s in a small terminal head, 4 facing outwards, 1 upwards; usually yellowish-green and approx. 5 mm across. Topmost flower has 4 petals, the others have 5 petal lobes. Stem erect. Basal leaves have long petioles, doubly trifoliate.
H: Needs ground rich in nutrients. Damp woodland, hedgerows and rock ledges. Widespread but nowhere common.
AI: Freely translated *adoxa* means 'not worth mentioning'. When Linnaeus used this description he wished to convey the fact that he was not concerned about the variable number of petals on the flower.

Rannoch Rush
Scheuchzeria palustris
Arrow-brass family
Scheuchzeriaceae

May–July   10–30 cm   M; ♃

IM: 3–10 flowers in a lax raceme shorter than the leaves. Peduncles up to 1 cm long. The flowers themselves only approx. 5 mm long, yellowish-green. 6 stamens at least as long as the petals. Leaves rush-like, the basal sheath enlarged. Deciduous leaves from previous year form a circle of withered leaf sheaths at the end of the horizontal rootstock.
H: Pools in sphagnum bogs. Very rare.
Al: Distributed across entire northern hemisphere where climate is moderate to cold. Seeds of the plant have been found in deposits from between the Ice Ages.

Fritillary
Fritillaria meleagris
Lily family
Liliaceae

April–May   20–50 cm   M; ♃; +

IM: Stem erect, with 3–6 very narrow deciduous leaves; these are grooved and blue-green. Flowers solitary (rarely in pairs) drooping, campanulate, up to 4 cm long and 2 cm wide, white and purple chequered like a chess-board, rarely creamy.
H: Very local, in low-lying water meadows rich in nutrients, often flooded in spring. S., E., and C. England. Often only planted.
Al: Often cultivated in gardens and then sometimes escaping. Formerly quite widespread but now disappearing.

Herb Paris
Paris quadrifolia
Lily family
Liliaceae

May–June   15–30 cm   M; ♃; +

IM: Only 1 terminal flower; up to 5 cm across. Peduncle which carries the 4-petalled flower above the whorl of deciduous leaves is always leafless. Leaf whorl consists of 4 leaves. Fruit is a bluish-black berry about the size of a cherry.
H: Needs shade and a somewhat damp soil rich in nutrients. Woodland. Widespread.
AI: Often individual plants in a larger number will have more leaves in the whorl (frequently 5, more rarely 6) or the number of petals varies. It is not yet clear how far this is determined by genetics or by environmental influences.

Alpine Leek
Allium victorialis
Lily family
Liliaceae

July–Aug.   30–60 cm   M; ♃

IM: Globular inflorescence. Petals approx. 5 mm long, somewhat blunt. Before opening, inflorescence is often drooping, surrounded by a white membraneous bract. Stem rounded, 2–3 leaves in lower ½. Leaves elliptical-lanceolate, 2–3 cm wide, with short petioles.
H: Not British. Alps. Needs moist soil containing nutrients. Grows in woods, thickets and stony places.
AI: Rootstock often Mandrake-like in shape. It has always been associated with mystical concepts, for example the possessor of the Mandrake is said to be invulnerable.

Broad-leaved Helleborine
Epipactis helleborine
Orchid family
Orchidaceae

June–Aug.   20–70 cm   M; ♃

IM: 15–30 flowers in a lax raceme. Lip does not have a spur; apex constricted laterally and therefore conspicuously bilobed. Petals noticeably campanulate, light green or slightly tinged with brown. Leaves ovate, 1.5–3 times as long as they are wide, always 2–3 times longer than the stem section between 2 leaves.
H: Needs loamy soil. Woodland, hedgebanks. Scattered throughout Britain.
Al: Similar: *E. purpurata*: flower spread out, hardly campanulate in formation; lip without spur; inflorescence 15–25 cm long, dense, with many flowers. Entire plant tinged with violet. Limy soil. Woodland. Rare.
372

Common Twayblade
Listera ovata
Orchid family
Orchidaceae

May–June   20–65 cm   M; ♃

IM: 20–40 flowers in a long lax raceme. Flowers green. Labellum long, pendulous, bilobed, without spur, up to 1 cm long, remaining petals considerably shorter and forming a helmet shape. Stem has only 2 opposite leaves which are leathery, wide ovate and up to 10 cm long.
H: Woodland, damp grassland and dunes. Common and widespread.
Al: Similar: Lesser Twayblade (*L. cordata*): much smaller, never over 20 cm, flower green, labellum reddish. Inflorescence has only 5–10 flowers. Labellum 4–8 mm long, usually with pointed lobes. Only 2 opposite cordiform leaves. Coniferous woodland and peaty moors. Commonest in Scotland, not in south-east England.

Bird's-nest Orchid
Neottia nidus-avis
Orchid family
Orchidaceae

June–July   20–45 cm   M; ♃

IM: Entire plant yellowish-brown. Tough stem with narrow-ovoid leaves. Raceme with many flowers, cylindrical. Flowers do not have a spur. Labellum bilobed, upper perianth-segments coming together to form a head.
H: In deciduous and mixed woodland, especially in beechwoods. Likes loamy soils rich in lime and nutrients and absorbs organic material in the mull with the help of fungi. Throughout Britain but easily overlooked.
AI: The rootstock under the ground bears many tightly interwoven roots. Their nest-like appearance gave the plant its name.

Frog Orchid
Coeloglossum viride
Orchid family
Orchidaceae

May–June   10–30 cm   M; ♃

IM: Inflorescence 3–10 cm long and relatively dense. Upper petals in a helmet formation approx. 5 mm across. Lip drooping, approx. 8 mm long, undivided, tongue-shaped, with 3 teeth only at the apex. Spur is short. Stem angular, with 2–5 alternate leaves.
H: Grasslands and pastures especially on chalky soils, also on moist hillsides to 1000 m in Scotland.
AI: Similar: Musk Orchid (*Herminium monorchis*): only 5–10 cm high, 10–30 small flowers which smell distinctly of honey. Lip is barely 5 mm long, trilobed. Stem usually has 2 narrow ovoid leaves. Limy grassland. Rare. Only in southern England.

Ophrys holosericea
Orchid family
Orchidaceae

June–July   15–30 cm   M; ♃

IM: Few flowers, very lax in an almost 1-sided spike. Marginal petals spread out, white or red. Lip without spur, covered with velvety hairs, slightly convex and approx. as wide as long. Lip a mixture of purple, brown and red to deep brown, with yellow markings; at the top an upwardly-curved 'beak'. Leaves elongate-ovate, alternate.
H: Not British. In Europe semi-dry turf, meadows with poor soil, glades in dry woodland. Needs a warm climate.
Al: When this plant appears together with other species of the same family, hybrids quite frequently occur.

Early Spider Orchid
Ophyrs sphegodes
Orchid family
Orchidaceae

May–June   15–30 cm   M; ♃

IM: Only 2–3 flowers (rarely as many as 8) in a lax and almost 1-sided spike. Marginal petals spread out, green or greenish-yellow. Lip without spur, covered with velvety hairs, pronouncedly convex, about as wide as long. Lip dark brown with blue markings which resemble an H or a horse-shoe. Leaves elongate-ovate, alternate.
H: Limy grassland, meadows with poor soil, glades in dry woodland. Needs a warm climate. Rare.
Al: When the Early Spider Orchid appears together with other species of the same family, hybrids may occur.

374

Fly Orchid
Ophrys insectifera
Orchid family
Orchidaceae

May–July   10–40 cm   M; ♃

    ▽

IM: 2–15 flowers in a lax almost 1-sided spike. Marginal petals spread out, green to yellowish-green. Lip without spur, covered with velvety hairs, longer than wide, trilobed.
H: Limy grassland and light areas in dry woodland. Local.
AI: Flower appears to resemble an insect to the males of certain hymenoptera. The latter attempt to mate with the lower lip. In this way they assist in pollination. They do not however make clear distinctions between the different types of *Ophrys* and so hybrids frequently occur.

Bee Orchid
Ophrys apifera
Orchid family
Orchidaceae

June–July   15–30 cm   M; ♃

   ▽

IM: 1–10 flowers in a lax almost 1-sided spike. Marginal petals spread out, mauve to pink. Lip does not have spur, covered with velvety hairs and is longer than wide, convex, with a folded back 'beak' at the apex; brownish-red, with yellow markings. Deciduous leaves are narrow ovoid, alternate.
H: Semi-dry turf, light areas in dry woodland. Very rare.
AI: Bee Orchids are very erratic in their appearance, producing abundant seed in some years then not re-appearing for as long as a decade.

Man Orchid
Aceras anthropophorum
Orchid family
Orchidaceae

May–June   20–30 cm   M ; ♃

IM: Inflorescence a narrow spike usually 5–15 cm long. Flowers do not have spur. Outer petals form a helmet shape approx. 5 mm across. They are green with a red or violet vein and margin. Lip approx. 1 cm long, divided into narrow lobes like the human body.
H: Limey grassland, scrub and woodland. Thinly scattered though locally abundant in southern England.
AI: The scientific name (anthropophorum = carrying a man) indicates the shape.

Lizard Orchid
Himantoglossum hircinum
Orchid family
Orchidaceae

April–June   20–80 cm   M ; ♃

 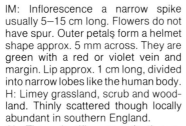

IM: Inflorescence a very lax spike 15–25 cm long. Outer petals light green, forming a helmet shape, often joined together along edges, with conspicuous red veins and margins. Lip is trilobed: lateral lobes 5–7 mm long, usually brown. Median lobe 5–7 cm long, bilobed at the apex, twisted.
H: Dry grassland and light woodland. Likes warmth. Very rare.
AI: In the Balkans there is the larger *H. calcaratum*: the lip is narrower and much more deeply divided.

Green Figwort
Scrophularia umbrosa
Figwort family
Scrophulariaceae

June–Aug.   20–120 cm   D; ♃; (+)

IM: Numerous small flowers in relatively dense pyramidal or ovoid panicles. Flowers approx. 7 mm long. Stem erect or ascending, broadly winged (wings measure a good ¹/₃ of the stem width). Leaves rounded at the base, small pinnate leaves absent from stem.
H: Ditches.
Al: Similar: Water Figwort (*S. auriculata*): flowers barely 1 cm long. Stem erect, with winged angles (wings barely ¹/₆–¹/₅ of stem width, only conspicuous membraneous rib). Leaves lobed: lobes resemble pinnate leaflets. Common by ponds, streams and in damp woods.

Common Figwort
Scrophularia nodosa
Figwort family
Scrophulariaceae

June–Sept.   60–140 cm   D; ♃; (+)

IM: Flowers in terminal panicle, approx. 8 mm long, dull brownish-red. Stem quadrangular but not winged. Leaves in opposite, alternate pairs and undivided.
H: Woodland on ground rich in nutrients. Scattered.
Al: Very rarely there are mutants in the flower colour of the Figwort. The flowers are then yellow, more rarely white. These variations can easily be distinguished from the yellowish-green flowered Yellow Figwort. The Yellow Figwort (*S. vernalis*) flowers in spring and has its flowers in axillary panicles. Naturalized in a few localities.

Spindle
Euonymus europaeus
Spindle family
Celastraceae

May   1–3 m   D; ♄; +

IM: Flowers usually have 4 petals, inconspicuous, green (without red spots) in small stalked axillary umbels. Branches green, 4 angled, leaves carried in opposite pairs are narrowly ovate and colour to a deep red in autumn. They are 3.5–5 cm in length. Capsule is carmine, 4-lobed, opening to show seeds with a fleshy orange-coloured aril.

H: Scrub and hedgerows usually on chalk. Also on dunes. Widespread and frequent, except in northern Scotland.

Al: Many species of *Euonymus* are cultivated.

Buckthorn
Rhamnus catharticus
Buckthorn family
Rhamnaceae

May–June   4–6 m   D; ♄; (+)

IM: Branches and leaves opposite. Leaves petiolate, ovoid; margin finely toothed. Many small branches terminating in pointed thorn. Flowers in sparse axillary clusters on the previous year's growth, yellowish-green, inconspicuous, pleasant smelling. Black berries, pea-sized, inedible (or have purging effect).

H: Hedges, dry thickets, oak and ash woods. Prefers calcareous soils. Scattered in England and Wales except for south-west areas, and Scotland.

Al: Similar: Rock Buckthorn, *R. saxatilis*, more delicate in every respect; leaves only 1–1.5 cm long. The Alder Buckthorn, *Frangula alnus* (see p. 379) has no thorns and leaves are alternate.

Alder Buckthorn
Frangula alnus
Buckthorn family
Rhamnaceae

May–June   1–4 m   D; ♄

IM: 2–10 flowers in small axillary clusters approx. 4 mm across; greenish-white. Branches always without thorns or thorny spikes. Leaves ovate, margin entire, 4–7 cm long and about ½ as wide, with 7–12 highly prominent lateral veins on the undersides. Berry-like drupe (only 1 seed), which is initially red, then later black.

H: Forest margins, clearings. Scattered.

Al: Like its close relative, Purging Buckthorn (*Rhamnus catharticus*), the fruit has strongly purgative properties.

Bilberry
Vaccinium myrtillus
Heath family
Ericaceae

May–June   15–40 cm   D; ♄

IM: Flowers solitary, occasionally in pairs in leaf axils, rounded, opening shortly at the mouth, greenish and usually tinged with red. Leaves deciduous, elongate-ovate, pointed, slightly crenate, green on both sides. Stem angular.

H: Needs ground low in nutrients and virtually free of lime. Common on heaths and moors especially in the west and north.

Al: Similar: Bog Bilberry (*V. uliginosum*): flowers rounded to ovoid, usually in terminal clusters. Leaves blunt, with bluish-green undersides. Stem round. Moors and peaty woodland. Scattered. Berries edible in small quantities.

Mountain Currant
Ribes alpinium
Saxifrage family
Saxifragaceae

April–June   1–2.5 m   D; ♄

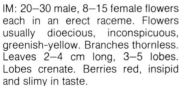

IM: 20–30 male, 8–15 female flowers each in an erect raceme. Flowers usually dioecious, inconspicuous, greenish-yellow. Branches thornless. Leaves 2–4 cm long, 3–5 lobes. Lobes crenate. Berries red, insipid and slimy in taste.
H: Needs stony calcareous ground. Grows in both dry and relatively moist woods on limestone, also on cliffs. Only in northern England and in Wales. Local.
Al: Mountain Currant is widespread, though never common in the mountains of Europe, as far east as Bulgaria and also in the Atlas in north Africa.

Gooseberry
Ribes uva-crispa
Saxifrage family
Saxifragaceae

April–May   50–120 cm   D; ♄

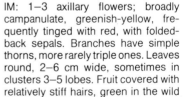

IM: 1–3 axillary flowers; broadly campanulate, greenish-yellow, frequently tinged with red, with folded-back sepals. Branches have simple thorns, more rarely triple ones. Leaves round, 2–6 cm wide, sometimes in clusters 3–5 lobes. Fruit covered with relatively stiff hairs, green in the wild form, red or yellow in the cultivated form.
H: Woods and hedges, frequent except in the far north of Scotland.
Al: There are numerous cultivated types. These originate in some cases from hybridization, hence growth forms and other characteristics may vary considerably. These may escape onto waste ground.

Sycamore
Acer pseudoplatanus
Maple family
Aceraceae

April   20–30 m   D; ♄

IM: Flowers pendulous in a raceme 5–15 cm long, containing up to 100 flowers. Flowers may be male, female or bisexual in one inflorescence. Flowers usually less than 1 cm across. Leaves 7–16 cm long, with 5 lobes. Lobes notched but not with a long point. Their stalk is usually reddish. The fruits are winged on one side.
H: Found throughout Britain but never native. Self sows itself freely.
AI: Although introduced less than 400 years ago, the Sycamore behaves like a native tree. It grows best on deep moist soils where it makes a broad crowned tree, but also flourishes on moorland to 500 m.

Ivy
Hedera helix
Ivy family
Araliaceae

Sept.–Nov.   50 cm–30 m   D; ♄; +

IM: Flowers greenish-yellow, in large globular umbels in clusters at the ends of the climbing stems. Leaves evergreen. Lobed leaves on sterile growth along the ground or when climbing, but develop entire, ovate ones on flowering stems; the margin of these is entire. Fruit is a bluish-black berry.
H: Likes half-shade and humid climate. Deciduous woodland, hedgerows. Scattered, locally in conspicuous abundance.
AI: The flowering and non-flowering branches of the Ivy plant differ considerably from one another.

GLOSSARY

Achene Dry fruit which does not split open to release the single seed.
Amplexicaul With the base clasping the stem.
Apex Tip of a stem or other organ.
Ascending Directed upwards at a shallow angle.
Auricle Ear-shaped lobe or appendage at the base of a leaf.
Awn Stiff, bristle-like organ.
Axil The angle between the stem and a branch, leaf or bract.
Axillary Arising from an axil.
Balk Open grassy land.
Bifid Deeply notched or cleft.
Bipinnate A pinnate leaf with leaflets that are themselves pinnate.
Bract (Usually) modified leaf with a flower or inflorescence in its axil.
Bulb Underground storage organ formed of fleshy leaves or scales.
Calcareous Containing calcium carbonate.
Calcicolous Needing or preferring soils high in calcium carbonate.
Calcifugous Intolerant of soils high in calcium carbonate.
Calyx All the sepals of a flower (see Sepal).
Campanulate Shaped like a bell.
Capitulum Condensed head of flowers, especially of *Compositae*.
Capsule Dry fruit which splits open to release the seeds.
Cauline Borne on the stem.
Compound Leaf composed of a number of leaflets.
Cordate Heart-shaped.
Corolla All the petals of a flower (see Petal).
Corymb A raceme with the lower pedicels longer that the upper so that the flowers are all borne at more or less the same level.
Crenate With blunt or rounded teeth.
Cuneate Wedge-shaped.
Cyme An inflorescence formed by a stem terminating in a flower, subsequent flowers being produced below it so that the oldest flower is at the top (or centre) of the inflorescence.
Deciduous Shed annually, usually in the autumn.
Decurrent Extended downwards, as a leaf extending to form a wing on the stem.
Decussate Arranged in alternating pairs, each pair at 90° to the next.
Dentate Toothed.
Dichasium A cyme in which the first flower is flanked by 2 younger ones, which in turn are flanked by 2 even younger ones, and so on.
Dichotomous Regular, repeated division by forking into 2 equal branches.
Digitate Composed of 5 leaflets.
Dioecious With separate male and female flowers borne on different plants.
Distichous Arranged in 2 vertical rows.
Drupe Fleshy fruit with stony seed(s).
Entire Even, not toothed or lobed.
Epicalyx An additional whorl similar to, but outside, the true calyx.
Fascicle A bundle.

Fen carr Wet woodland growing over peat.

Follicle Dry fruit which splits open on 1 side only.

Fusiform Elongated, tapering at both ends.

Halophyte Plant able to tolerate salty conditions.

Hastate Spear-shaped.

Imparipinnate Leaf with the leaflets paired except for the terminal one.

Inflorescence The arrangement of all a plant's flowers.

Internode Section of stem between 2 nodes.

Involucre Whorl of bracts beneath an inflorescence or capitulum: adj. involucral.

Keel Boat-shaped lower petal(s) of a Pea flower.

Labiate Lipped, e.g. shaped like the flower of a Deadnettle.

Lamina The blade of a leaf.

Lanceolate Narrow and tapering at both ends.

Legume Seed-pod characteristic of the Pea family.

Ligule Strap-like extension of the corolla of a floret.

Linear Very narrow, with parallel sides.

-merous Having so many parts, e.g. 6-merous.

Monoecious With separate male and female flowers borne on the same plants.

Node Stem joint bearing a leaf.

Nut Dry fruit containing a single seed within a woody shell.

Obovate Inverted egg-shape, widest above the middle.

Ovary Female part of the flower containing the ovule(s) from which the seeds develop.

Ovate See Ovoid.

Ovoid Egg-shaped, widest below the middle.

Palmate Composed of more than 3 leaflets or lobes arising from a central point.

Panicle A branched raceme with sessile flowers.

Papilionaceous Butterfly-like, e.g. shaped like the flower of a Pea.

Pappus Parachute of hairs (sometimes reduced to scales) on a fruit, especially of *Compositae*.

Pedicel Individual flower stalk.

Peduncle Stalk of an inflorescence.

Peltate Circular, flat leaf with the petiole attached in the centre.

Perianth The sepals and petals together, especially when not distinguishable as calyx and corolla (see Tepal).

Petal One segment of a whorl of floral leaves, usually brightly coloured (see Corolla).

Petiolate Having a petiole (see below).

Petiole Stalk of a leaf.

Pinnate Leaf composed of several pairs of leaflets.

Prostrate Lying close to the ground.

Raceme An inflorescence formed by a stem producing a flower then growing further before producing the next, so that the youngest flowers are at the top of the stem; all pedicels are of equal length.

Radical Arising from the roots.

Receptacle Flat, domed or dished part of the stem to which the floral parts are attached.

Reniform Kidney-shaped.

Rhizome Underground, creeping stem producing roots and shoots.

Rhomboid Diamond-shaped.

Ruderal Plant typically found on wasteland and rubbish tips.

Saggitate Arrow-shaped.

Samara Dry fruit with part of the wall extended to form a wing.

Scape Leafless flower-stalk arising from the rootstock.

Scarious Dry, membranous.

Scorpioid Curved or coiled like the tail of a scorpion.

Scree Unstable slope of small, loose stones.

Sepal One segment of the whorl of floral parts (usually green) outside in petals (see Calyx).

Serrate Sharply toothed like a saw.

Sessile Without a stalk.

Silicula Seed-pod which is broader than long, with a central partition wich persists after the seeds are released; characteristic of some members of the cabbage family.

Siliqua Like a silicula but longer than broad; characteristic of the remaining members of the cabbage family.

Spadix Inflorescence in which sessile flowers are borne on a thickened, fleshy axis.

Spathe Large bract, often brightly coloured, which encloses a spadix.

Spatulate Spoon-shaped.

Spike A simple raceme with sessile flowers.

Stamen Male reproductive organ bearing pollen.

Standard The posterior petal of a Pea flower.

Stigma Part of the flower receptive to pollen.

Stipule Leaf-like organ at the base of a petiole.

Stolon Creeping overground stem rooting at intervals.

Style Usually elongated organ connecting the ovary and stigma.

Synanthropic Associated with man.

Tepal Term for 1 segment of the perianth when calyx and corolla are indistinguishable.

Trifoliate Composed of 3 leaflets.

Tuber Underground storage organ derived from a stem.

Umbel Umbrella-shaped inflorescence with all the pedicels arising from the same point.

Undulate Wavy.

Unilateral Arranged on 1 side.

Verticillaster Dichasial arrangement of flowers giving the appearance of a whorl.

Violaceous Flower shaped like that of a Pansy.

Wings The lateral petals of a Pea flower.

INDEX

Page references in italics
indicate illustrations.

B

J

Jack-by-the-Hedge 36
Jack-in-the-Pulpit 34, 352
Jenny, Creeping *151*
Jersey Orchid 256
Jerusalem Artichoke *162*
Jupiter's Distaff *192*

K

Kidney Vetch *184*
Knapweed, Brown *248*
Common *248*
Greater *249*
Mountain *327*
Knautia arvensis 349
K. dipsacifolia 349
Knawel, Annual *366*
Knotgrass *49, 214*

L

Labrador-Tea 114
Lactuca muralis 174
L. perennis 329
L. scariola 176
L. serriola 176
Lady Orchid *256*
Lady's Bedstraw *131*
Lady's Mantle *360*
Lady's-slipper *178*
Lady's-tresses, Creeping *95*
Lamiastrum galeobdolon 192
ssp. *galeobdolon*
192
ssp. *flavidium* 192
ssp. *montanum* 192
Lamium album 100
L. amplexicaule 275
L. galeobdolon 192
ssp. *flavidum* 192
L. hybridum 275
L. maculatum 274
L. purpureum 275
Lapsana communis 174
Large Bellflower 318
Large Birdweed 74
Large Bitter-cress 41
Large Hop Trefoil *184*
Large Self-heal *343*
Large White Buttercup 57
Large Yellow Foxglove *196*
Large-flowered Hemp-nettle
191

Large-flowered Mullein *155*
Large-leaved Lime 201
Larkspur, Forking *330*
Lathraea squamaria 281
Lathyrus aphaca 188
L. japonicus 267
L. liniifolius 269, 333
L. niger 268
L. pratensis 188
ssp. *angustifolium* 267
ssp. *platyphyllos* 267
ssp. *sylvestris* 267
L. tuberosus 268
L. vernus 269, 333
Lavender, Sea *307*
Leafy Lousewort *194*
Leafy Spurge 129
Least Bur-reed 118, 350
Least Water-lily 132
Ledum palustre 114
Leek, Alpine *371*
Houseleek *240*
Round-headed Leek 239
Legousia hybrida 320
L. speculum-veneris 320
Lembotropis nigricans 204
Lemna gibba 351
L. minor 351
L. trisulca 351
Leontodon autumnalis 171
L. hispidus 171
Lesser Birdweed *233*
Lesser Burdock *250*
Lesser Butterfly-orchid *94*
Lesser Celandine *158*
Lesser Grape Hyacinth *322*
Lesser Periwinkle *307*
Lesser Reedmace 350
Lesser Skullcap *342*
Lesser Spearwort *137*
Lesser Stitchwort *50*
Lesser Trefoil *185*
Lesser Twayblade 372
Lettuce, Blue *329*
Prickly *176*
Red Hare's *251*
Wall *174*
Leucantheum corymbosum
93
L. vulgare 93
Leucojum aestivum 83
L. vernum 83
Ligustrum ovalifolium 105
L. vulgare 105
Lilium martagon 239
Lily, Branched St Bernard's
79
Martagon *239*
May *35*
St Bernard's *79*

Lily-of-the-valley *82*
Lime, Long-leaved 201
Small-leaved *201*
Limestone Woundwort *276,*
277
Limodore *330*
Limodorum abortivum 330
Limonium vulgare 307
Linaria alpina 346
L. minor 347
L. vulgaris 197
Linum catharticum 65
Liquorice, Wild *182*
Listera cordata 372
L. ovata 372
Lithospermum arvense 74
L. officinale 74
Little Mouse-ear 52
Livelong Saxifrage *61*
Lizard Orchid *261, 376*
Long-flowered Primrose 230
Long-headed Poppy 208
Long-stalked Crane's-bill
224
Lonicera caprifolium 117
L. periclymenum 117
L. ruprechtiana 116, 205
L. xylosteum 116, 205
Loosestrife, Dotted 150
Purple *241*
Slender 241
Tufted *150*
Yellow *150*
Lords and Ladies *34, 352*
Lotus corniculatus 186
L. pedunculatus 186
L. siliquosus 187
L. uliginosus 186
Lousewort *281*
Leafy *194*
Marsh 281
Whorled *280*
Lucerne 183, *332*
Lunaria annua 293
L. rediviva 293
Lungwort 235
Soft *311*
Lupinum polyphyllus 331
Lychnis flos-cuculi 220
L. viscaria 220
•*Lycopsis arvensis* 314
Lysimachia nemorum 151
L. nummularia 151
L. punctata 150
L. thyrsiflora 150
L. vulgaris 150
Lythrum salicaria 241
L. virgatum 241

M

Madder, Field *302*
Mahonia aquifolium 104
Maianthemum bifolium 35
Maiden Pink 217
Malus domesticus 106, 286
    M. sylvestris 106, 286
Malva alcea 228
    M. moschata 228
    M. neglecta 229
    M. pusilla 229
    M. sylvestris 228
Man Orchid *261, 376*
Mandrake 371
Maple, Field *200*
Mare's-tail *364*
Marguerite 93
Marigold, Field *169*
    Marsh Marigold *132*
    Pot Marigold 169
Marjoram *278*
Marsh Bedstraw, Common
    47
Marsh Cinquefoil *223*
Marsh Crane's-bill *226*
Marsh Gentian *308*
Marsh Gladiolus *252*
Marsh Helleborine *94*
Marsh Lousewort 281
Marsh-marigold *132*
Marsh Pennywort *70*
Marsh Stitchwort 51
Marsh Thistle 173, *246*
Marsh Valerian *237*
Marsh Woundwort *277*
Martagon Lily *239*
Matricaria corymbosum 93
    M. inodora 90
    M. maritimum 90
    M. matricarioides 163
    M. perforata 90
    M. suaveolens 163
May Lily *35*
Mayweed, Scented *90*
    Scentless *90*
    Sea Mayweed 90
Meadow Buttercup *134*
Meadow Crane's-bill *305*
Meadow Rue, Columbine-
    leaved 292
    Common Meadow Rue
        118
Meadow Saffron *238*
Meadow Sage *344*
Meadow Saxifrage *60*
Meadow Vetchling *188*
Meadowsweet *64*
Medicago falcata 332
    M. lupulina 183

M. sativa 332
    ssp. *falcata* 183
Medick, Black *183*
    Sickle Medick *183*, 332
Medlar *107*
Melampyrum arvense 279
    M. pratense 192
    M. sylvaticum 193
Melandrium album 54
    M. dioicum 219
    M. rubicum 219
Melilot, Ribbed *182*
    Tall Melilot 182
    White Melilot *99*
Melilotus alba 99
    M. altissima 182
    M. officinalis 182
Mellitis melissophyllum 102,
    272
Mentha aquatica 213, 296
    M. arvensis 296
    M. spicata 296
    M. × piperita 213
Menyanthese trifoliata 73
Mercurialis annua 363
    M. perennis 363
Mercury, Annual *363*
    Dog's Mercury *363*
Mespil, Snowy *107*
Mespilus germanica 107
Mezereon *282*
Midland Hawthorn 109
Mignonette, Wild *126, 159*
Military Orchid *255*
Milk-parsley, Cambridge 69
Milkweed Gentian *308*
Milkwhite Rock-jasmine *72*
Milkwort, Bitter 336
    Common 270, *336*
    Dwarf *336*
    Heath *337*
    Sea *231*
    Shrubby *205*
    Tufted *270*
Mint, Corn *296*
    Water Mint 213, *296*
Mistletoe *198*
Moehringia trinervia 53
Moneses uniflora 70
Monkey Orchid *257*
Monk's-hood *331*
Monk's Rhubarb *356*
Monotropa hypopitys 130
    ssp. *hypophegea* 130
Moon Daisy 93
Moor-king *194*
Moschatel *369*
Moss Campion *219*
Moth Mullein 154
Mountain Ash 109, *326*

Mountain Avens *86*
Mountain Clover *99*
Mountain Currant *380*
Mountain Everlasting *244*
Mountain Knapweed *327*
Mountain Valerian *236*
Mouse-ear *52*
    Field Mouse-ear *52*
    Grey 52
    Little 52
    Sticky 52
Mouse-ear Hawkweed *176*
Mugwort *164*, 234
Mullein, Dark *154*
    Large-flowered *155*
    Moth 154
    White *75*, 154
Muscari botryoides 322
    M. comosum 322
    M. neglectum 322
    M. racemosum 322
Musk Mallow *228*
Musk Orchid 373
Musk Thistle *245*
Mustard, Black 121
    Garlic *36*
    Hare's-ear *38*
    Hedge *121*
    Tower 38, 121
    Treacle *121*
Mycelis muralis 174
Myosotis alpestris 313
    M. arvensis 312
    M. scorpioides 312
    M. secunda 312
    M. sylvatica 312, 313
Myosoton aquaticum 51

N

Narcissus-flowered
    Anemone *56*
Narrow-leaved Bitter-cress
    40, 208, 294
Narrow-leaved Everlasting
    Pea *267*
Narrow-leaved Helleborine
    95
Narrow-leaved Water-
    plantain 32, 206
Narrow-leaved Yellow-rattle
    195
Narthecium ossifragum 156
Nasturtium microphyllum 41
    N. officinale 41
Neottia nidus-avis 179, 373
Neslia paniculata 123
Nettle 234
    Common *354*